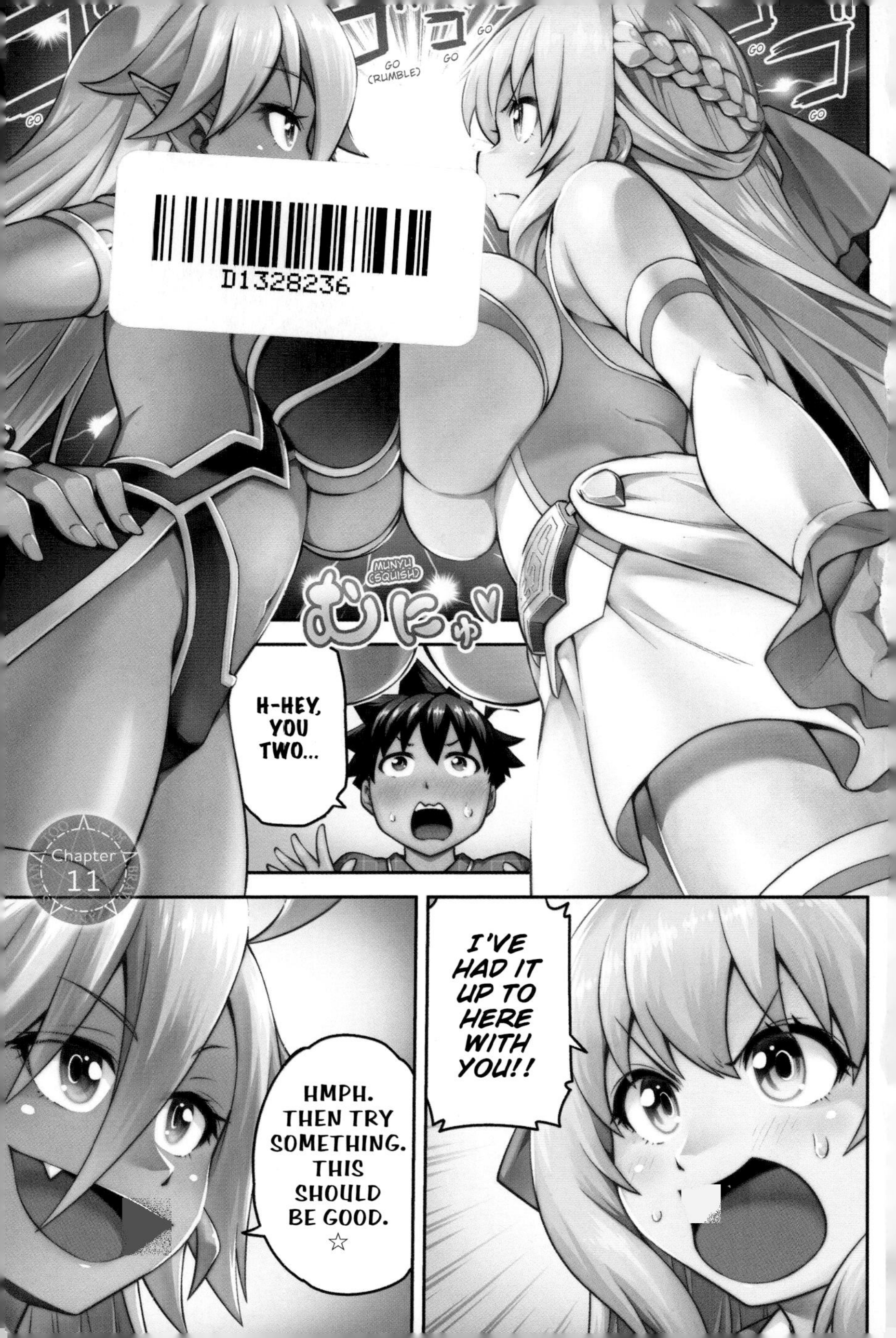
GO
GO
GO
(RUMBLE)
GO
GO
GO
MUNYU (SQUISH)
むにゅ♥
H-HEY, YOU TWO...
Chapter 11
I'VE HAD IT UP TO HERE WITH YOU!!
HMPH. THEN TRY SOMETHING. THIS SHOULD BE GOOD. ☆

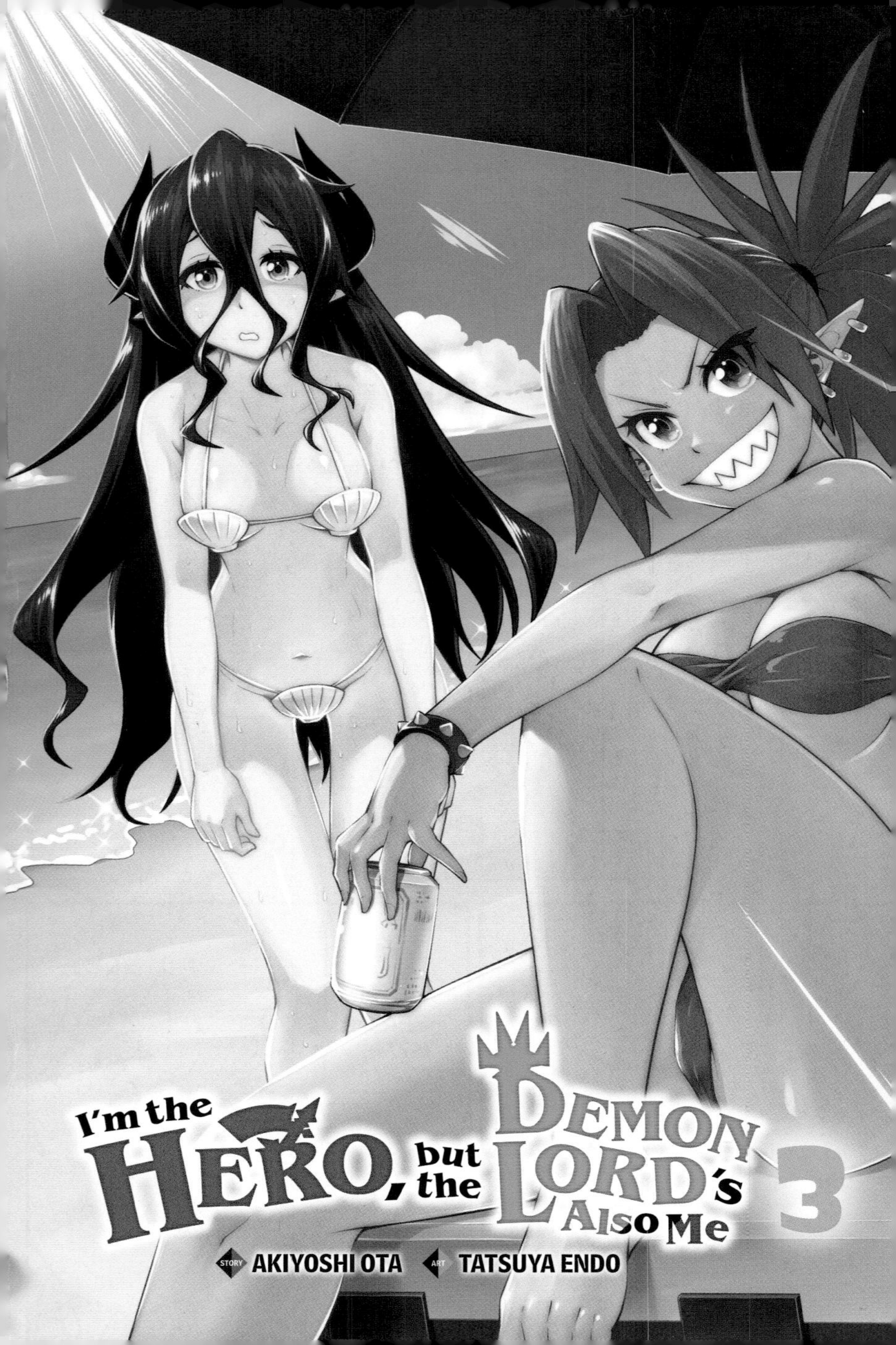
I'm the HERO, but the DEMON LORD's Also Me
3
STORY AKIYOSHI OTA
ART TATSUYA ENDO

# Contents



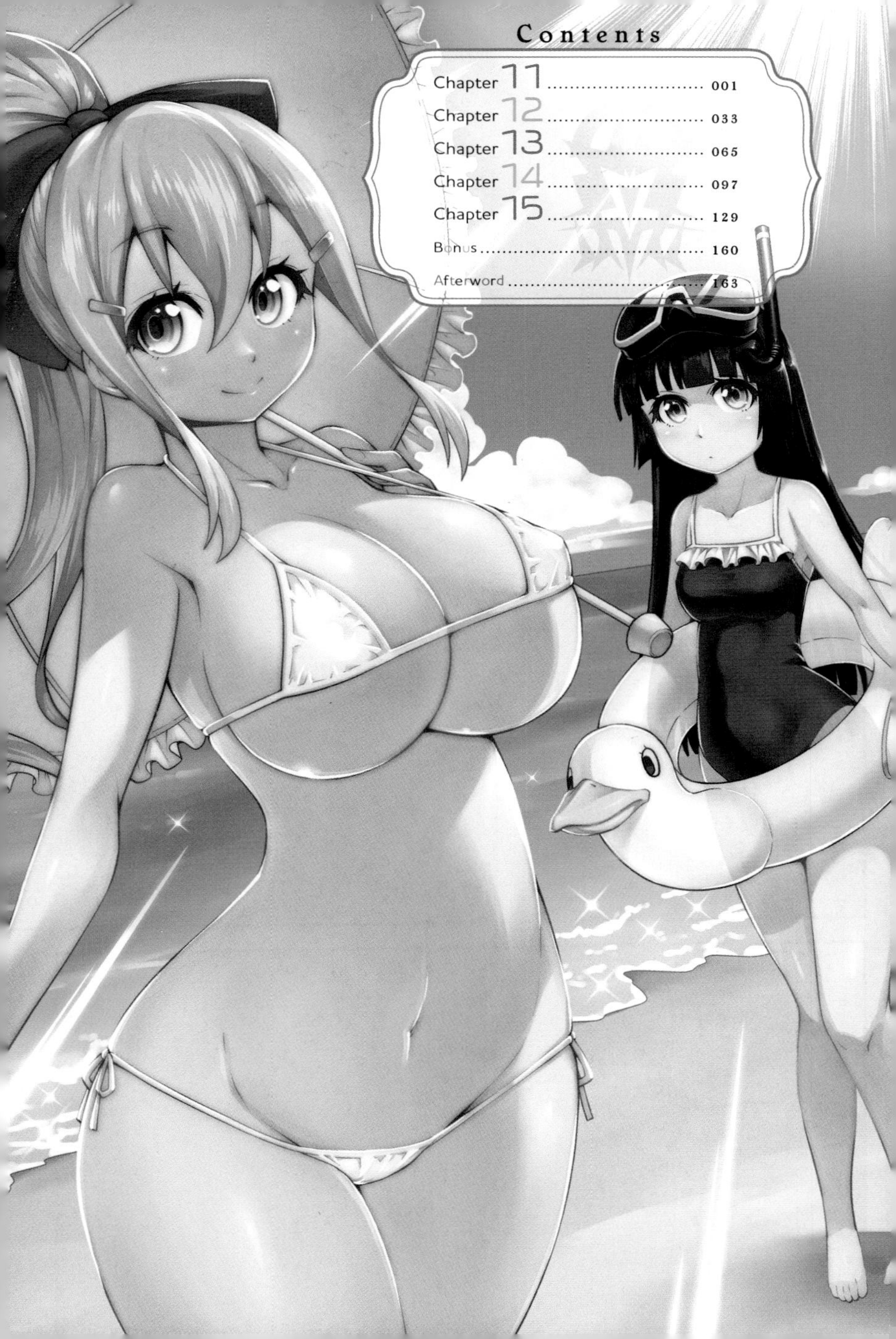

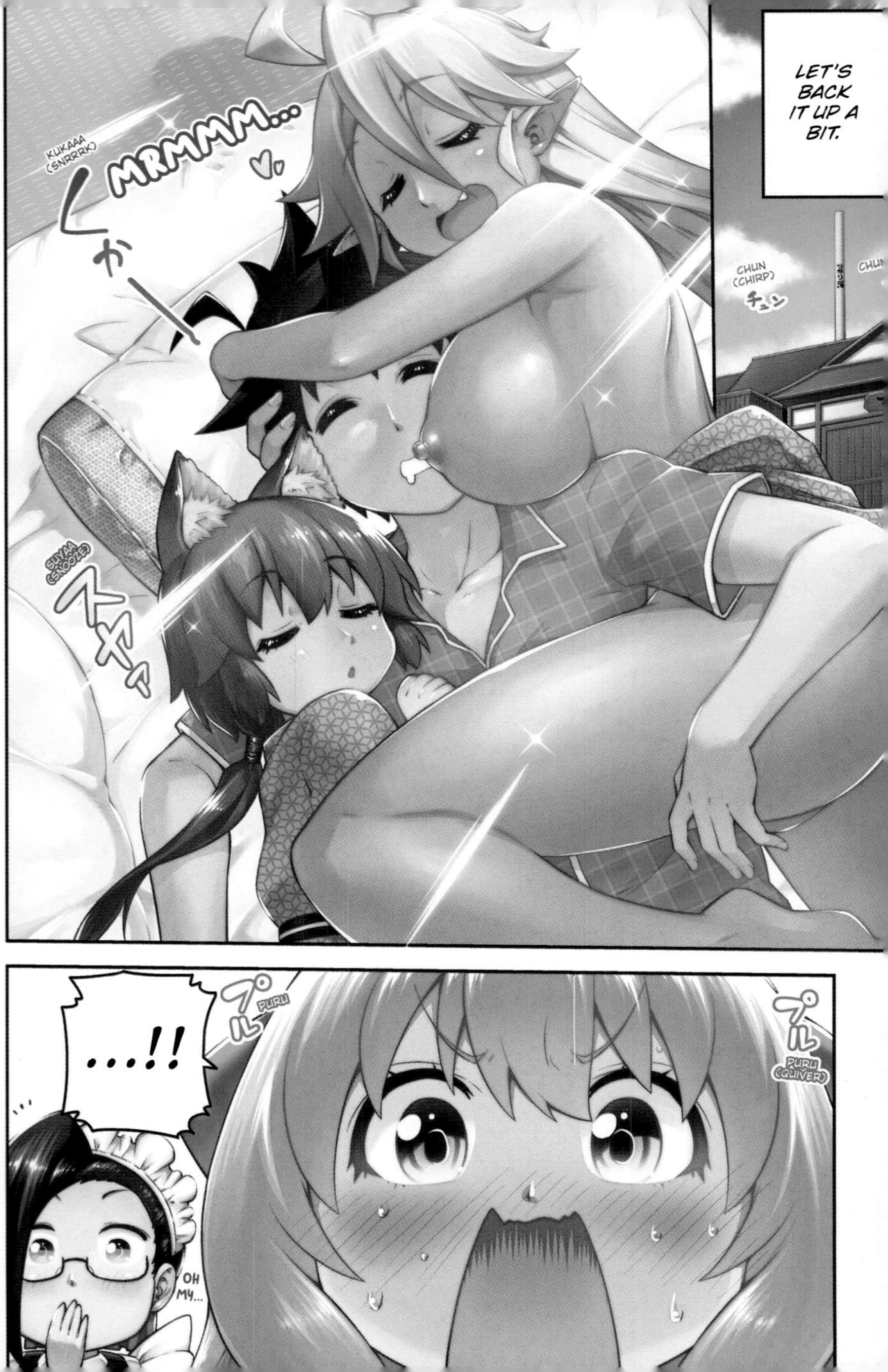

LET'S BACK IT UP A BIT.
CHUN (CHIRP)
チュン
CHUN
MRMMM...
KUKAAA (SNRRRK)
くかー
SUYAA (SNOOZE)
スヤァ
PURU (QUIVER)
プル
PURU
プル
...!!
...
OH MY...

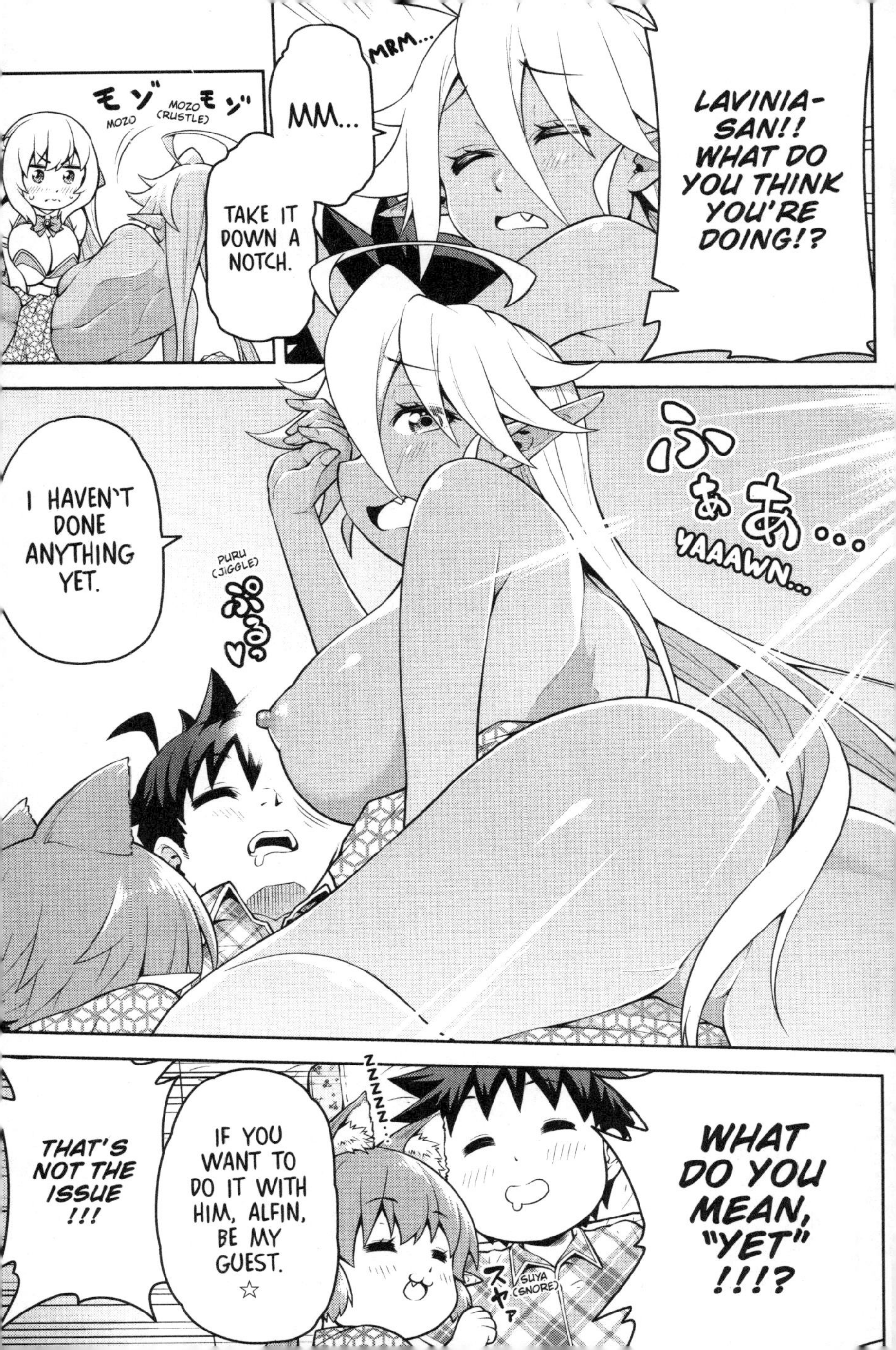
LAVINIA-SAN!! WHAT DO YOU THINK YOU'RE DOING!?
MRM...
MM...
TAKE IT DOWN A NOTCH.
モゾ MOZO モゾ MOZO (RUSTLE)
ふぁあ... YAAAWN...
I HAVEN'T DONE ANYTHING YET.
ぷるっ♥ PURU (JIGGLE)
WHAT DO YOU MEAN, "YET"!!!?
ZZZZZ...
IF YOU WANT TO DO IT WITH HIM, ALFIN, BE MY GUEST. ☆
スヤァ SUYA (SNORE)
THAT'S NOT THE ISSUE!!!

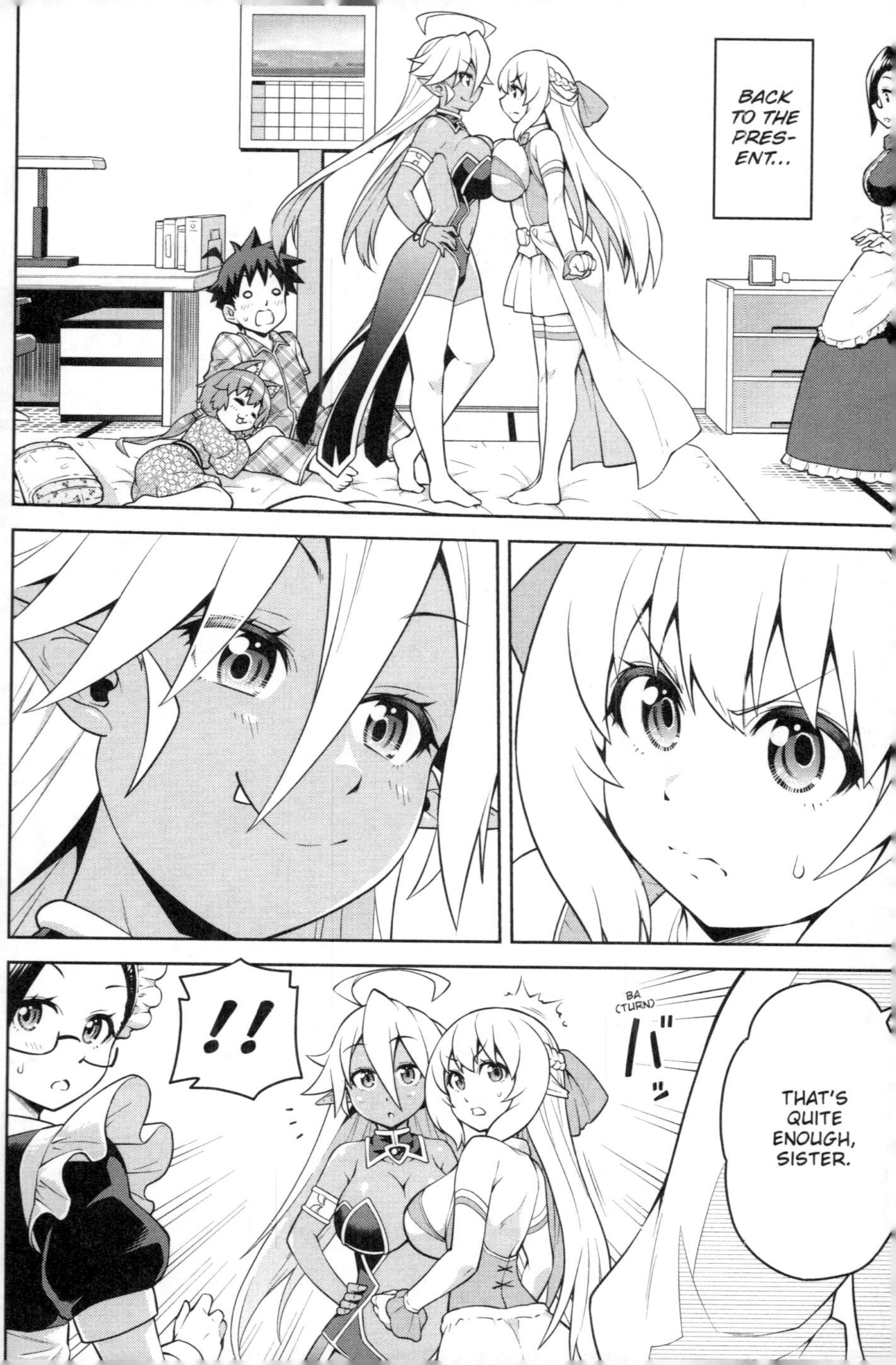
BACK TO THE PRES-ENT...
THAT'S QUITE ENOUGH, SISTER.
BA (TURN)
!!

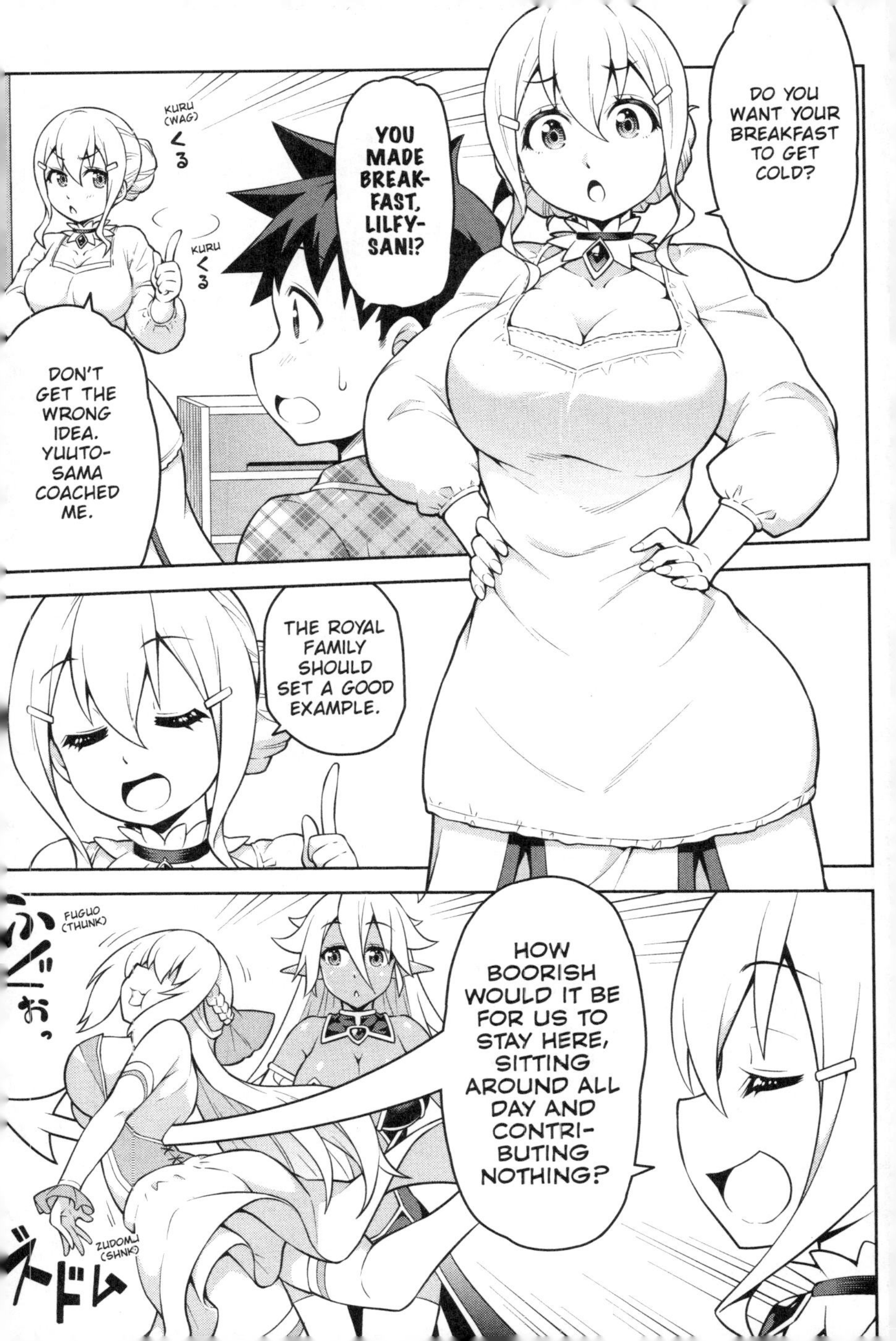
DO YOU WANT YOUR BREAKFAST TO GET COLD?
YOU MADE BREAKFAST, LILFY-SAN!?
KURU (WAG)
くる
KURU
くる
DON'T GET THE WRONG IDEA. YUUTO-SAMA COACHED ME.
THE ROYAL FAMILY SHOULD SET A GOOD EXAMPLE.
HOW BOORISH WOULD IT BE FOR US TO STAY HERE, SITTING AROUND ALL DAY AND CONTRI-BUTING NOTHING?
FUGUO (THUNK)
ふぐぉっ
ZUDOMU (SHNK)
ズドム

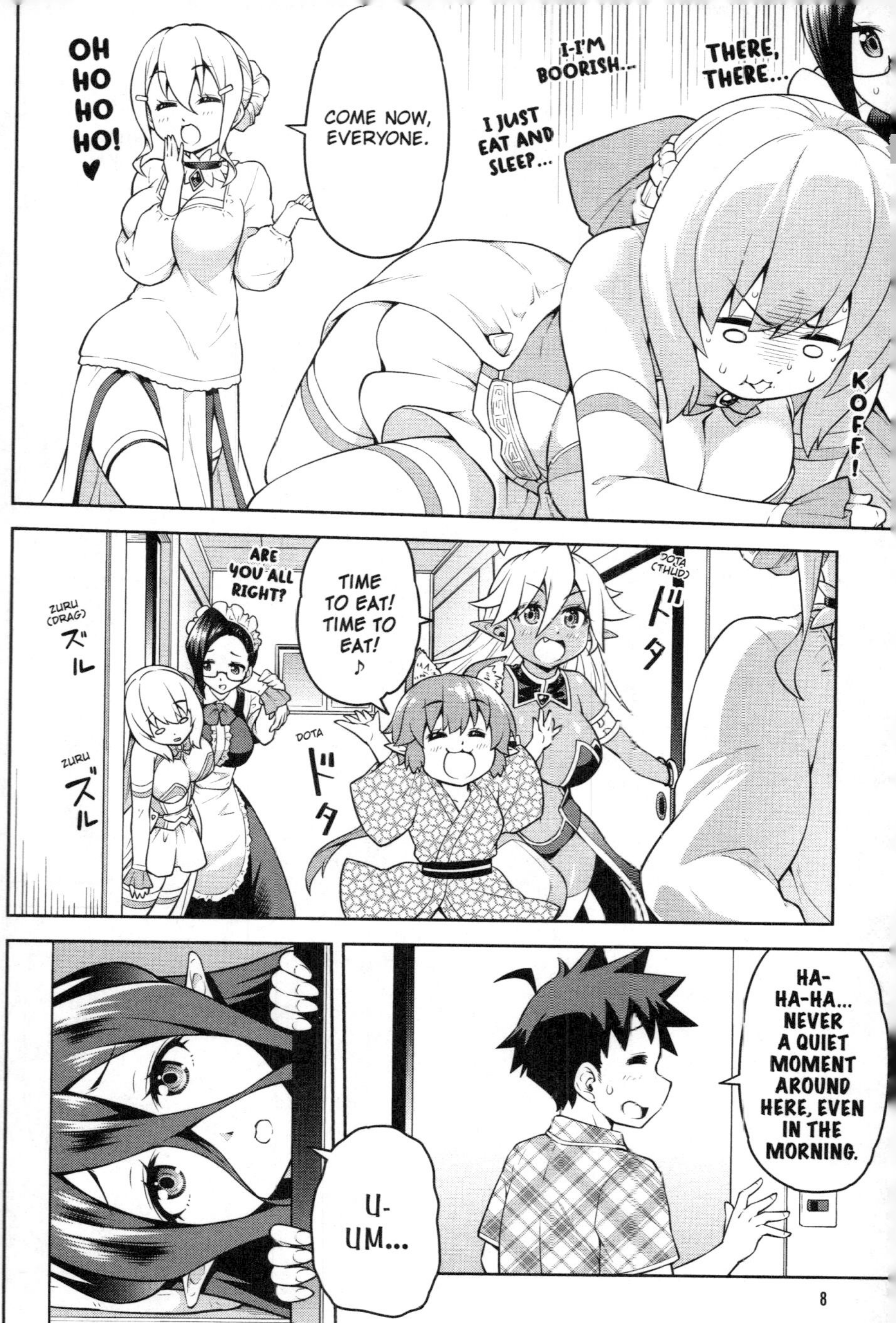
THERE, THERE...
I-I'M BOORISH...
I JUST EAT AND SLEEP...
KOFF!
COME NOW, EVERYONE.
OH HO HO HO! ♥
DOTA (THUD)
ドタ
TIME TO EAT! TIME TO EAT! ♪
DOTA
ドタ
ARE YOU ALL RIGHT?
ZURU (DRAG)
ズル
ZURU
ズル
HA-HA-HA... NEVER A QUIET MOMENT AROUND HERE, EVEN IN THE MORNING.
U-UM...

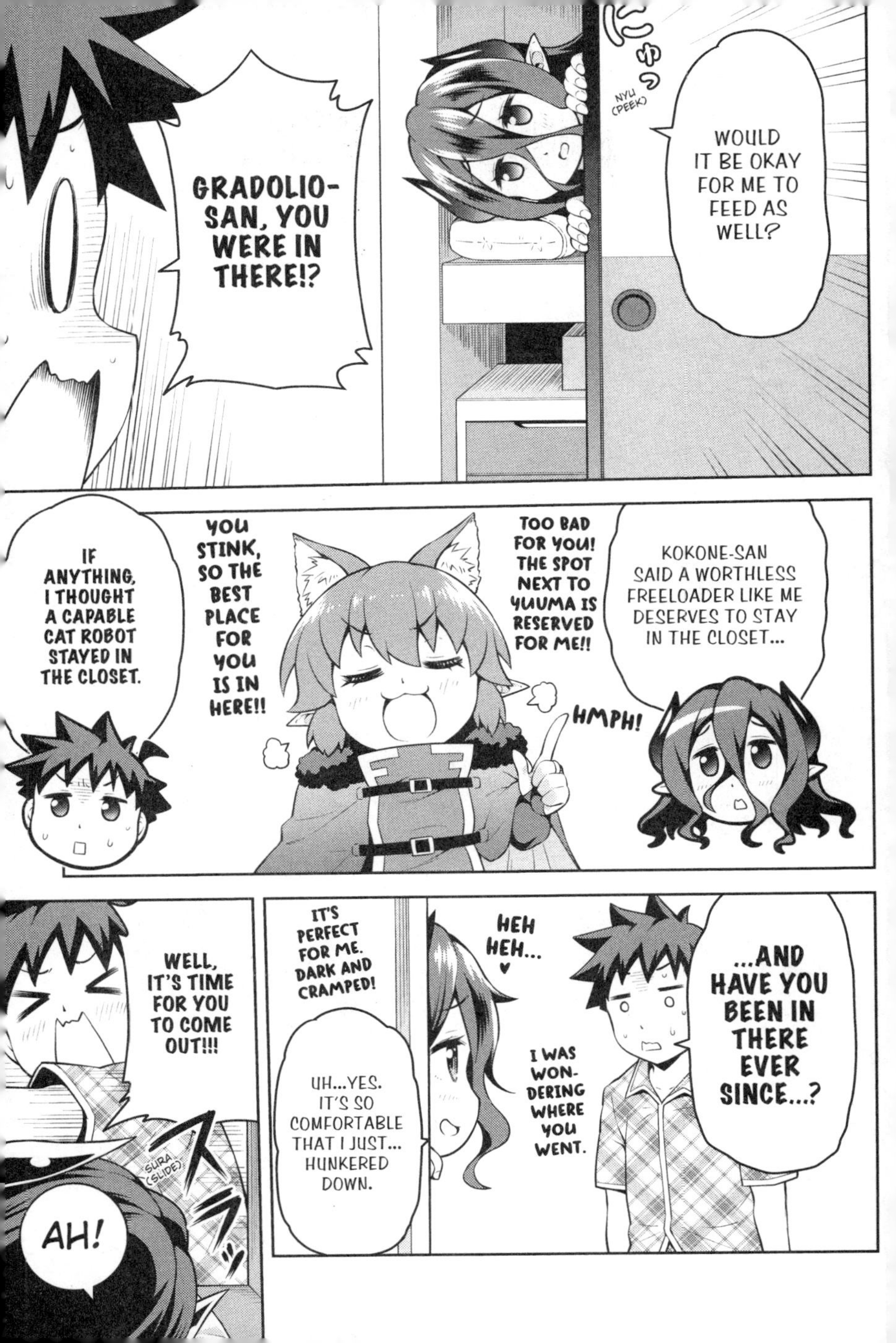
にゅっ
NYU (PEEK)
WOULD IT BE OKAY FOR ME TO FEED AS WELL?
GRADOLIO-SAN, YOU WERE IN THERE!?
KOKONE-SAN SAID A WORTHLESS FREELOADER LIKE ME DESERVES TO STAY IN THE CLOSET...
HMPH!
TOO BAD FOR YOU! THE SPOT NEXT TO YUUMA IS RESERVED FOR ME!!
YOU STINK, SO THE BEST PLACE FOR YOU IS IN HERE!!
IF ANYTHING, I THOUGHT A CAPABLE CAT ROBOT STAYED IN THE CLOSET.
...AND HAVE YOU BEEN IN THERE EVER SINCE...?
I WAS WONDERING WHERE YOU WENT.
HEH HEH...♥
UH...YES. IT'S SO COMFORTABLE THAT I JUST... HUNKERED DOWN.
IT'S PERFECT FOR ME. DARK AND CRAMPED!
WELL, IT'S TIME FOR YOU TO COME OUT!!!
SURA (SLIDE)
AH!

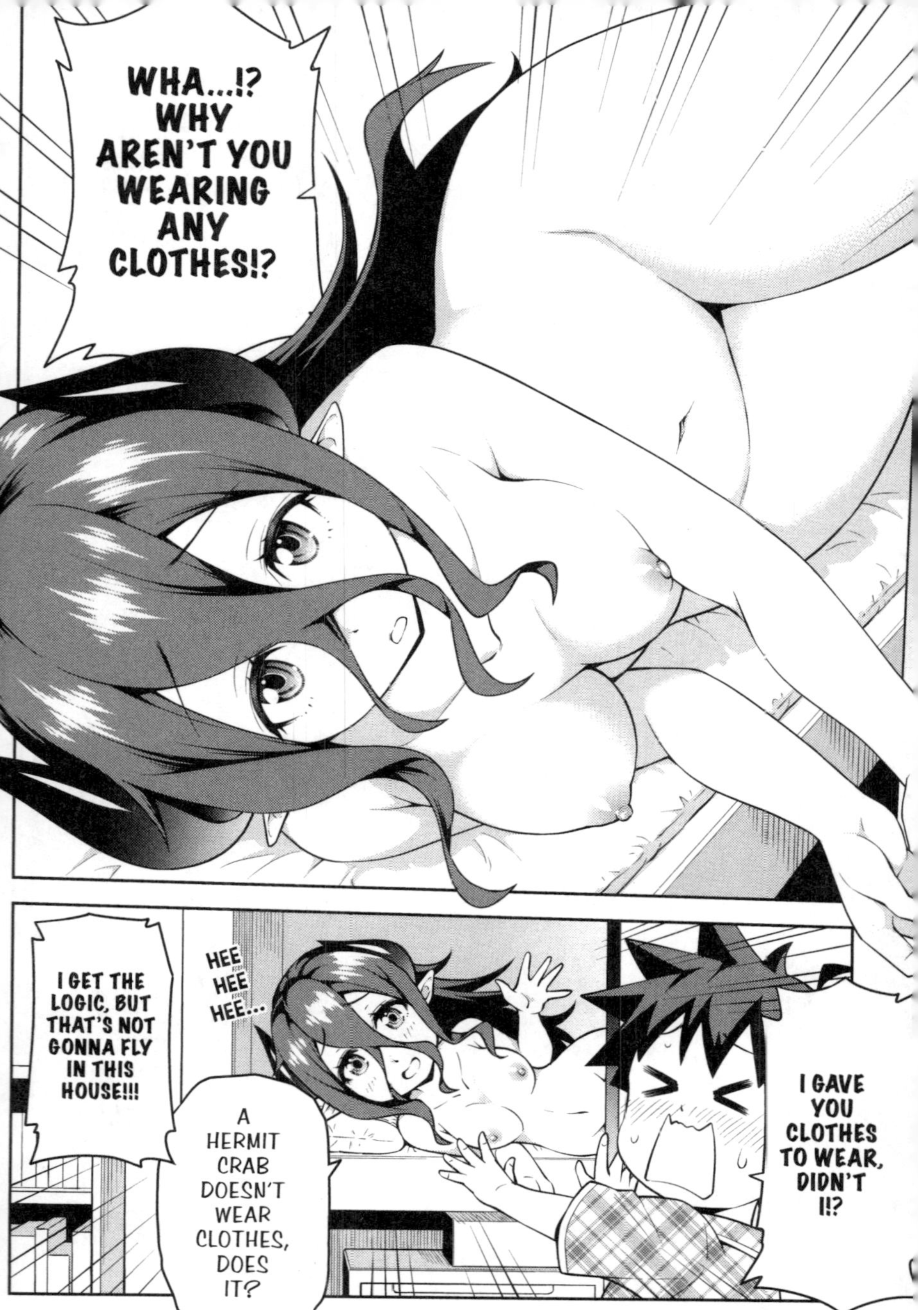
WHA...!? WHY AREN'T YOU WEARING ANY CLOTHES!?
I GAVE YOU CLOTHES TO WEAR, DIDN'T I!?
HEE HEE HEE...
A HERMIT CRAB DOESN'T WEAR CLOTHES, DOES IT?
I GET THE LOGIC, BUT THAT'S NOT GONNA FLY IN THIS HOUSE!!!

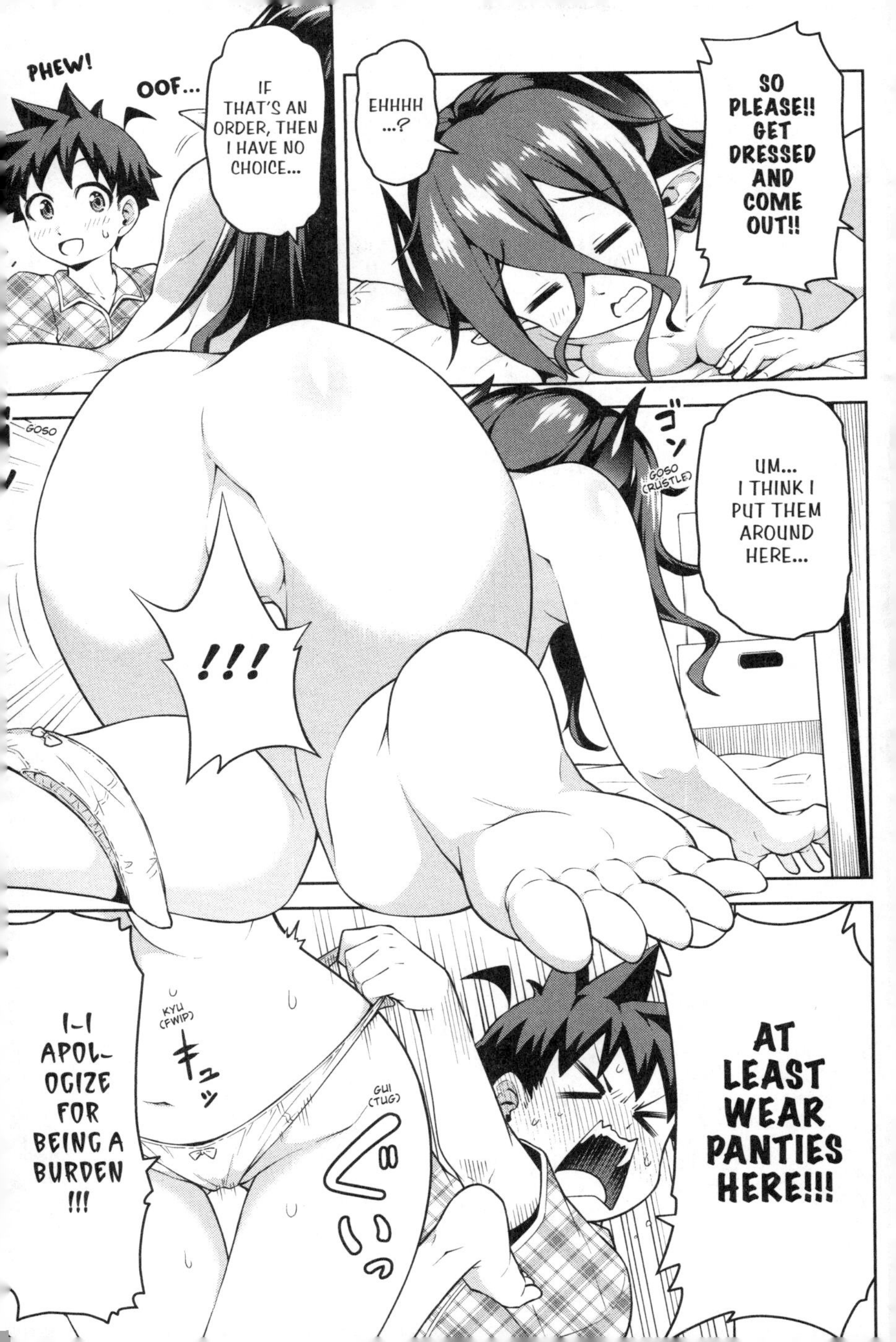
SO PLEASE!! GET DRESSED AND COME OUT!!
EHHHH ...?
IF THAT'S AN ORDER, THEN I HAVE NO CHOICE...
OOF...
PHEW!
ゴン
GOSO (RUSTLE)
UM... I THINK I PUT THEM AROUND HERE...
GOSO
!!!
AT LEAST WEAR PANTIES HERE!!!
GUI (TUG)
KYU (FWIP)
キュッ
I-I APOLOGIZE FOR BEING A BURDEN!!!

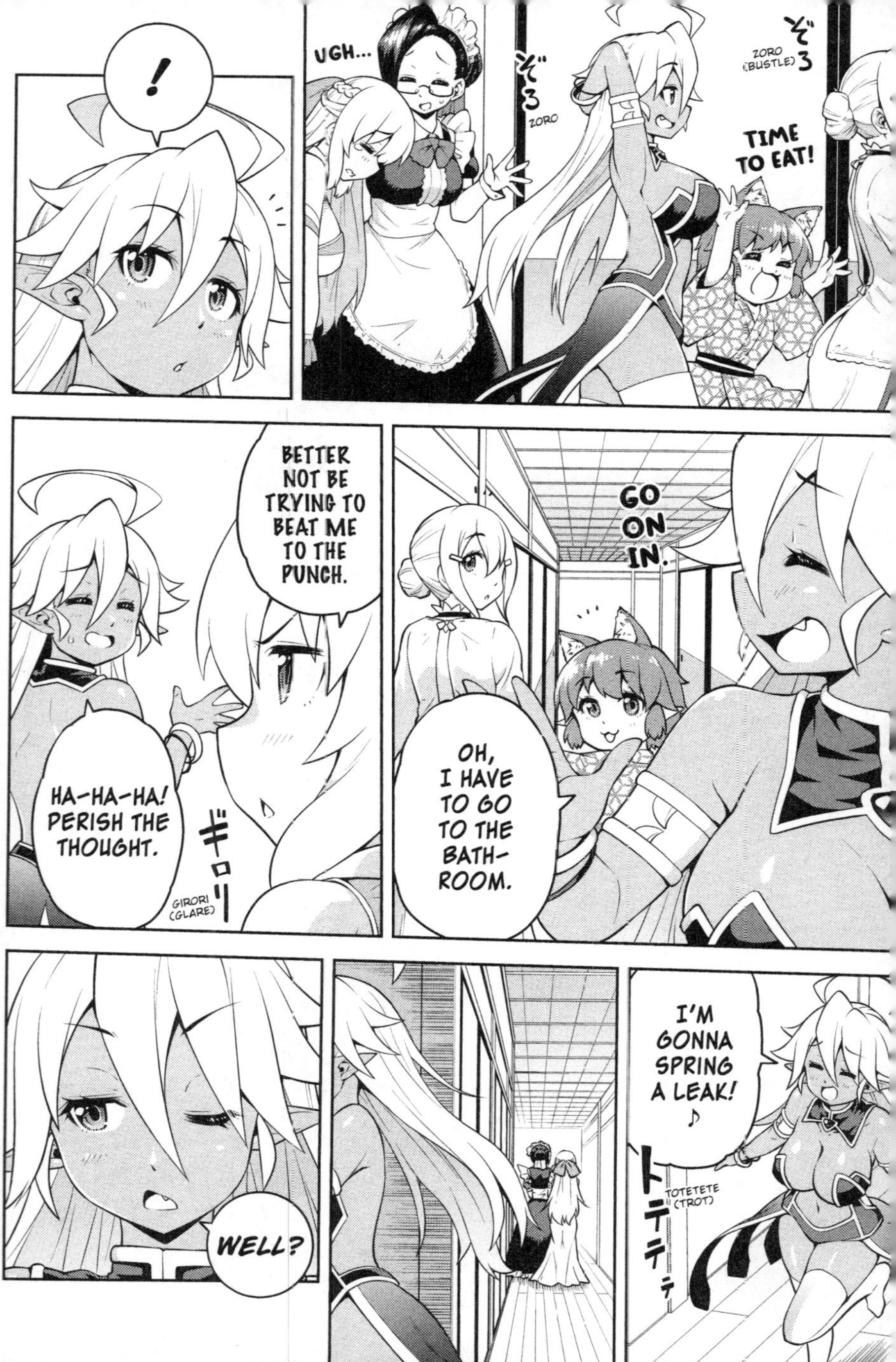
ぞろ
ZORO (BUSTLE)
TIME TO EAT!
ぞろ
ZORO
UGH...
!
GO ON IN.
OH, I HAVE TO GO TO THE BATH-ROOM.
BETTER NOT BE TRYING TO BEAT ME TO THE PUNCH.
HA-HA-HA! PERISH THE THOUGHT.
ギロリ
GIRORI (GLARE)
I'M GONNA SPRING A LEAK! ♪
トテテテ
TOTETETE (TROT)
WELL?

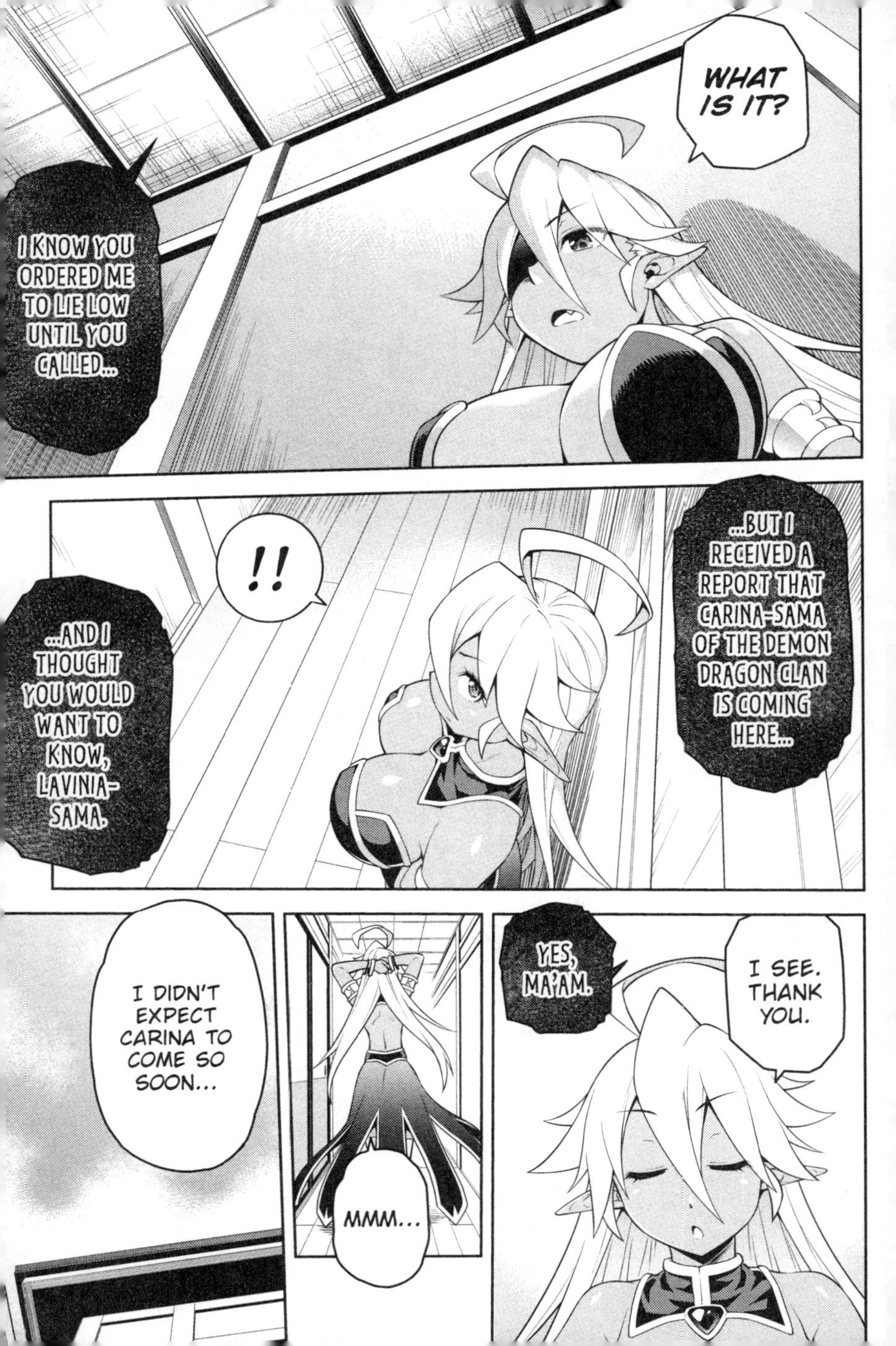
WHAT IS IT?
I KNOW YOU ORDERED ME TO LIE LOW UNTIL YOU CALLED...
...BUT I RECEIVED A REPORT THAT CARINA-SAMA OF THE DEMON DRAGON CLAN IS COMING HERE...
!!
...AND I THOUGHT YOU WOULD WANT TO KNOW, LAVINIA-SAMA.
I SEE. THANK YOU.
YES, MA'AM.
MMM...
I DIDN'T EXPECT CARINA TO COME SO SOON...

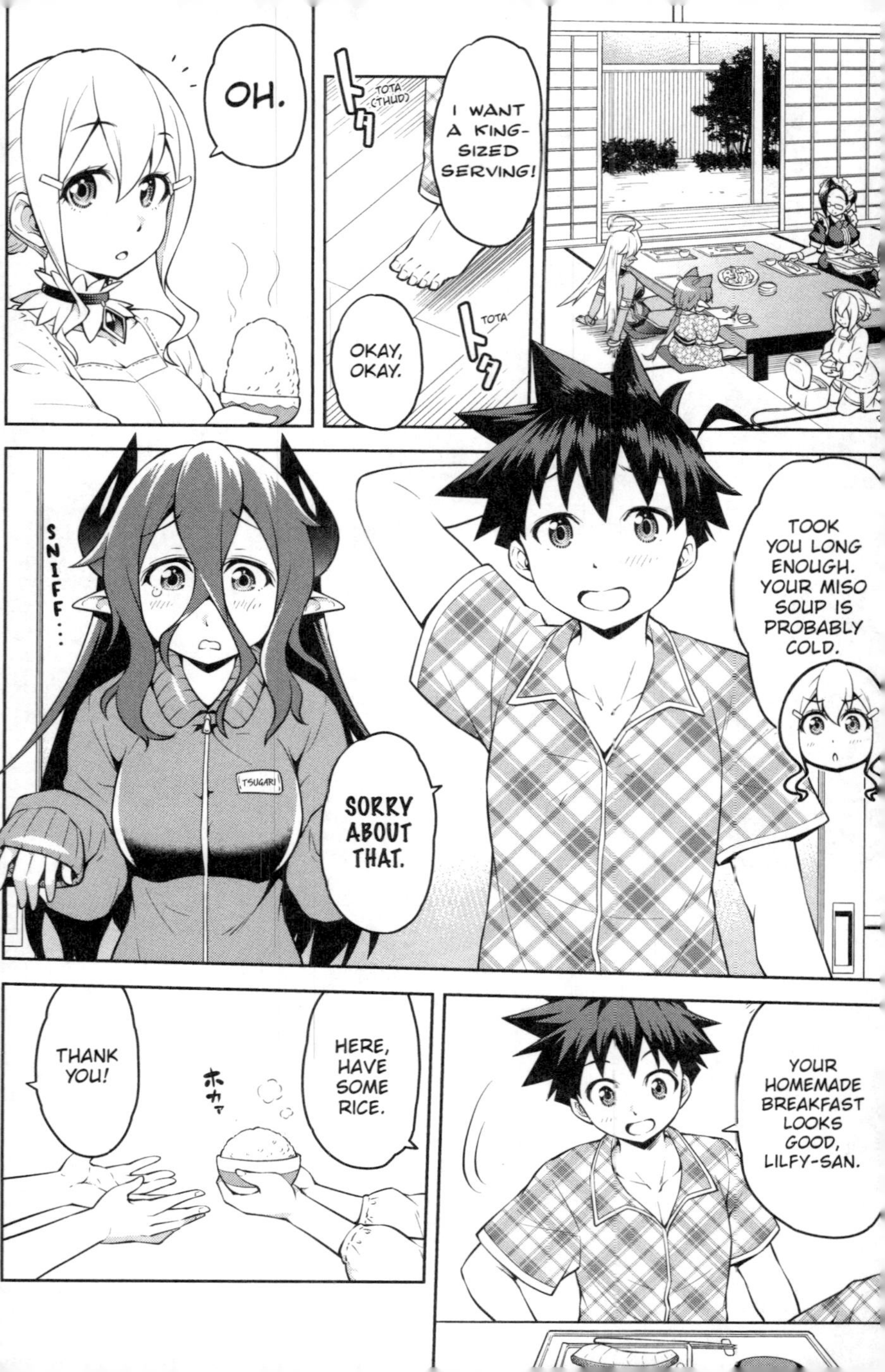
トタ
TOTA (THUD)
I WANT A KING-SIZED SERVING!
トタ
TOTA
OKAY, OKAY.
OH.
TOOK YOU LONG ENOUGH. YOUR MISO SOUP IS PROBABLY COLD.
SORRY ABOUT THAT.
TSUGARI
SNIFF...
YOUR HOMEMADE BREAKFAST LOOKS GOOD, LILFY-SAN.
HERE, HAVE SOME RICE.
ホカァ
THANK YOU!

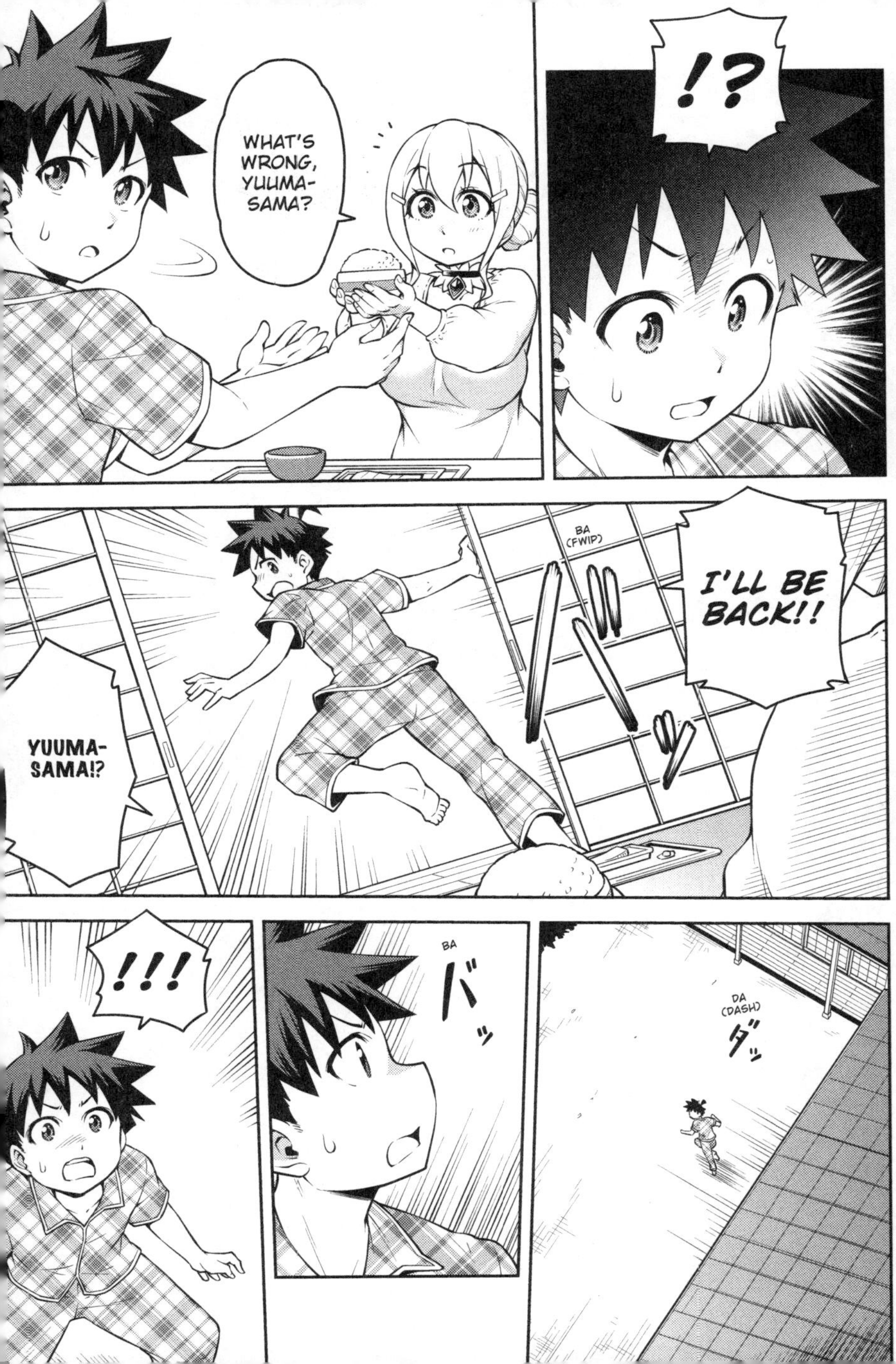
!?
WHAT'S WRONG, YUUMA-SAMA?
I'LL BE BACK!!
BA (FWIP)
YUUMA-SAMA!?
DA (DASH)
ダッ
BA
バッ
!!!

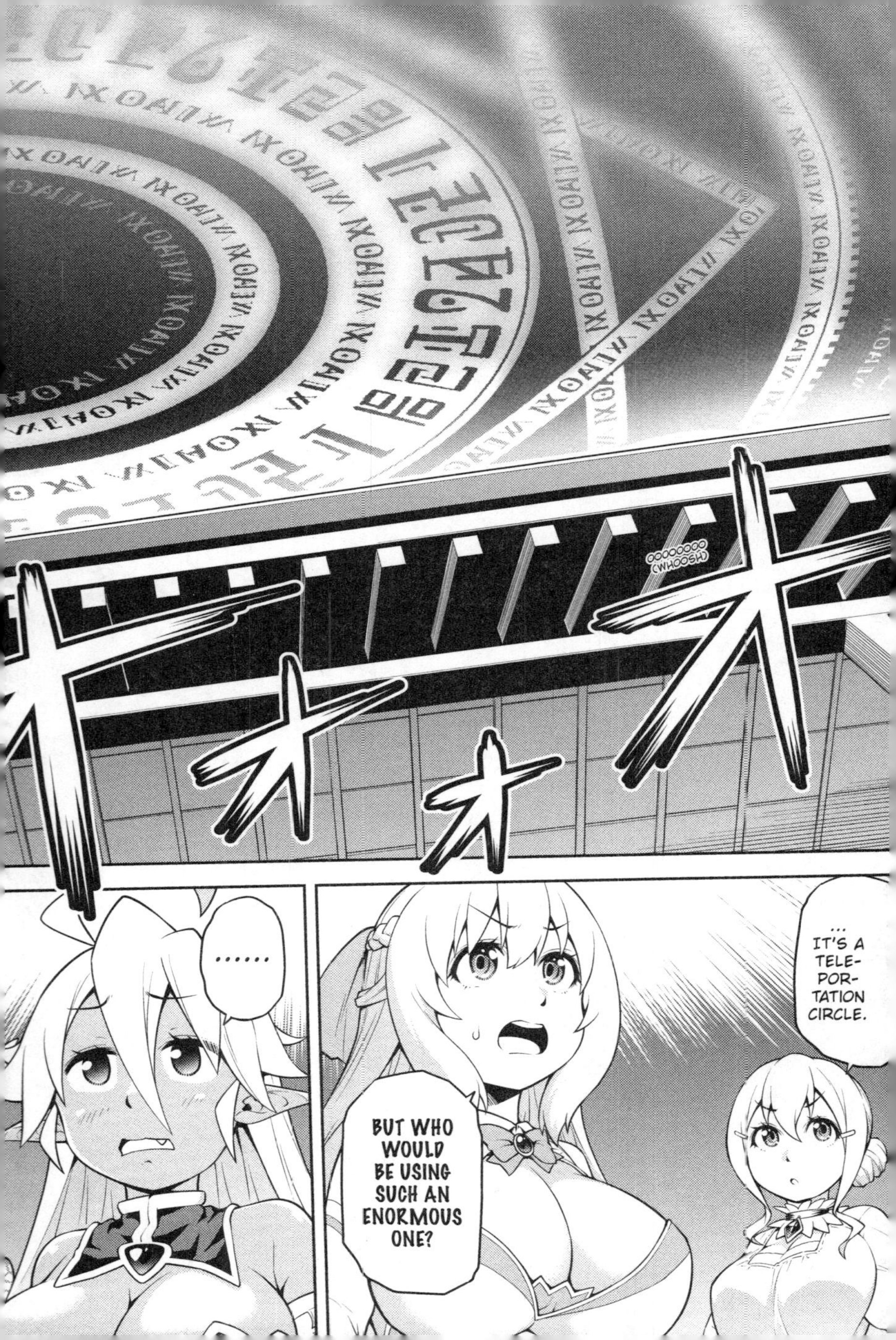
OOOOOOOO
(WHOOSH)
... IT'S A TELE-POR-TATION CIRCLE.
BUT WHO WOULD BE USING SUCH AN ENORMOUS ONE?
......

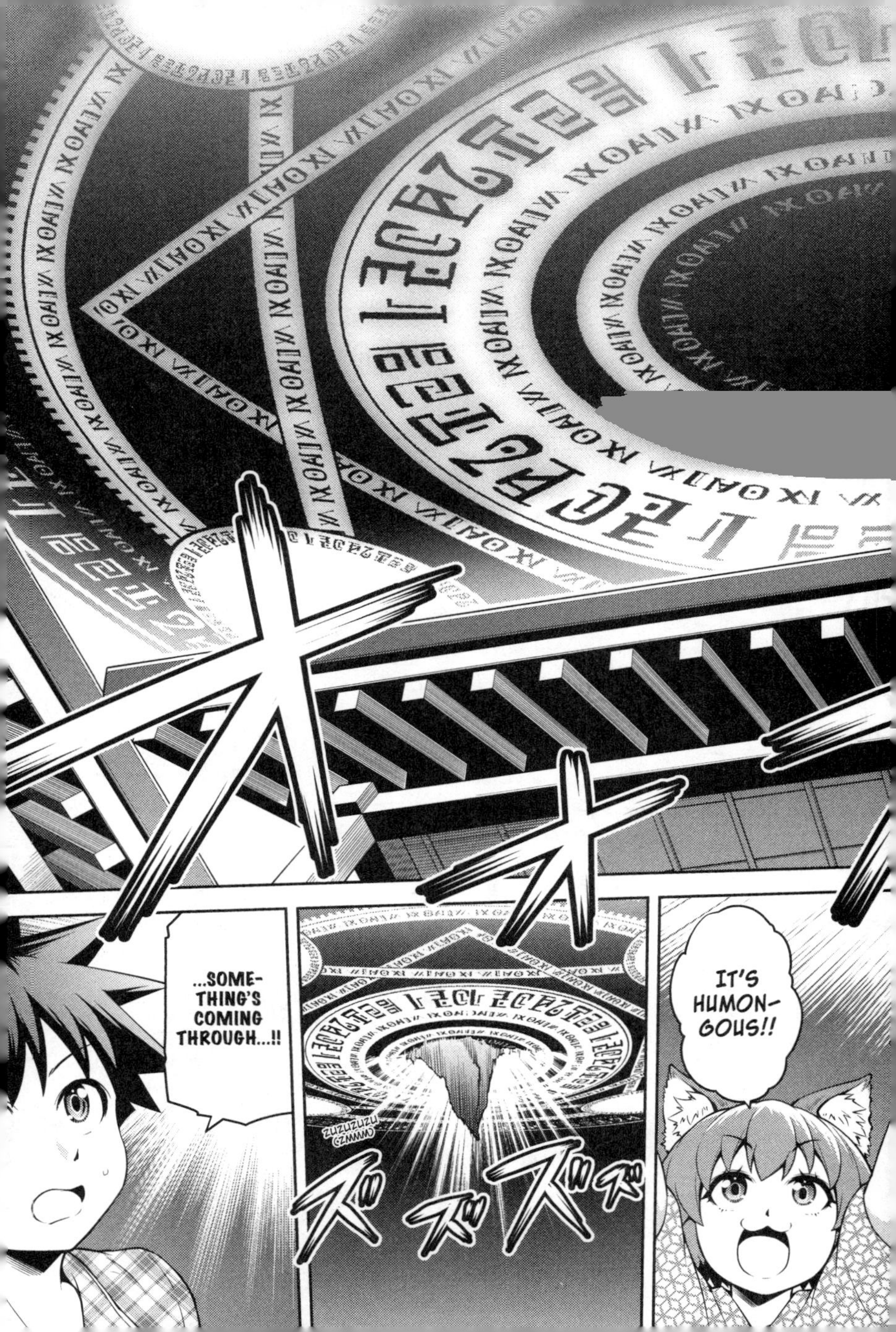
IT'S HUMON-GOUS!!
ZUZUZUZU (ZMMMM)
...SOME-THING'S COMING THROUGH...!!

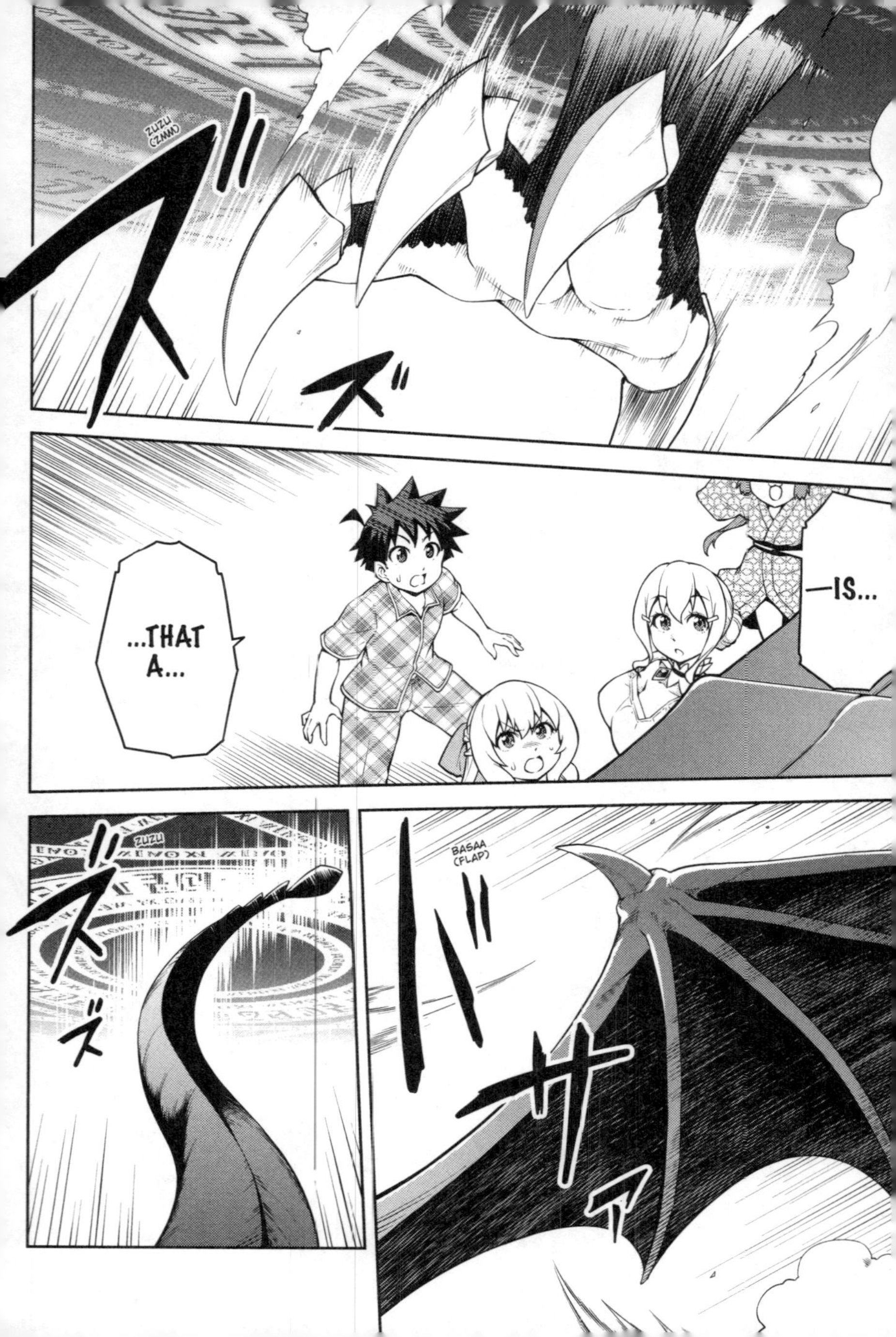
ZUZU (ZMM)
—IS...
...THAT A...
BASAA (FLAP)
ZUZU

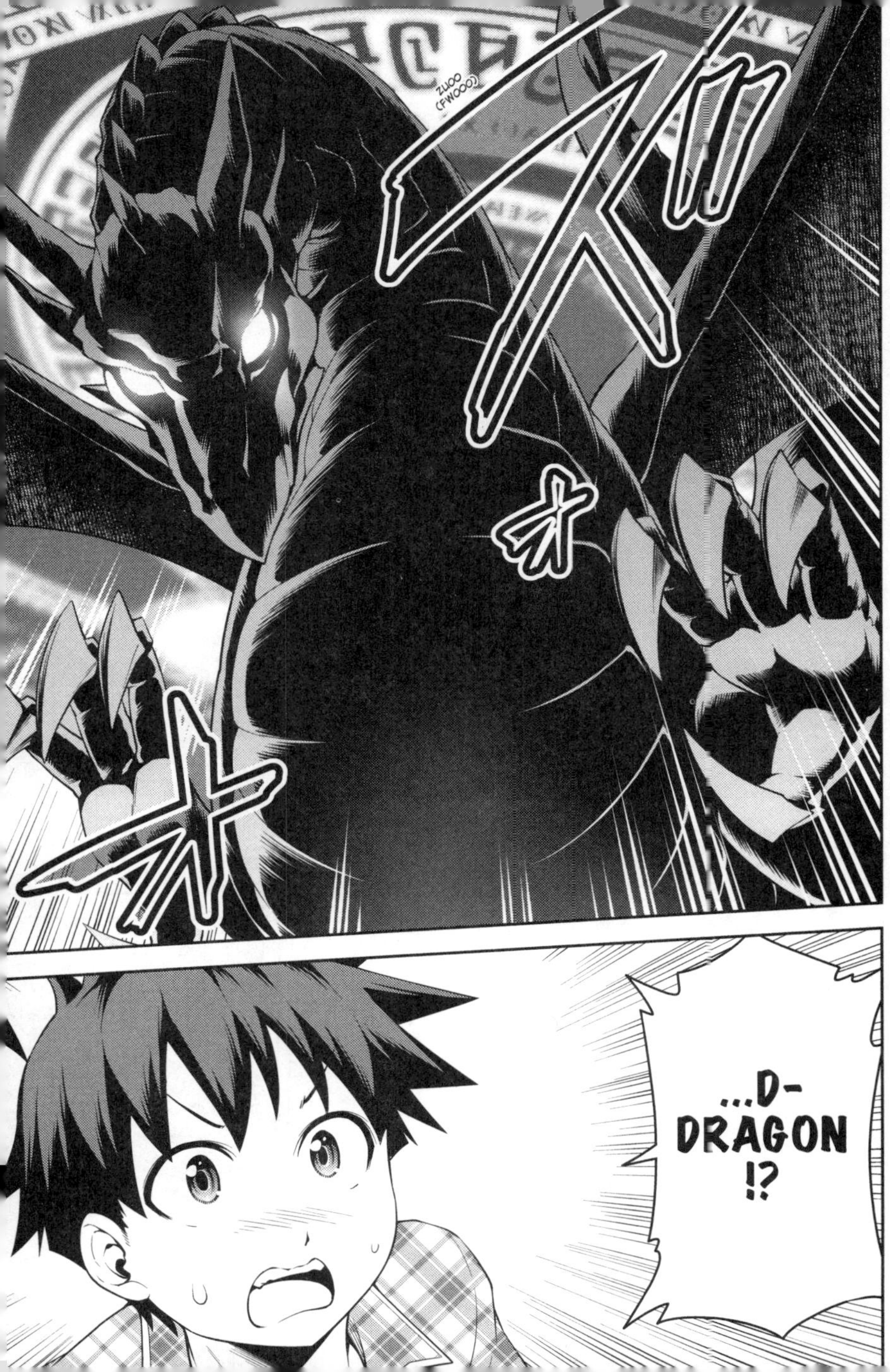
ZUOO
(FWOOO)
...D-
DRAGON
!?

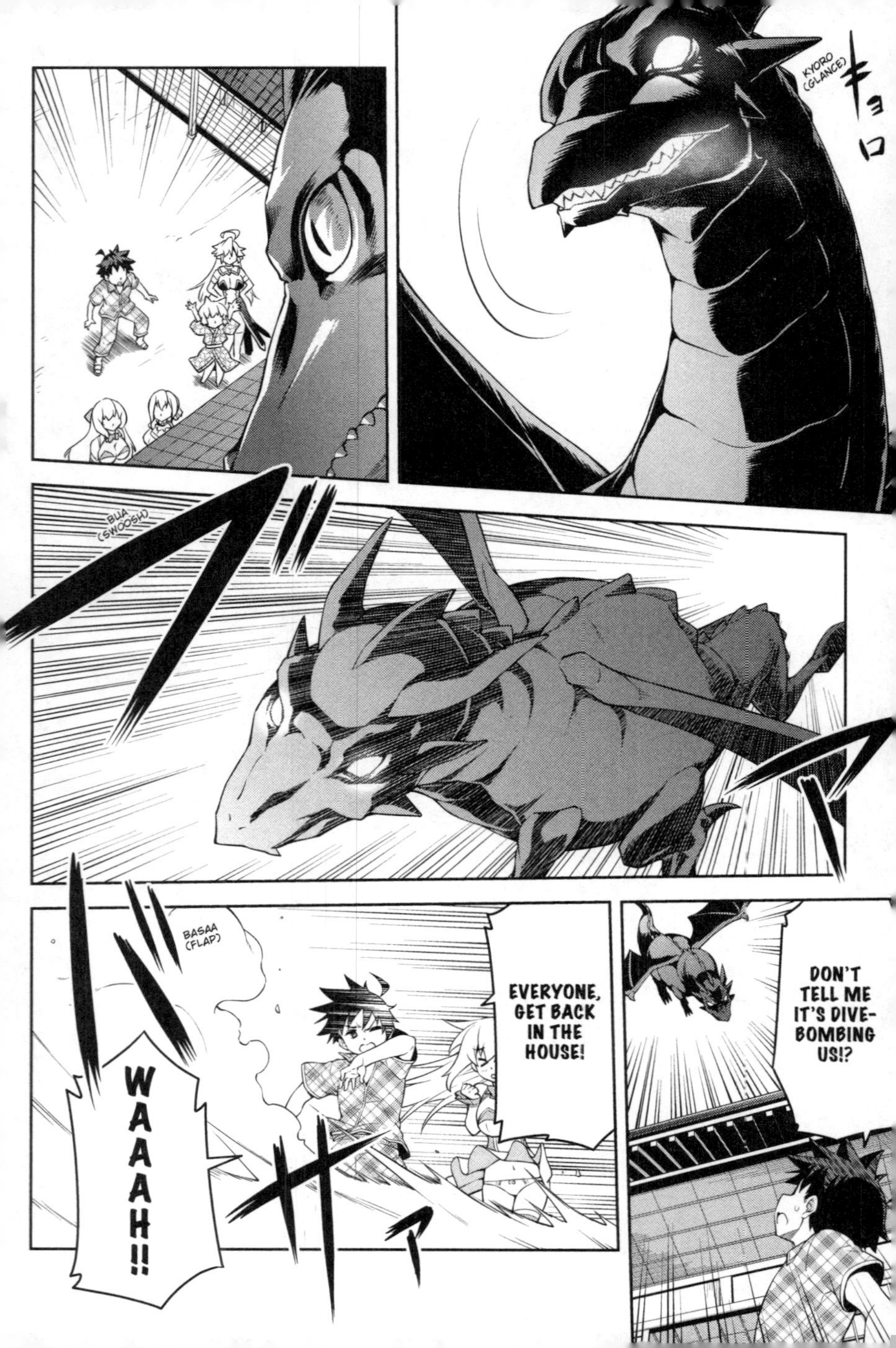
キョロ
KYORO (GLANCE)
BUA (SWOOSH)
DON'T TELL ME IT'S DIVE-BOMBING US!?
EVERYONE, GET BACK IN THE HOUSE!
BASAA (FLAP)
WAAAAH!!

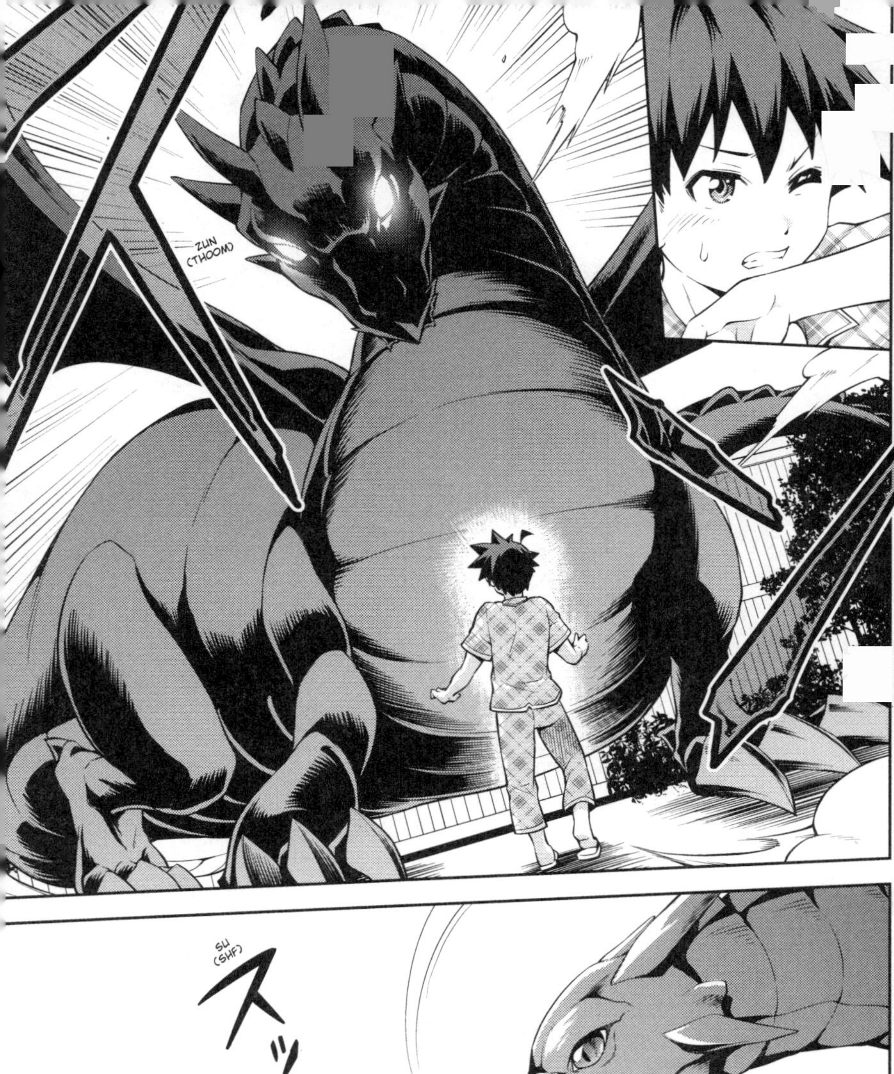
ZUN
(THOOM)
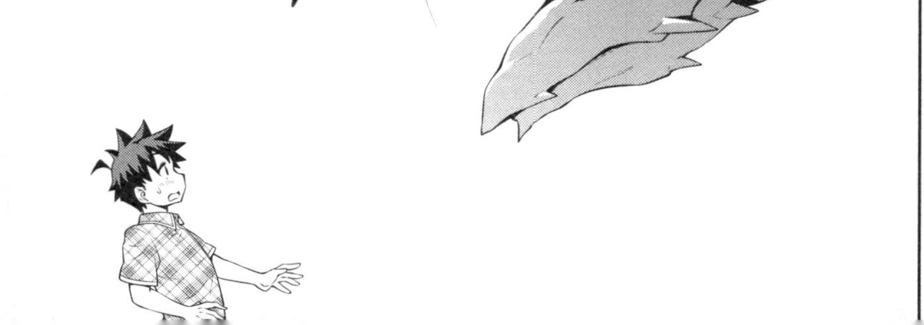
SU
(SHF)
スッ

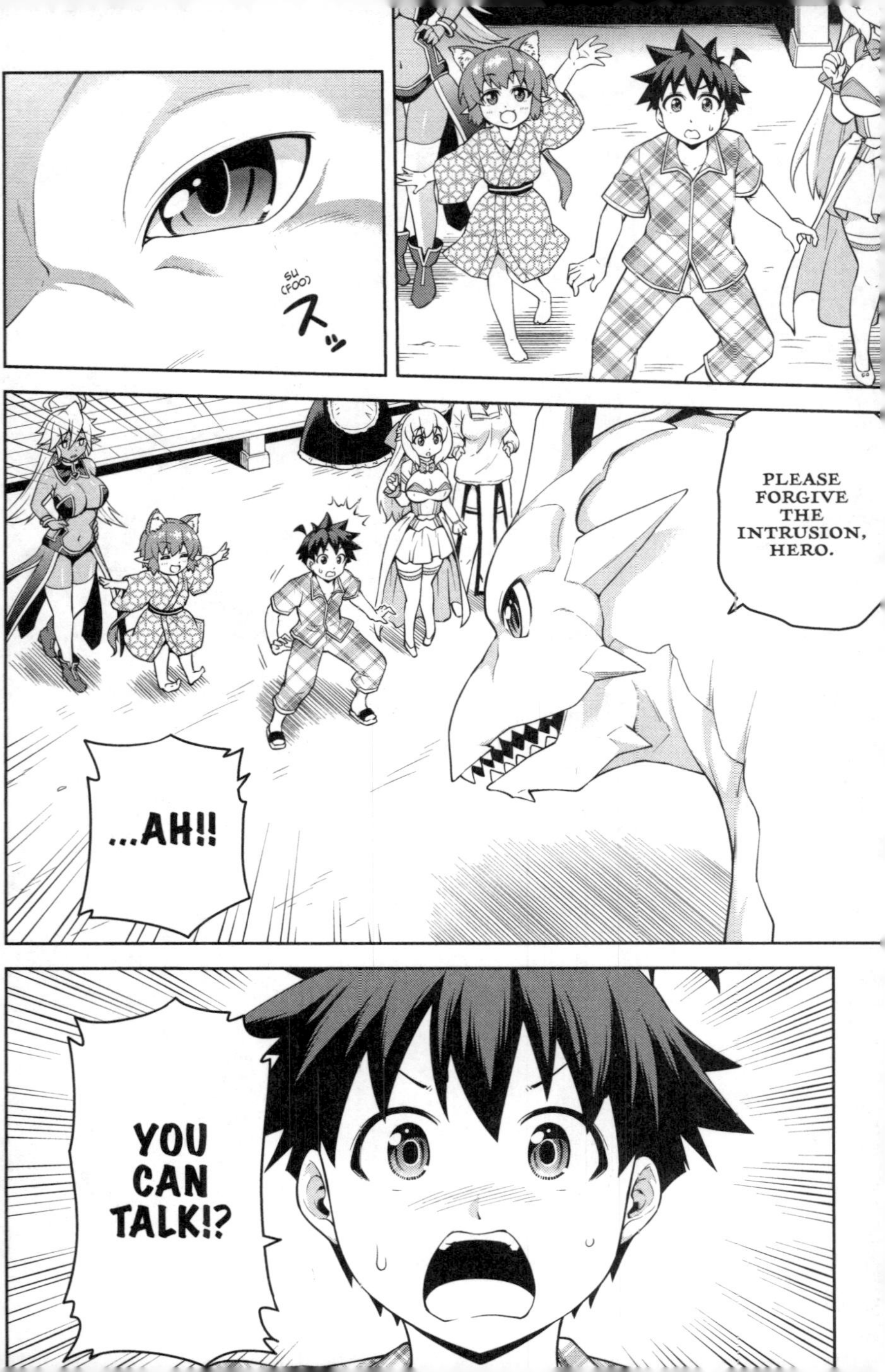
SU (FOO)
スッ
PLEASE FORGIVE THE INTRUSION, HERO.
...AH!!
YOU CAN TALK!?

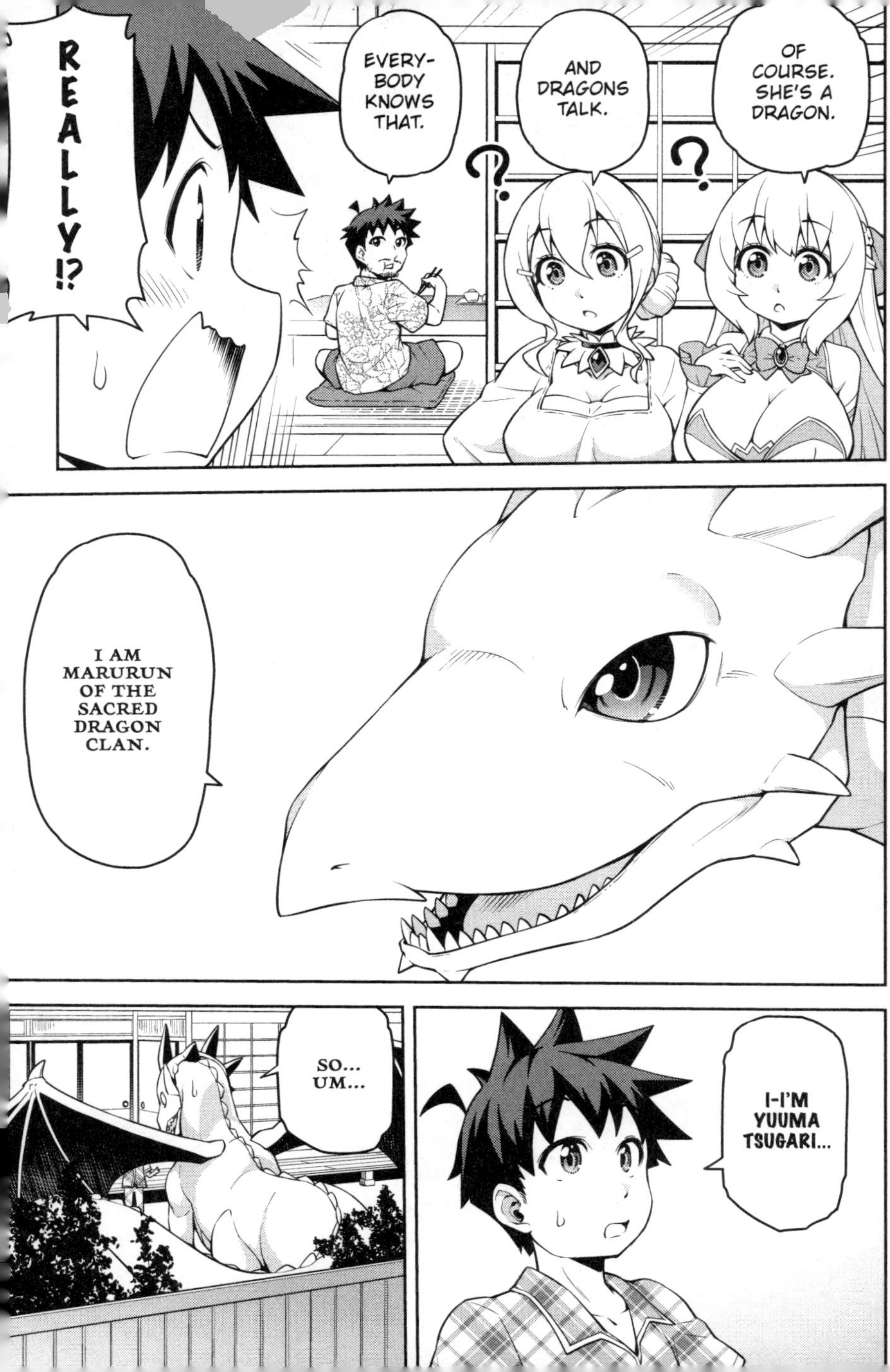
OF COURSE. SHE'S A DRAGON.
AND DRAGONS TALK.
EVERY-BODY KNOWS THAT.
REALLY!?
I AM MARURUN OF THE SACRED DRAGON CLAN.
I-I'M YUUMA TSUGARI...
SO... UM...

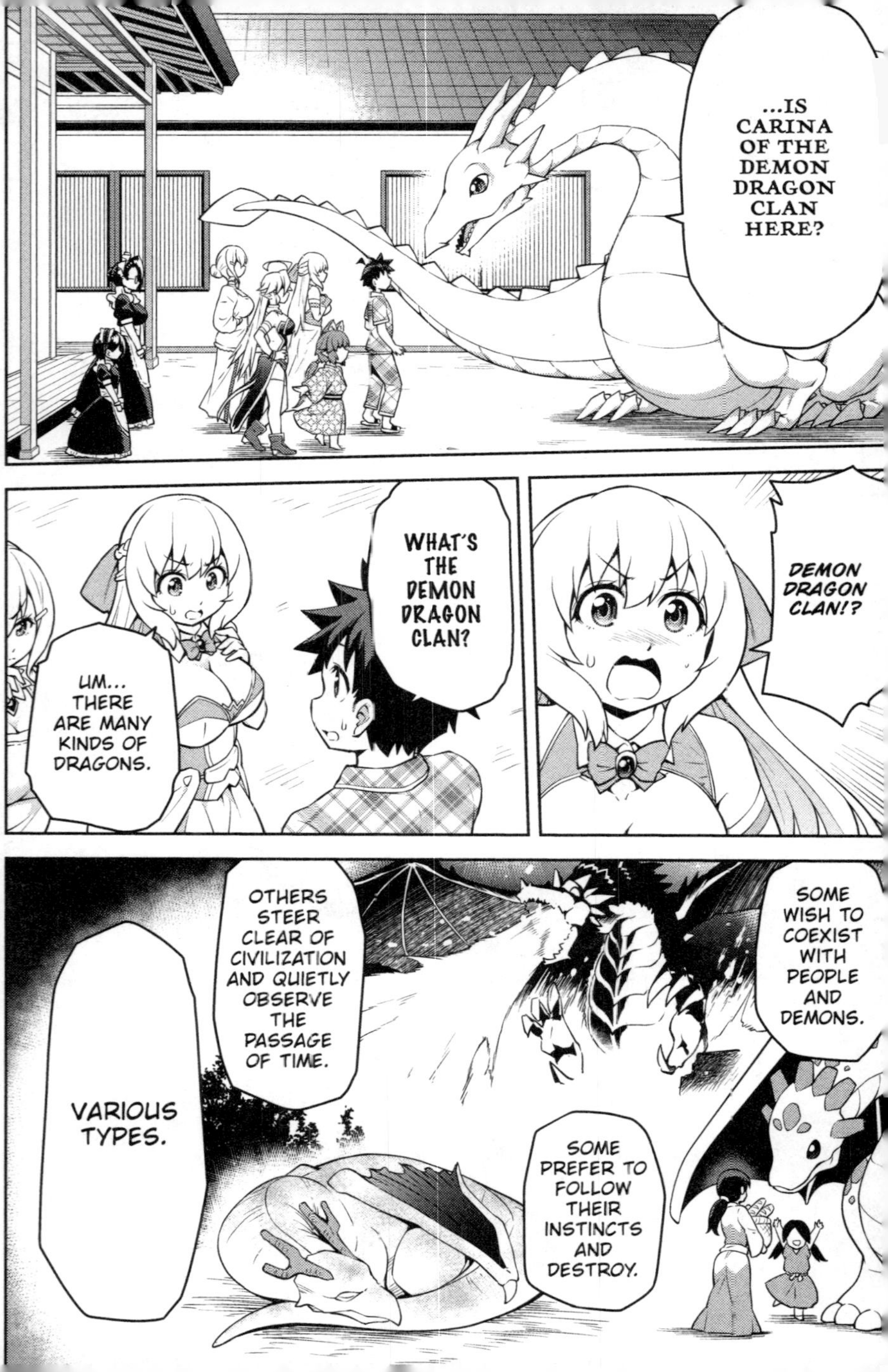
...IS CARINA OF THE DEMON DRAGON CLAN HERE?
DEMON DRAGON CLAN!?
WHAT'S THE DEMON DRAGON CLAN?
UM... THERE ARE MANY KINDS OF DRAGONS.
SOME WISH TO COEXIST WITH PEOPLE AND DEMONS.
OTHERS STEER CLEAR OF CIVILIZATION AND QUIETLY OBSERVE THE PASSAGE OF TIME.
SOME PREFER TO FOLLOW THEIR INSTINCTS AND DESTROY.
VARIOUS TYPES.

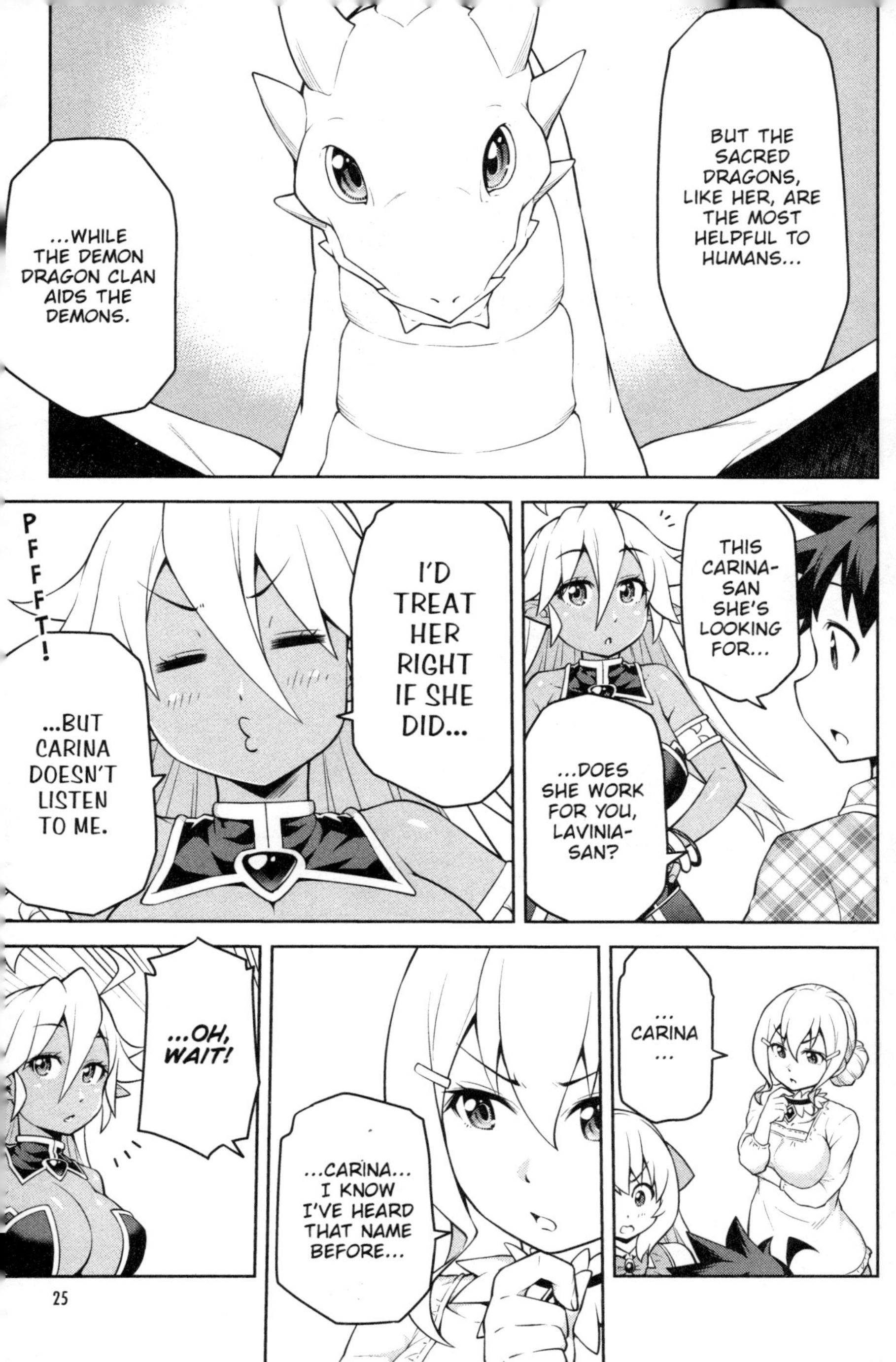
BUT THE SACRED DRAGONS, LIKE HER, ARE THE MOST HELPFUL TO HUMANS...
...WHILE THE DEMON DRAGON CLAN AIDS THE DEMONS.
THIS CARINA-SAN SHE'S LOOKING FOR...
...DOES SHE WORK FOR YOU, LAVINIA-SAN?
I'D TREAT HER RIGHT IF SHE DID...
PFFFT!
...BUT CARINA DOESN'T LISTEN TO ME.
... CARINA ...
...CARINA... I KNOW I'VE HEARD THAT NAME BEFORE...
...OH, WAIT!

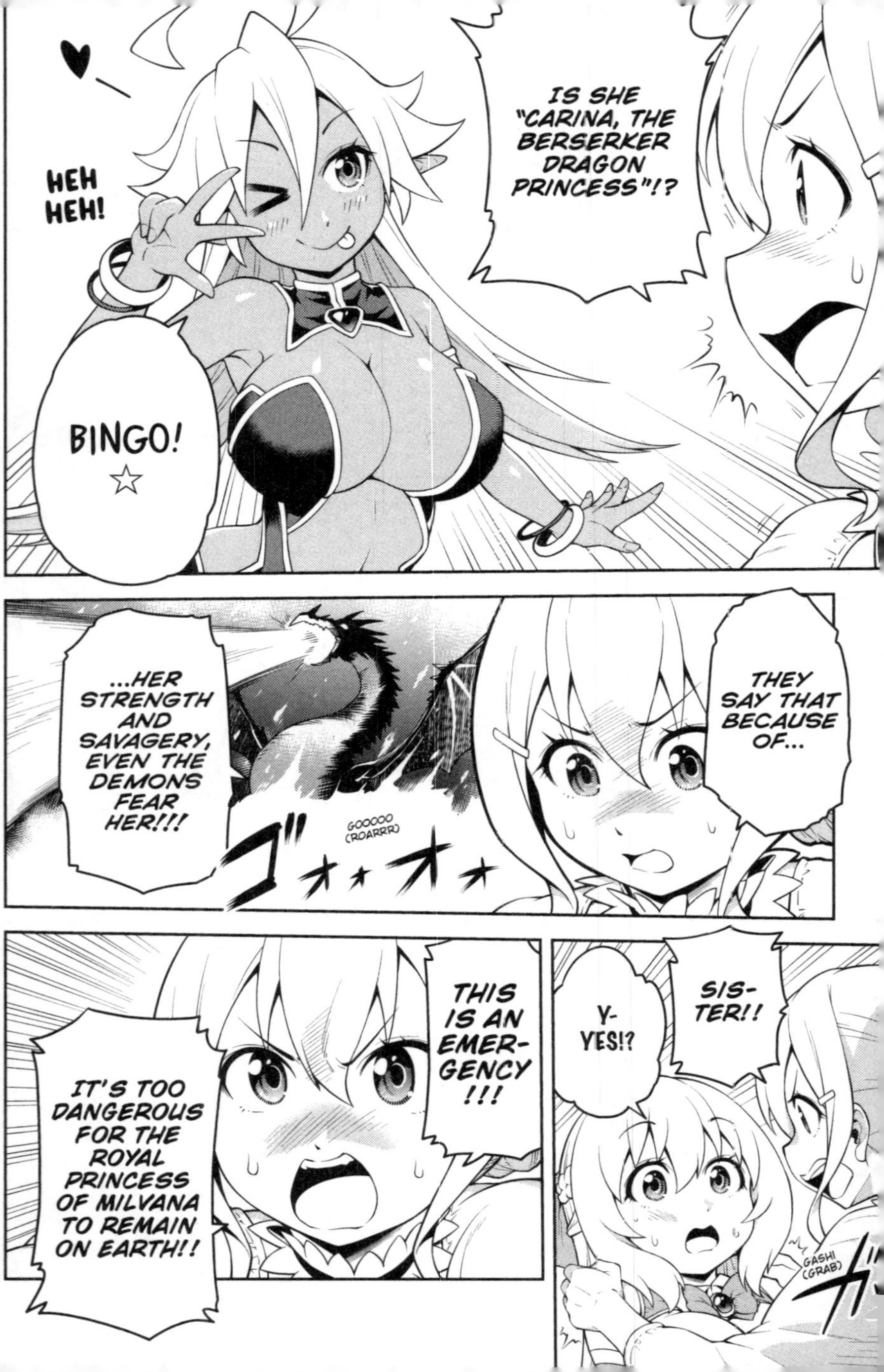
IS SHE "CARINA, THE BERSERKER DRAGON PRINCESS"!?
HEH HEH!
BINGO! ☆
THEY SAY THAT BECAUSE OF...
...HER STRENGTH AND SAVAGERY, EVEN THE DEMONS FEAR HER!!!
GOOOOO (ROARRR)
SIS-TER!!
Y-YES!?
GASHI (GRAB)
THIS IS AN EMERGENCY!!!
IT'S TOO DANGEROUS FOR THE ROYAL PRINCESS OF MILVANA TO REMAIN ON EARTH!!

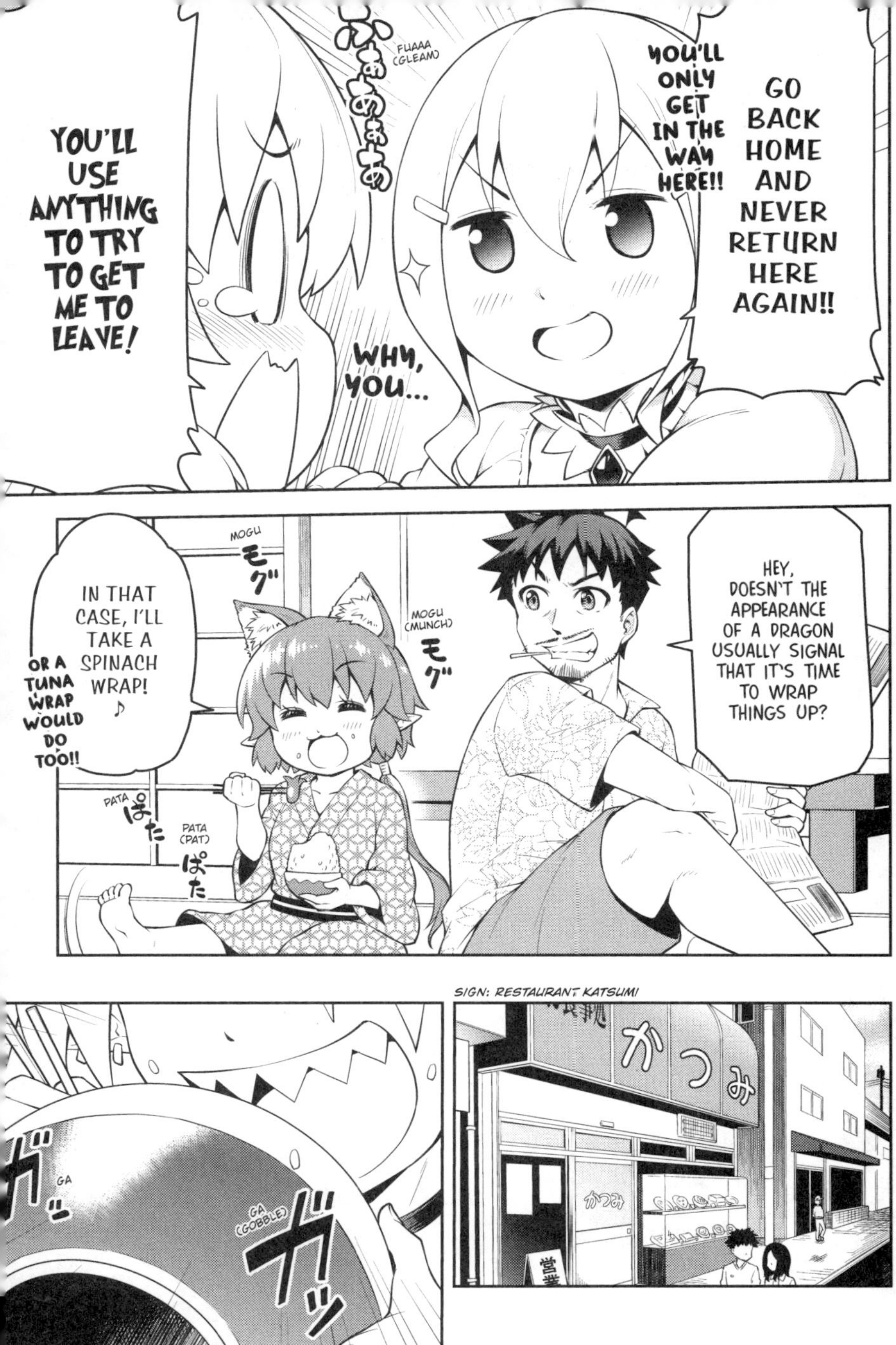
GO BACK HOME AND NEVER RETURN HERE AGAIN!!
YOU'LL ONLY GET IN THE WAY HERE!!
FUAAA (GLEAM)
WHY, YOU...
YOU'LL USE ANYTHING TO TRY TO GET ME TO LEAVE!
HEY, DOESN'T THE APPEARANCE OF A DRAGON USUALLY SIGNAL THAT IT'S TIME TO WRAP THINGS UP?
MOGU (MUNCH)
MOGU
IN THAT CASE, I'LL TAKE A SPINACH WRAP! ♪
OR A TUNA WRAP WOULD DO TOO!!
PATA (PAT)
PATA
SIGN: RESTAURANT KATSUMI
GA (GOBBLE)
GA

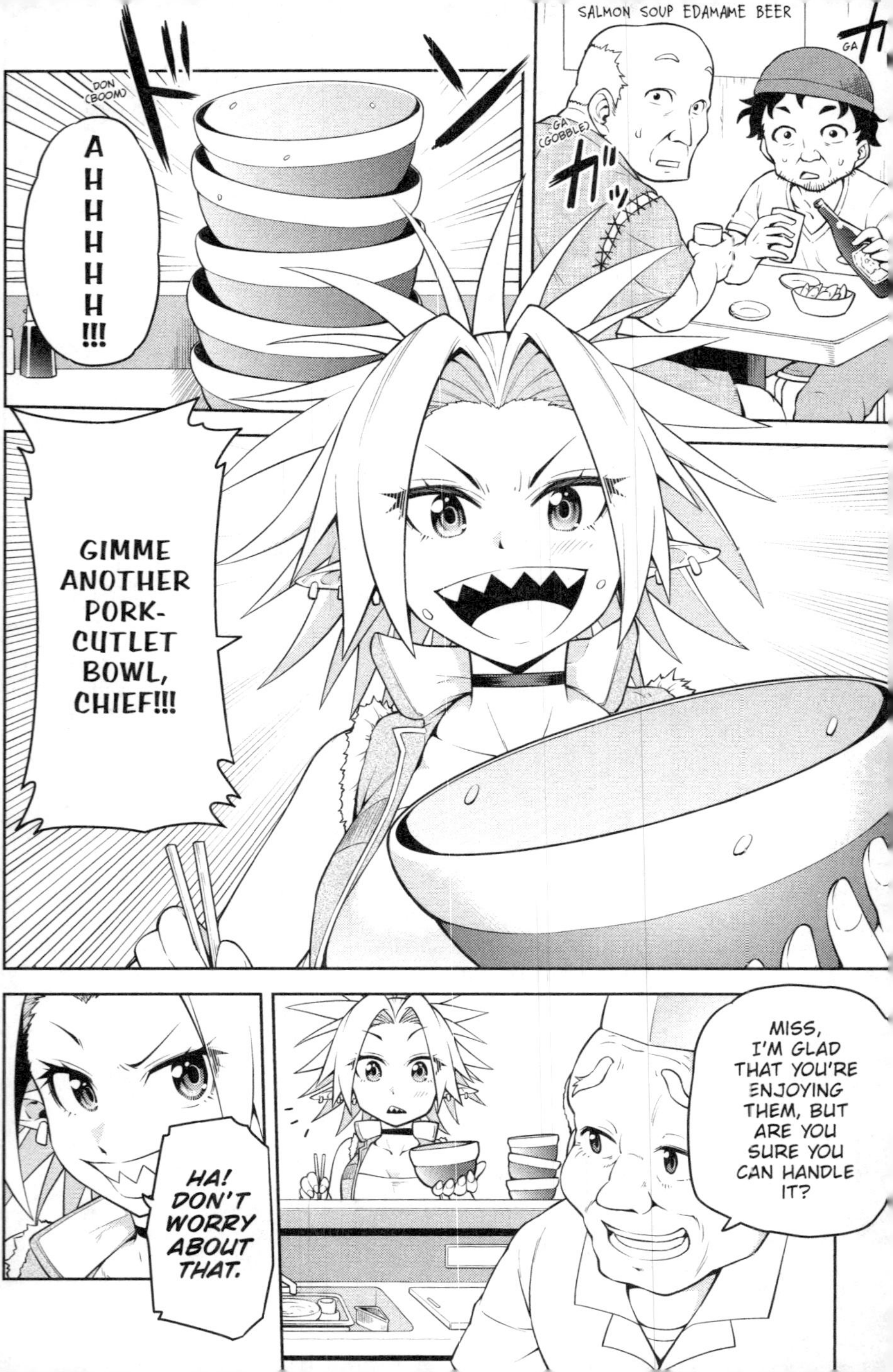
SALMON SOUP EDAMAME BEER
GA
GA (GOBBLE)
DON (BOOM)
AHHHHHH!!!
GIMME ANOTHER PORK-CUTLET BOWL, CHIEF!!!
MISS, I'M GLAD THAT YOU'RE ENJOYING THEM, BUT ARE YOU SURE YOU CAN HANDLE IT?
HA! DON'T WORRY ABOUT THAT.

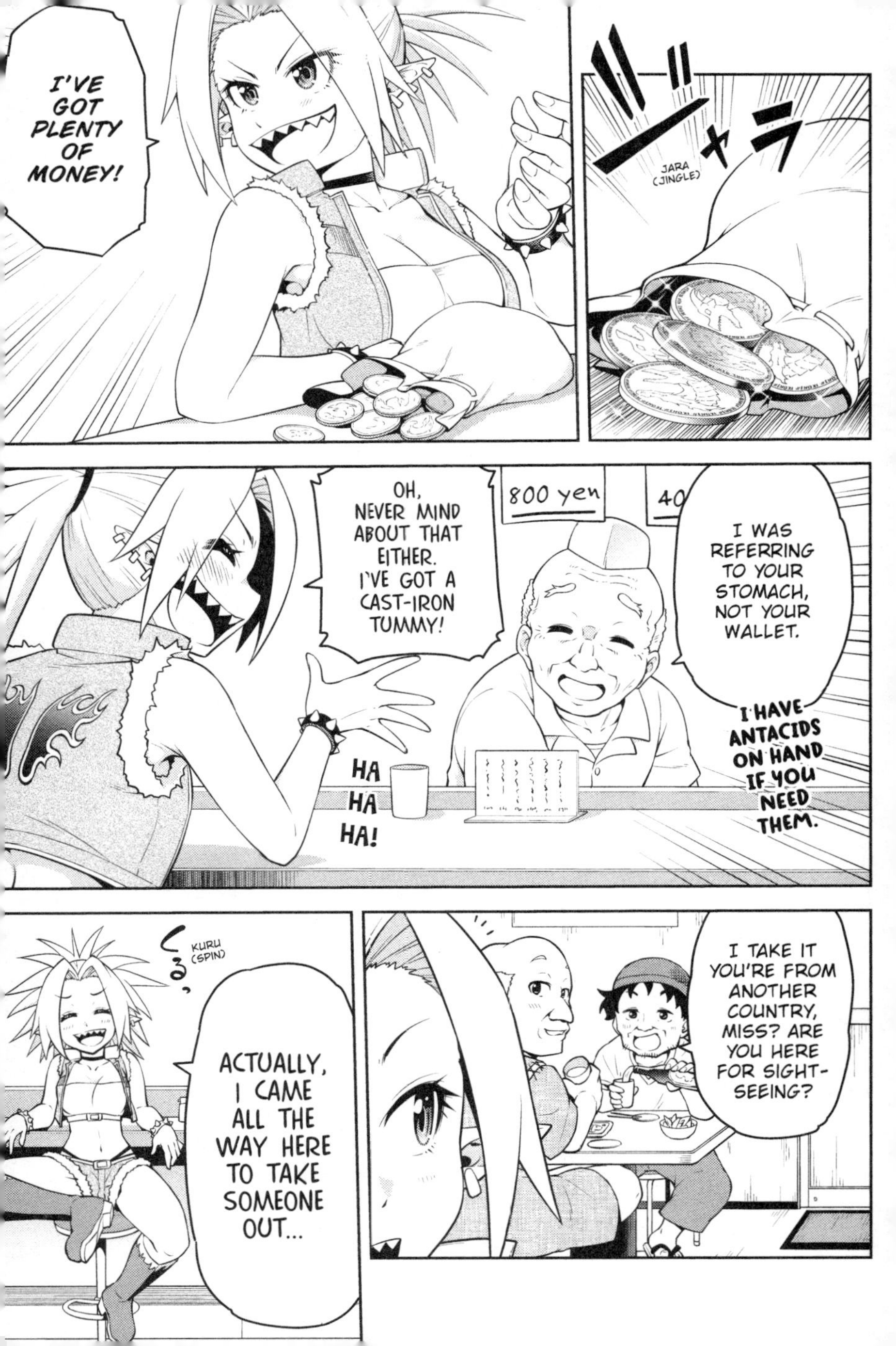
JARA (JINGLE)
I'VE GOT PLENTY OF MONEY!
800 yen
I WAS REFERRING TO YOUR STOMACH, NOT YOUR WALLET.
I HAVE ANTACIDS ON HAND IF YOU NEED THEM.
OH, NEVER MIND ABOUT THAT EITHER. I'VE GOT A CAST-IRON TUMMY!
HA HA HA!
I TAKE IT YOU'RE FROM ANOTHER COUNTRY, MISS? ARE YOU HERE FOR SIGHT-SEEING?
KURU (SPIN)
ACTUALLY, I CAME ALL THE WAY HERE TO TAKE SOMEONE OUT...

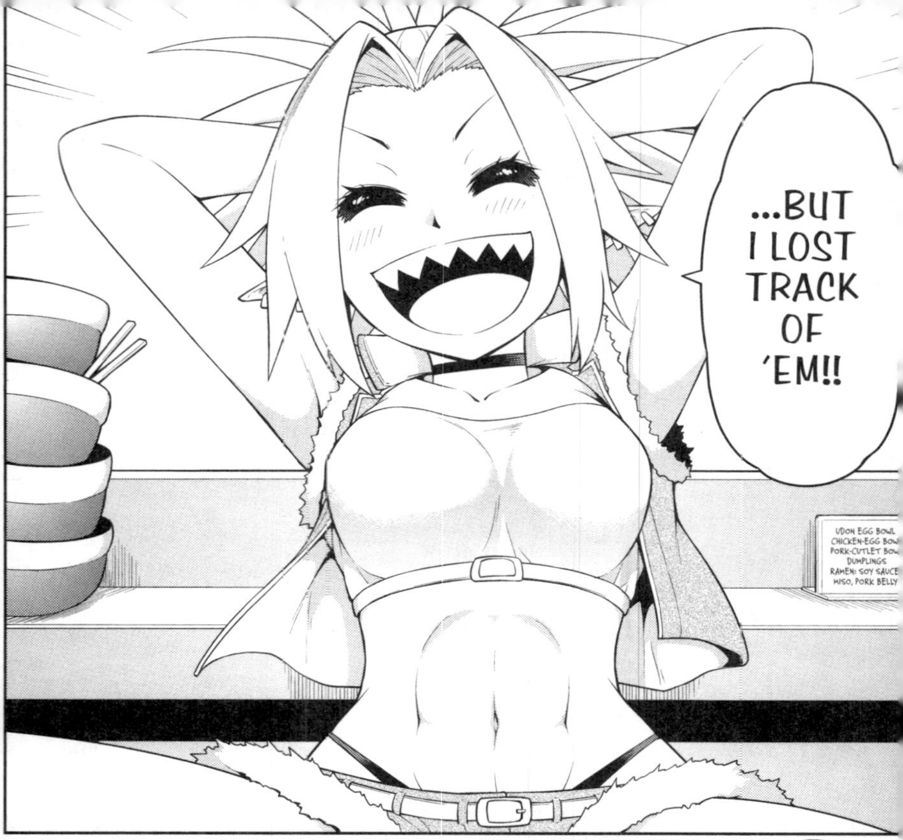
...BUT I LOST TRACK OF 'EM!!
UDON EGG BOWL
CHICKEN-EGG BOWL
PORK-CUTLET BOWL
DUMPLINGS
RAMEN: SOY SAUCE
MISO, PORK BELLY

SIGNS: RESTAURANT KATSUMI / OPEN

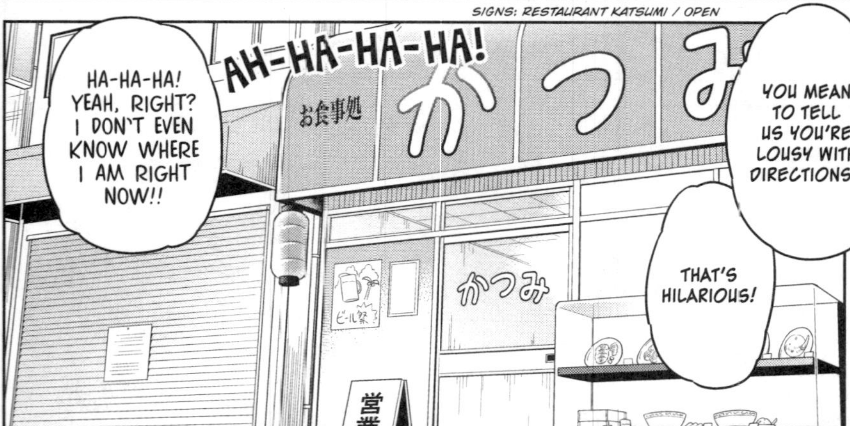
YOU MEAN TO TELL US YOU'RE LOUSY WITH DIRECTIONS?
THAT'S HILARIOUS!
お食事処
かつみ
AH-HA-HA-HA!
HA-HA-HA! YEAH, RIGHT? I DON'T EVEN KNOW WHERE I AM RIGHT NOW!!
かつみ
ビール祭
営業中

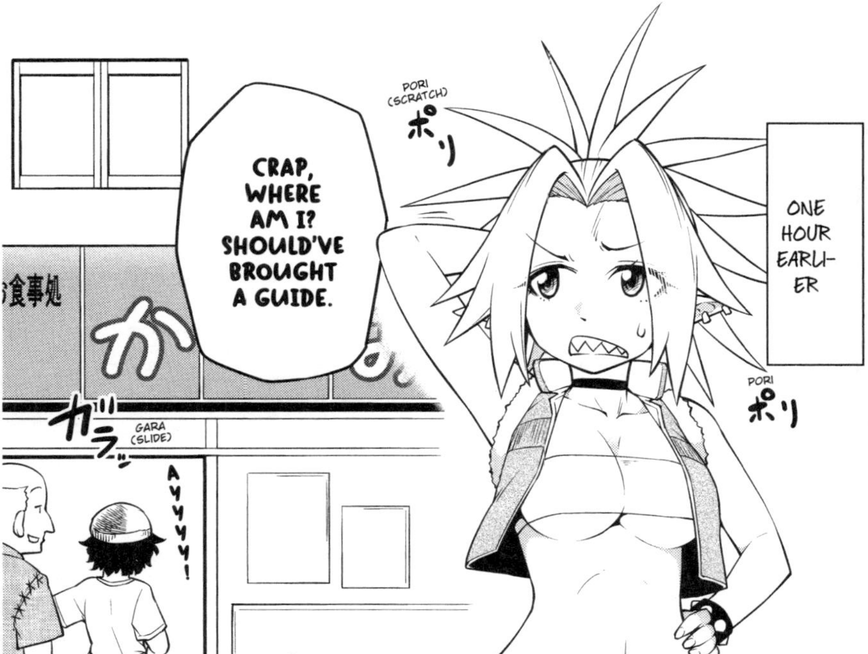
ONE HOUR EARLI-ER
PORI (SCRATCH)
ポリ
CRAP, WHERE AM I? SHOULD'VE BROUGHT A GUIDE.
PORI
ポリ
ガラ
GARA (SLIDE)
AYYYYY!

I'm the HERO, but the DEMON LORD's Also Me

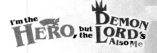

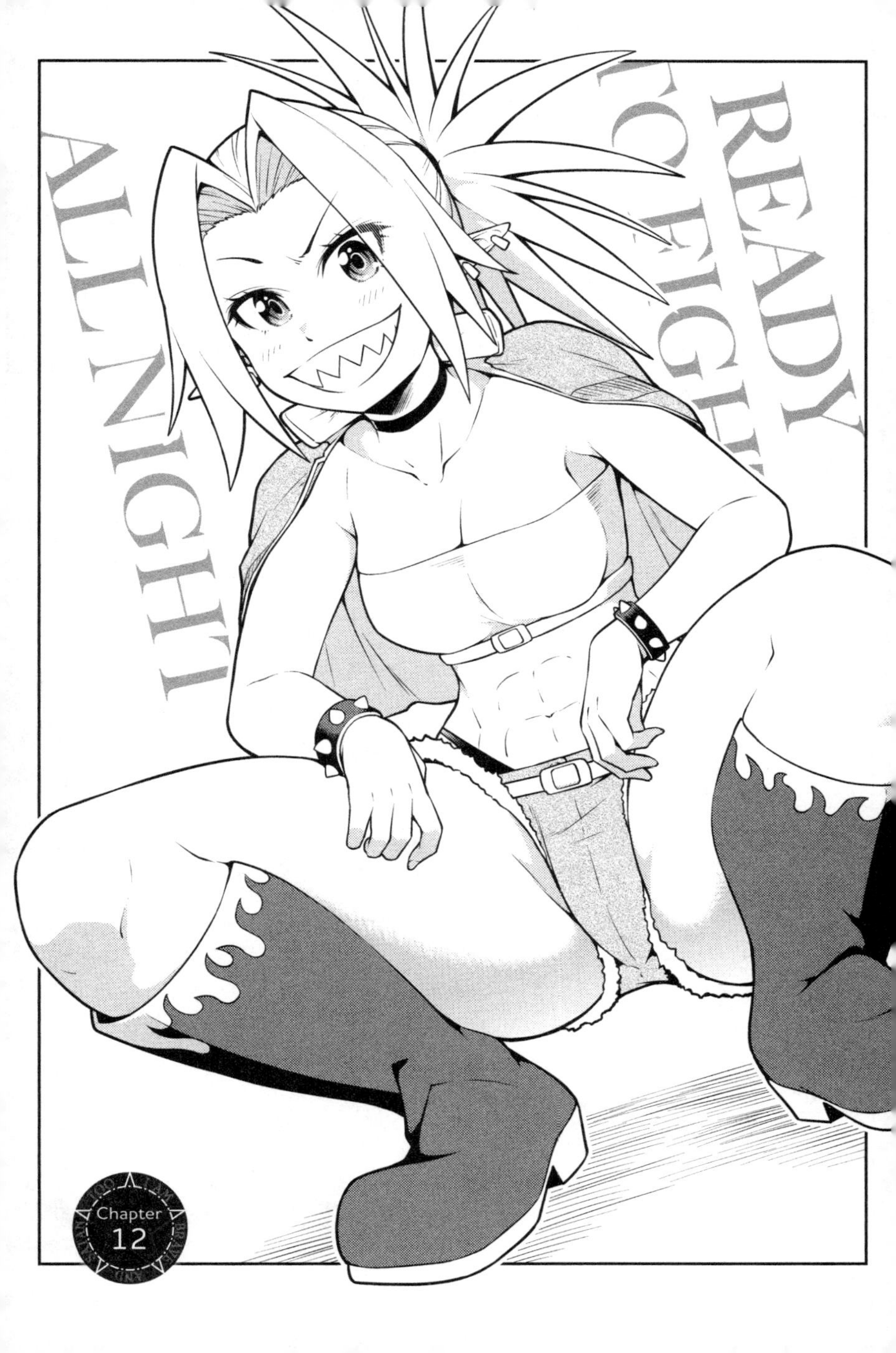
READY
TO FIGHT
ALL NIGHT
Chapter
12

I'M SORRY!!

BA
(BOW)

は゛

SIGN: RESTAURANT KATSUMI / OPEN

I SWEAR, I DIDN'T KNOW MY MONEY WAS NO GOOD HERE!

WHERE'D YOU STEAL IT FROM?

WHAT THE HELL IS THIS?

OF COURSE, WE'D NEVER BE IN THAT POSITION.

EVEN IF IT'S PURE GOLD, NOBODY'S GONNA TOUCH MONEY THAT'S NOT IN CIRCULA-TION.

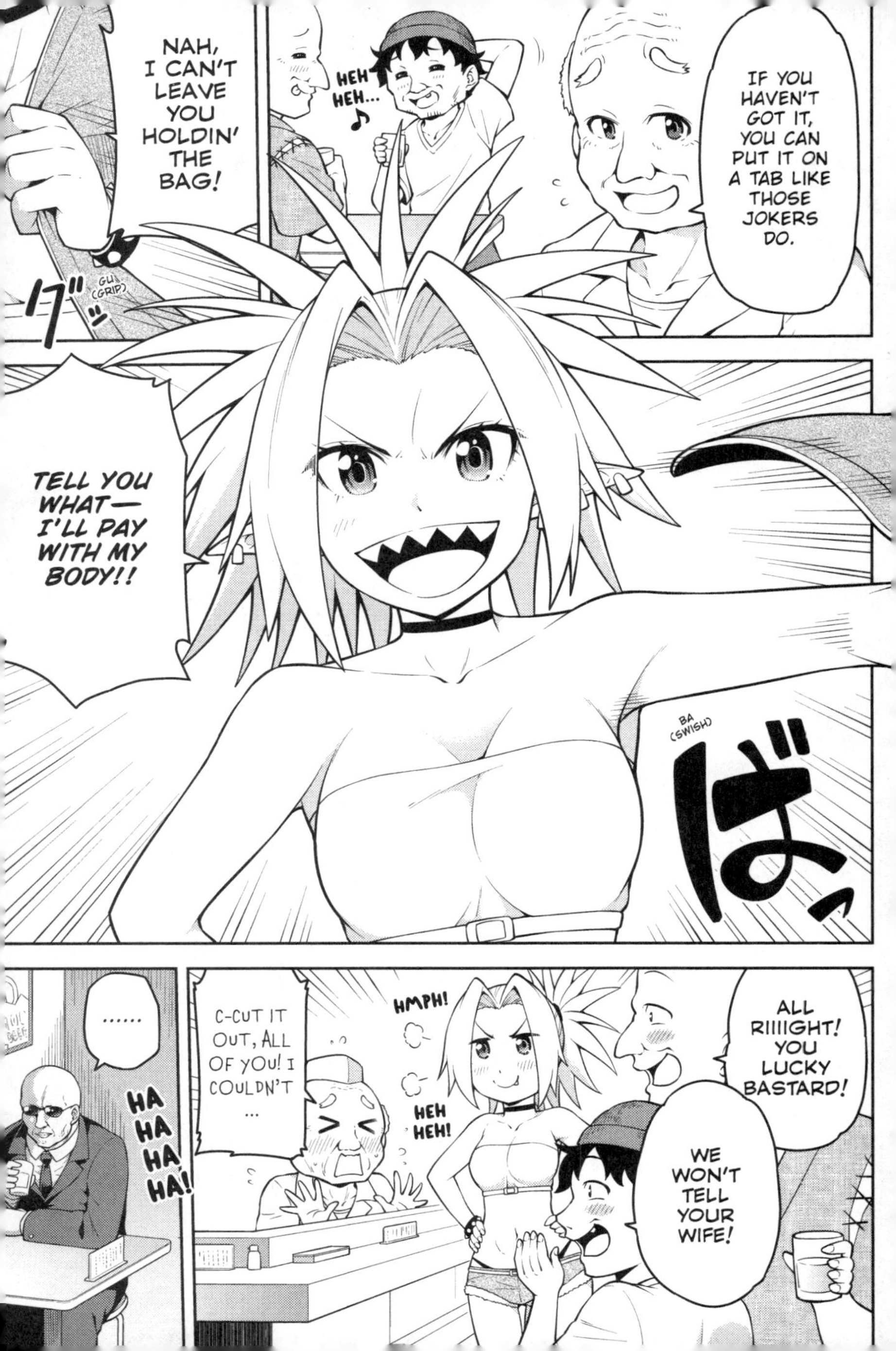
IF YOU HAVEN'T GOT IT, YOU CAN PUT IT ON A TAB LIKE THOSE JOKERS DO.
HEH HEH... ♪
NAH, I CAN'T LEAVE YOU HOLDIN' THE BAG!
GU (GRIP)
TELL YOU WHAT— I'LL PAY WITH MY BODY!!
BA (SWISH)
ばっ
ALL RIIIIGHT! YOU LUCKY BASTARD!
WE WON'T TELL YOUR WIFE!
HMPH!
HEH HEH!
C-CUT IT OUT, ALL OF YOU! I COULDN'T ...
......
HA HA HA HA!

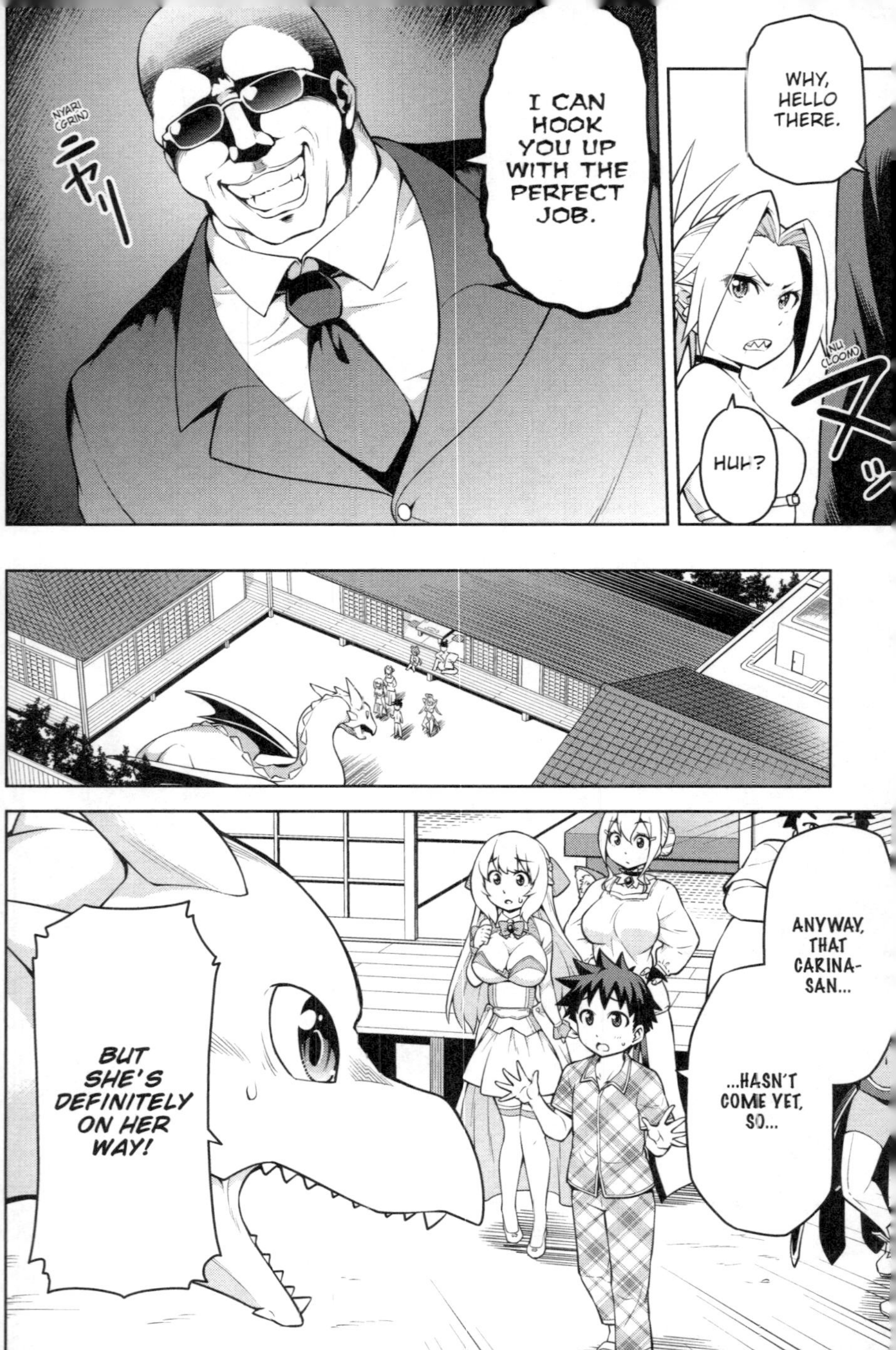
WHY, HELLO THERE.
NU (LOOM)
HUH?
I CAN HOOK YOU UP WITH THE PERFECT JOB.
NYARI (GRIN)
ANYWAY, THAT CARINA-SAN...
...HASN'T COME YET, SO...
BUT SHE'S DEFINITELY ON HER WAY!

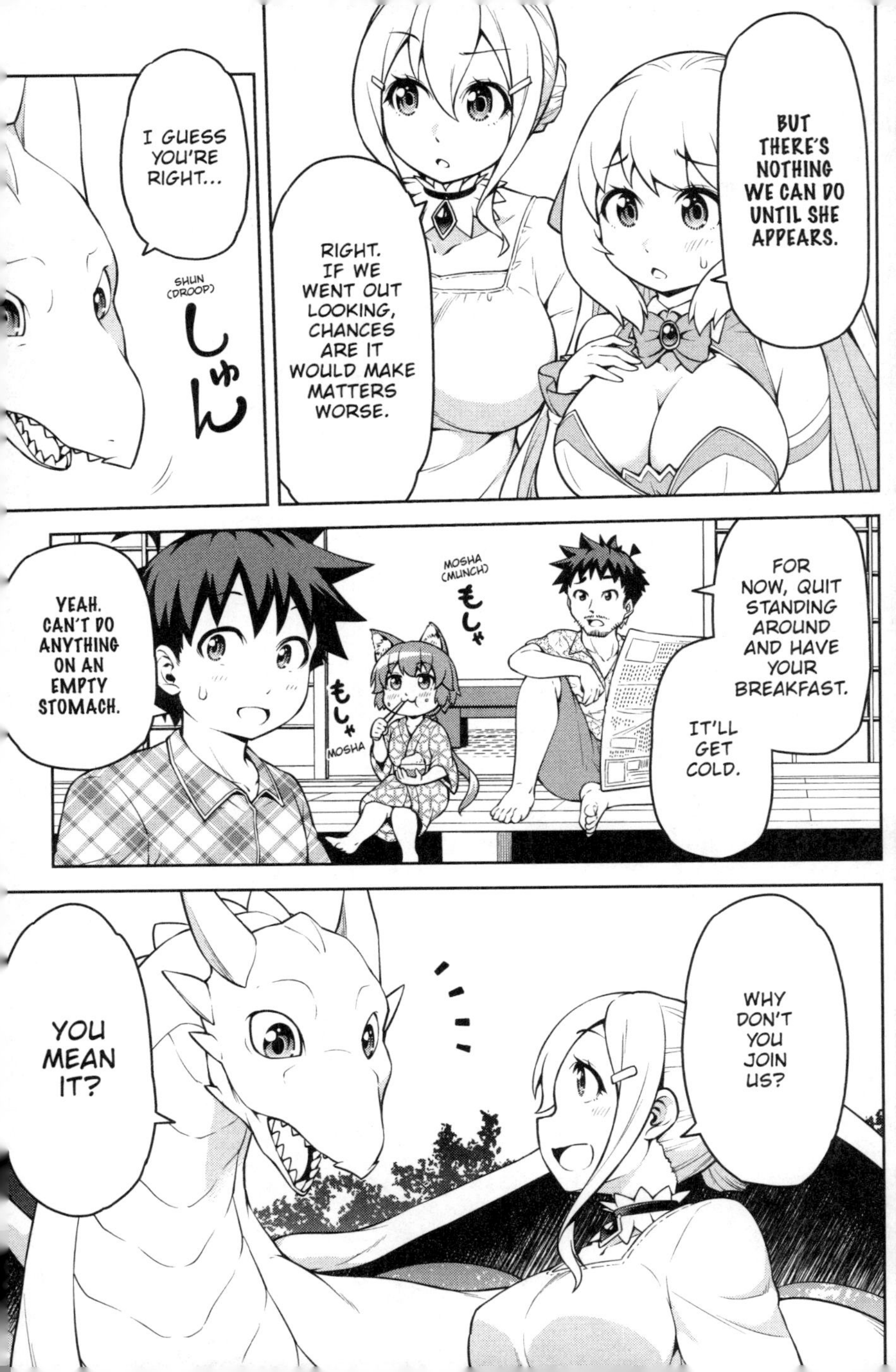
BUT THERE'S NOTHING WE CAN DO UNTIL SHE APPEARS.
RIGHT. IF WE WENT OUT LOOKING, CHANCES ARE IT WOULD MAKE MATTERS WORSE.
I GUESS YOU'RE RIGHT...
しゅん
SHUN (DROOP)
FOR NOW, QUIT STANDING AROUND AND HAVE YOUR BREAKFAST.
IT'LL GET COLD.
もしゃ
MOSHA (MUNCH)
もしゃ
MOSHA
YEAH. CAN'T DO ANYTHING ON AN EMPTY STOMACH.
WHY DON'T YOU JOIN US?
YOU MEAN IT?

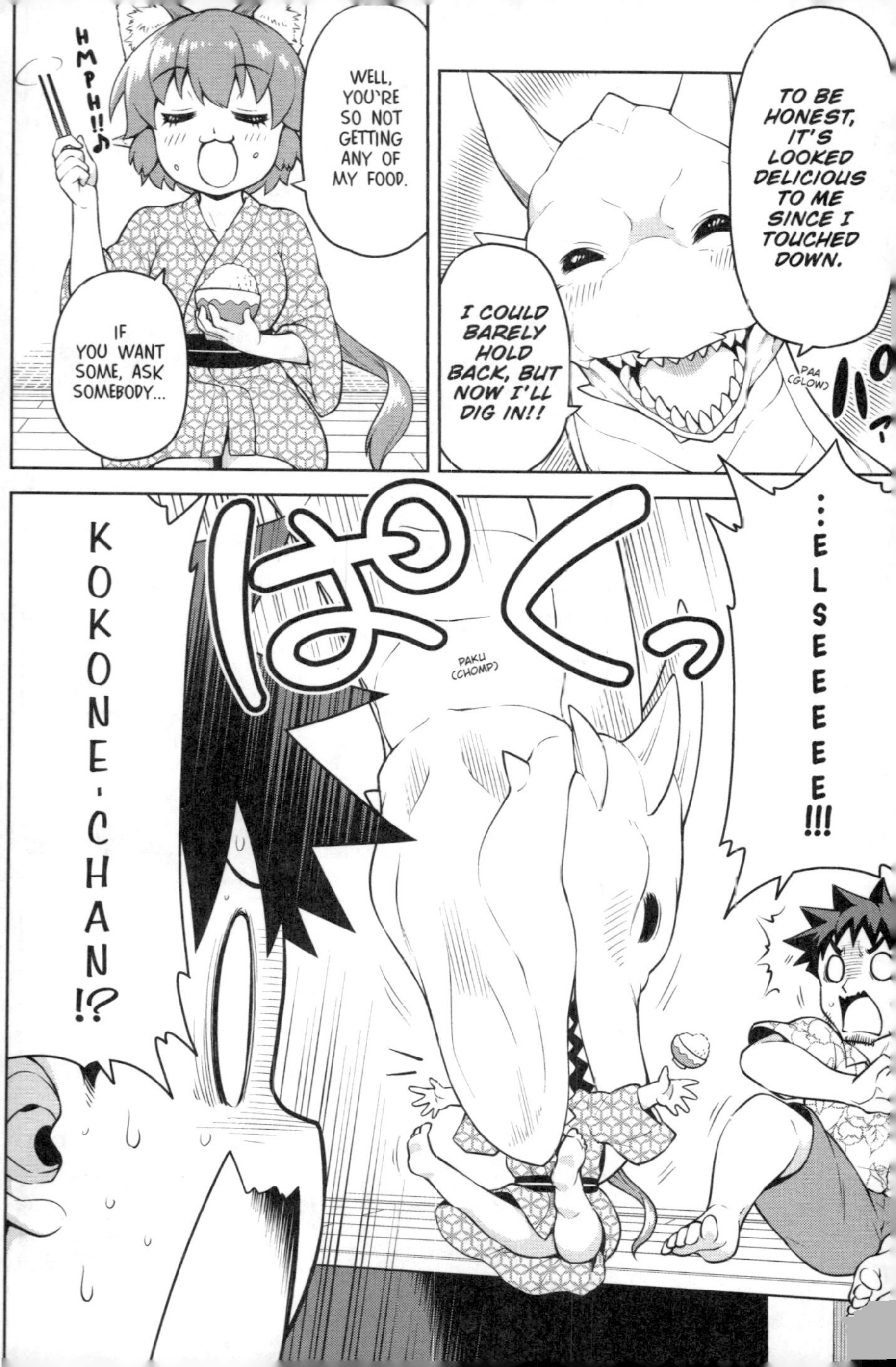

TO BE HONEST, IT'S LOOKED DELICIOUS TO ME SINCE I TOUCHED DOWN.
I COULD BARELY HOLD BACK, BUT NOW I'LL DIG IN!!
PAA (GLOW)
WELL, YOU'RE SO NOT GETTING ANY OF MY FOOD.
HMPH!!♪
IF YOU WANT SOME, ASK SOMEBODY...
...ELSEEEEEE!!!
ぱくっ
PAKU (CHOMP)
KOKONE-CHAN!?

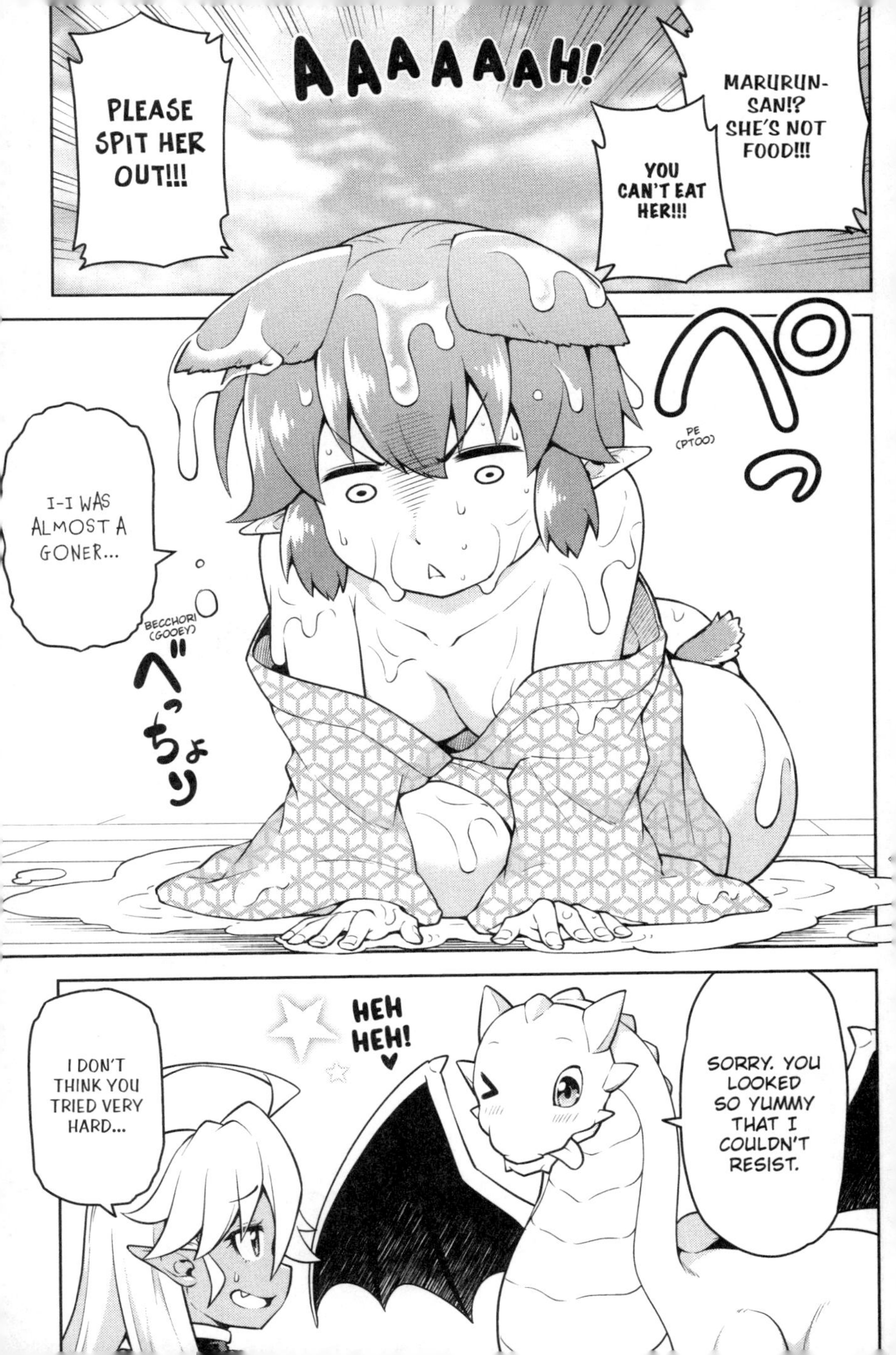
MARURUN-SAN!? SHE'S NOT FOOD!!!
YOU CAN'T EAT HER!!!
AAAAAAH!
PLEASE SPIT HER OUT!!!
ぺっ
PE (PTOO)
I-I WAS ALMOST A GONER...
BECCHORI (GOOEY)
べっちょり
SORRY. YOU LOOKED SO YUMMY THAT I COULDN'T RESIST.
HEH HEH!
I DON'T THINK YOU TRIED VERY HARD...

UM... YUUMA-KUN?

SU (SHF)
ス

HYOKO (PEEK)
ひょこ

HUH? IT'S THAT TIME ALREADY!?

WE'D BETTER GET GOING.

YIKES!!

STUDY HARD!

GOTCHA!

SORRY, EVERYONE! YOU HOLD THE FORT!

DA (DASH)
ダッ

LEAVE THIS TO US. YOU GO TO SCHOOL.

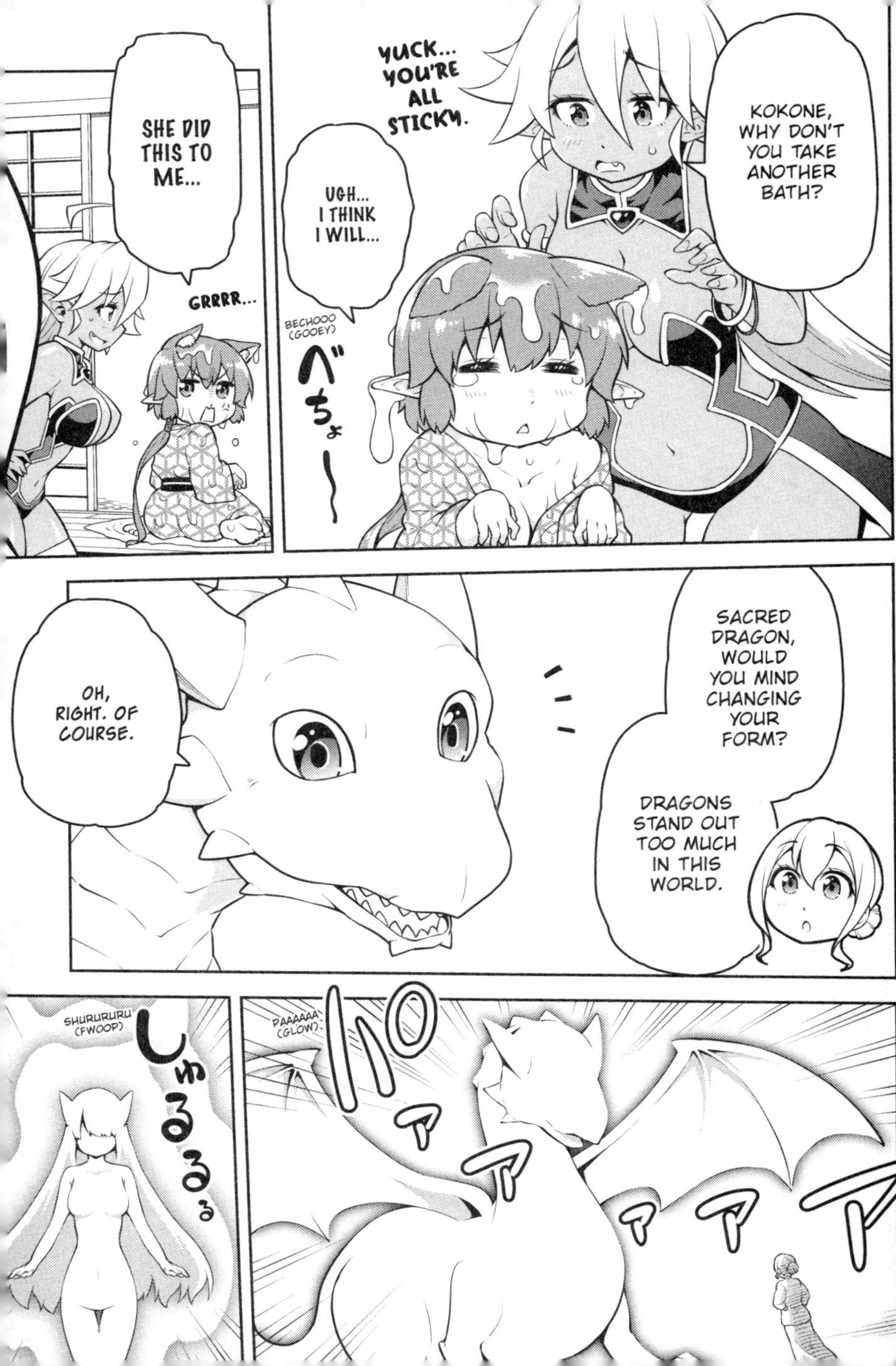
KOKONE, WHY DON'T YOU TAKE ANOTHER BATH?
YUCK... YOU'RE ALL STICKY.
UGH... I THINK I WILL...
BECHOOO (GOOEY)
べちょ〜
SHE DID THIS TO ME...
GRRRR...
SACRED DRAGON, WOULD YOU MIND CHANGING YOUR FORM?
DRAGONS STAND OUT TOO MUCH IN THIS WORLD.
OH, RIGHT. OF COURSE.
PAAAAAA (GLOW)
SHURURURU (FWOOP)
しゅるるる

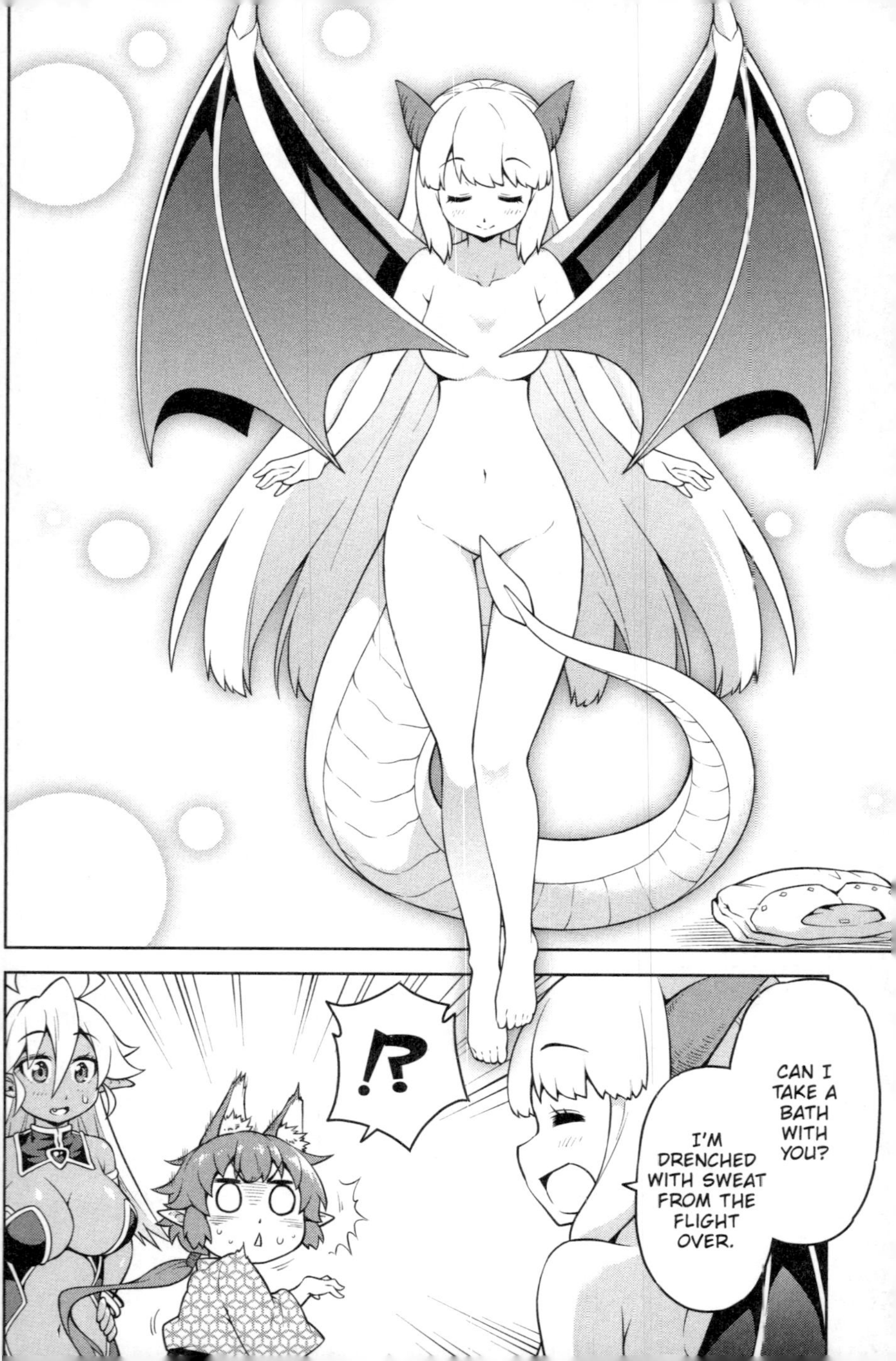
CAN I TAKE A BATH WITH YOU?
I'M DRENCHED WITH SWEAT FROM THE FLIGHT OVER.
!?

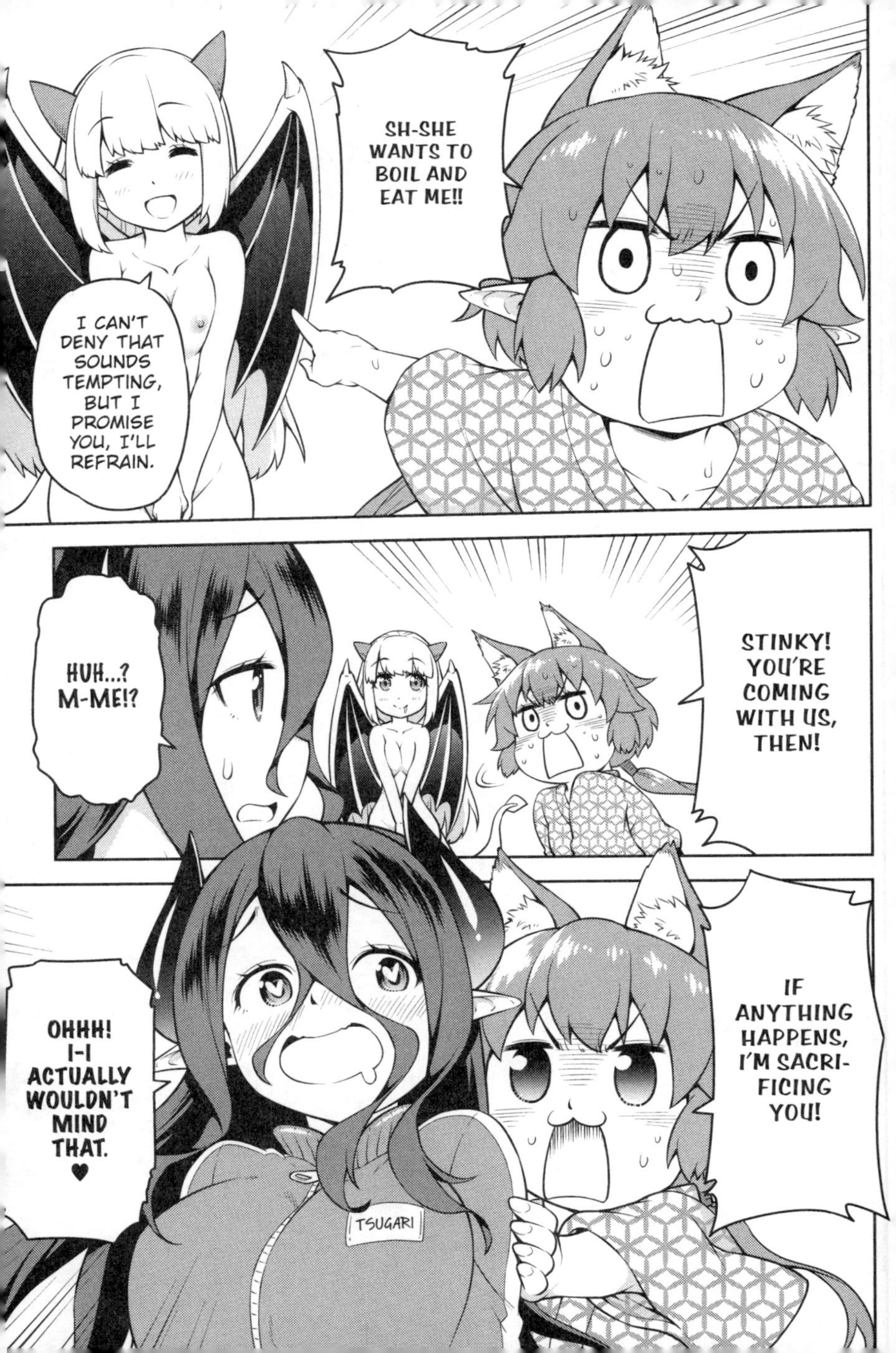
SH-SHE WANTS TO BOIL AND EAT ME!!
I CAN'T DENY THAT SOUNDS TEMPTING, BUT I PROMISE YOU, I'LL REFRAIN.
STINKY! YOU'RE COMING WITH US, THEN!
HUH...? M-ME!?
IF ANYTHING HAPPENS, I'M SACRI-FICING YOU!
OHHH! I-I ACTUALLY WOULDN'T MIND THAT. ♥
TSUGARI

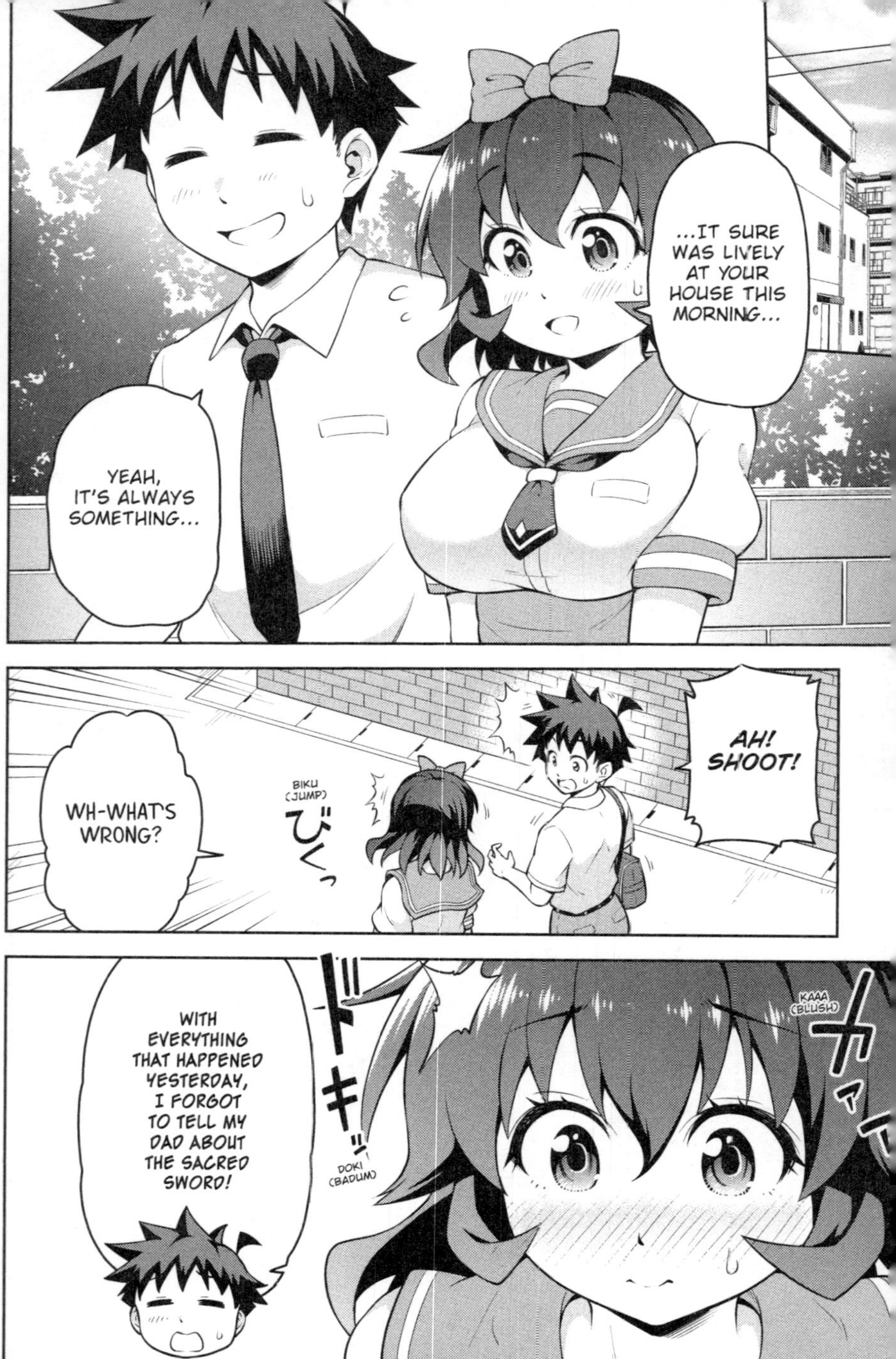
...IT SURE WAS LIVELY AT YOUR HOUSE THIS MORNING...
YEAH, IT'S ALWAYS SOMETHING...
AH! SHOOT!
BIKU (JUMP)
びくっ
WH-WHAT'S WRONG?
KAAA (BLUSH)
カァァ
DOKI (BADUM)
ドキッ
WITH EVERYTHING THAT HAPPENED YESTERDAY, I FORGOT TO TELL MY DAD ABOUT THE SACRED SWORD!

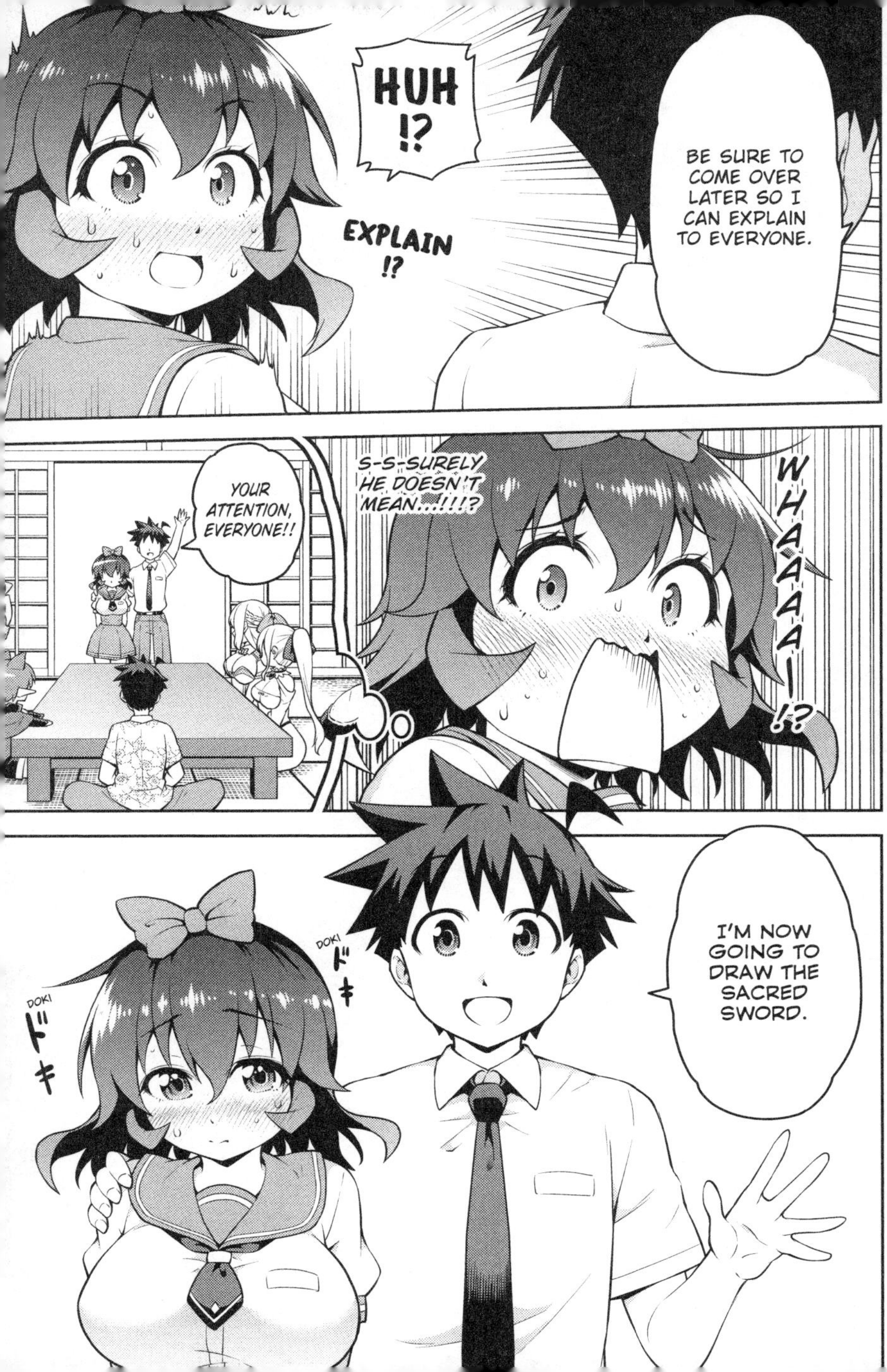
BE SURE TO COME OVER LATER SO I CAN EXPLAIN TO EVERYONE.
HUH!?
EXPLAIN!?
WHAAAAAI!?
S-S-SURELY HE DOESN'T MEAN...!!!!?
YOUR ATTENTION, EVERYONE!!
I'M NOW GOING TO DRAW THE SACRED SWORD.
DOKI ドキ
DOKI ドキ

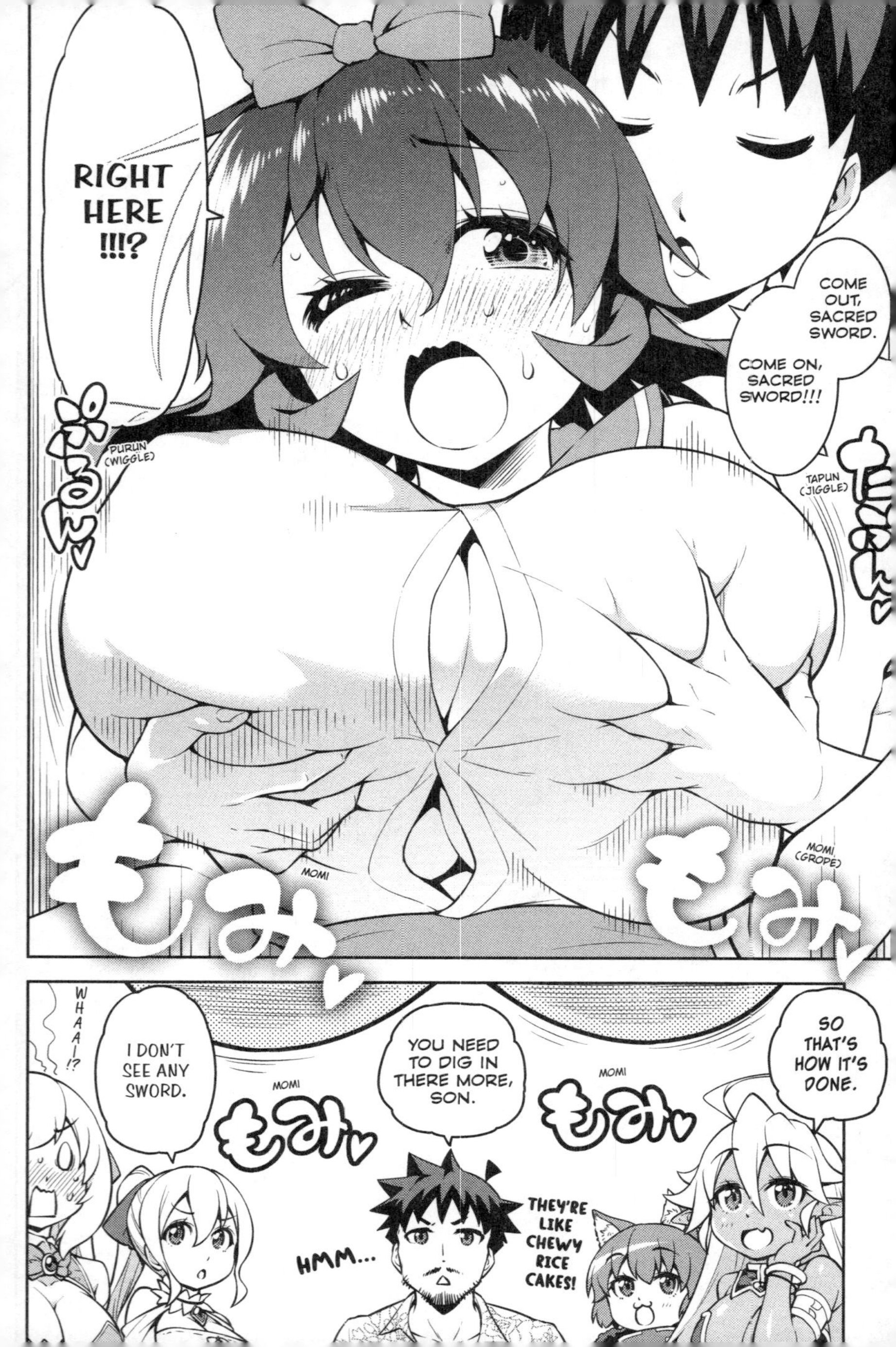
COME OUT, SACRED SWORD.
COME ON, SACRED SWORD!!!
TAPUN (JIGGLE)
たぷんっ♥
RIGHT HERE !!!?
PURUN (WIGGLE)
ぷるんっ♥
MOMI (GROPE)
もみ♥
MOMI
もみ♥
SO THAT'S HOW IT'S DONE.
MOMI
もみ♥
YOU NEED TO DIG IN THERE MORE, SON.
MOMI
もみ♥
I DON'T SEE ANY SWORD.
WHAAAI!?
THEY'RE LIKE CHEWY RICE CAKES!
HMM...

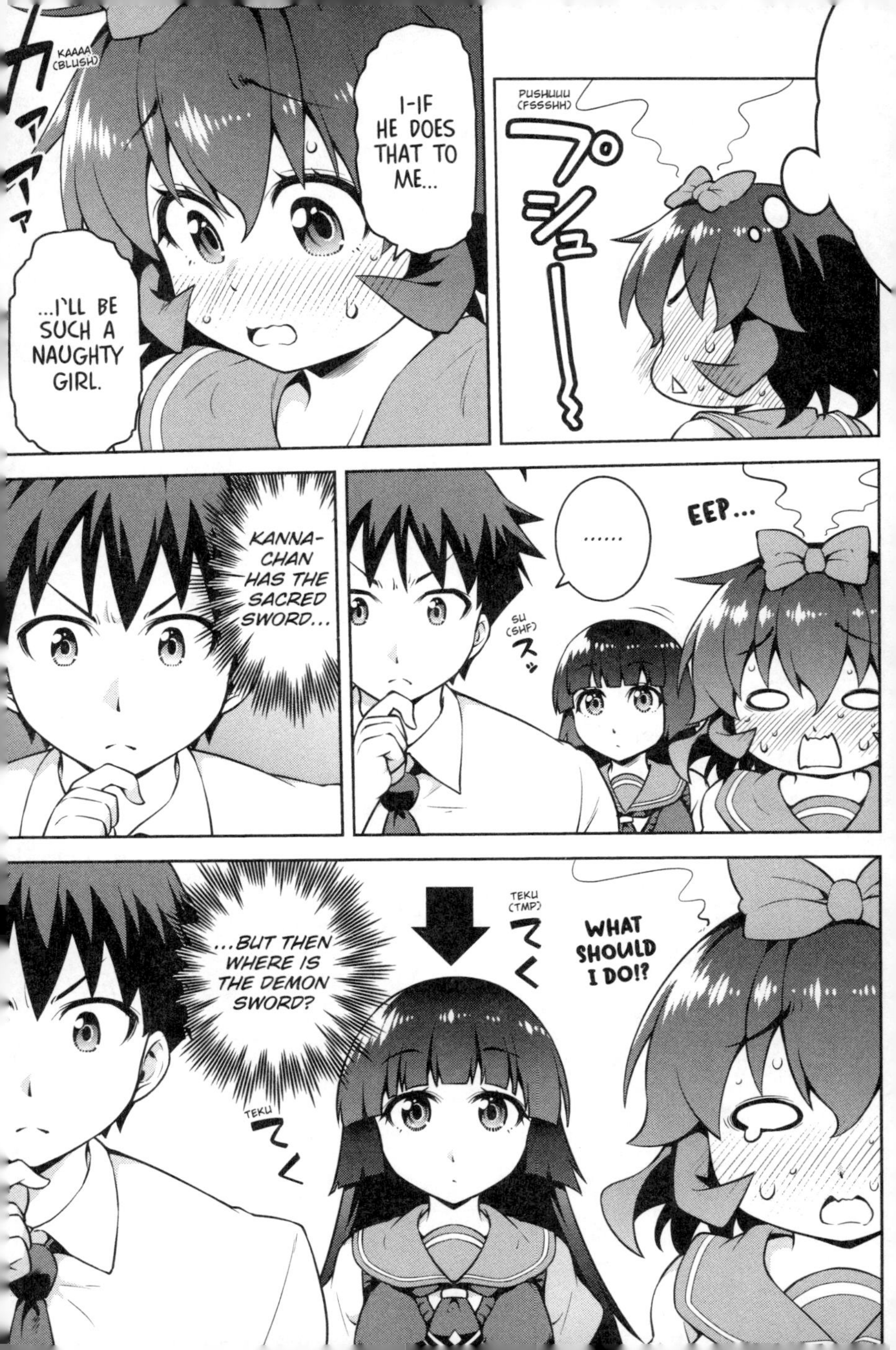
PUSHUUU (FSSSHH)
プシュ～
I-IF HE DOES THAT TO ME...
KAAAA (BLUSH)
カァァァ
...I'LL BE SUCH A NAUGHTY GIRL.
EEP...
......
SU (SHF)
スッ
KANNA-CHAN HAS THE SACRED SWORD...
WHAT SHOULD I DO!?
TEKU (TMP)
...BUT THEN WHERE IS THE DEMON SWORD?
TEKU

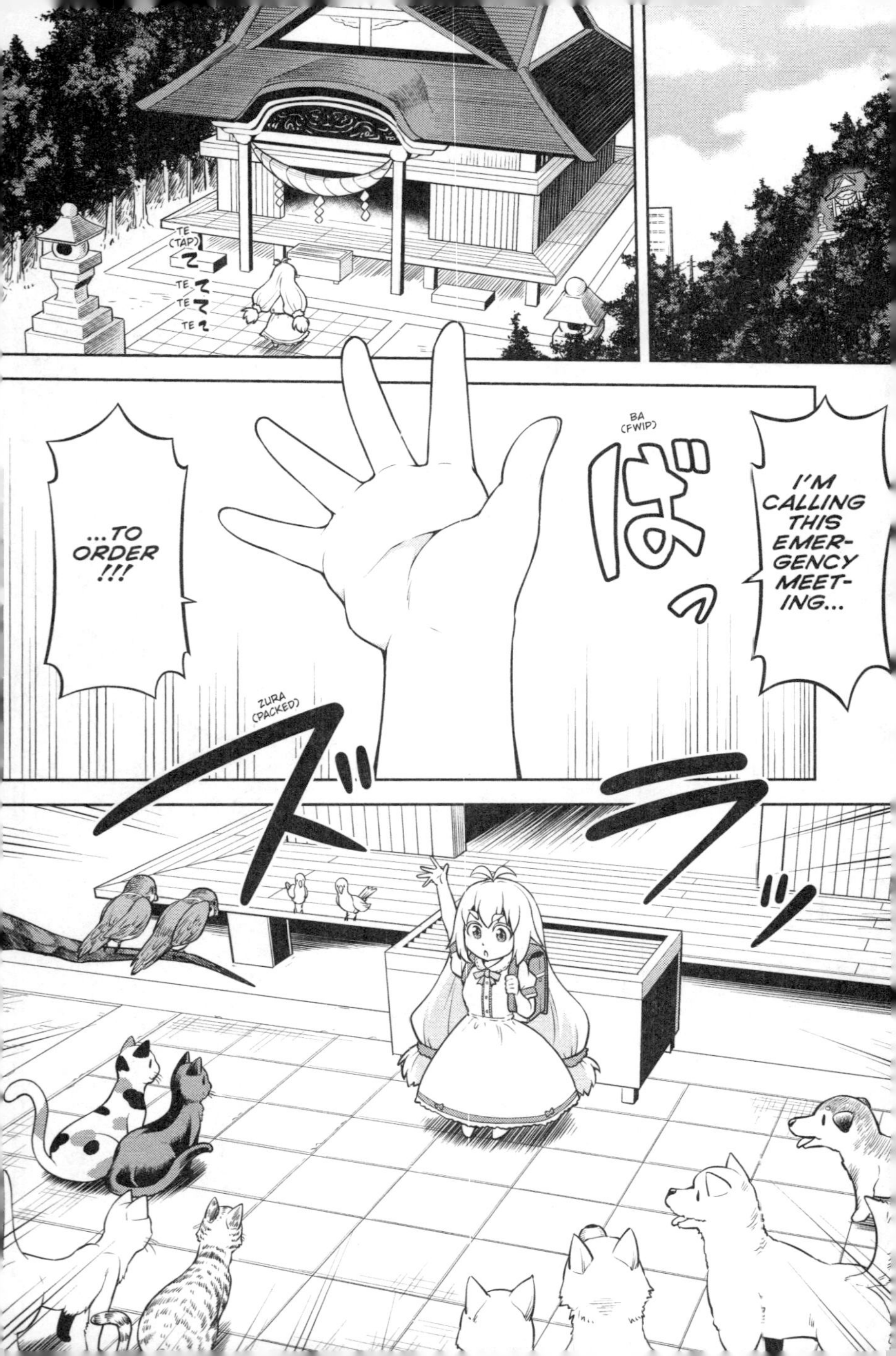
TE (TAP)
て
TE て
TE て
TE て
BA (FWIP)
ばっ
I'M CALLING THIS EMERGENCY MEETING...
...TO ORDER!!!
ZURA (PACKED)
ズラッ

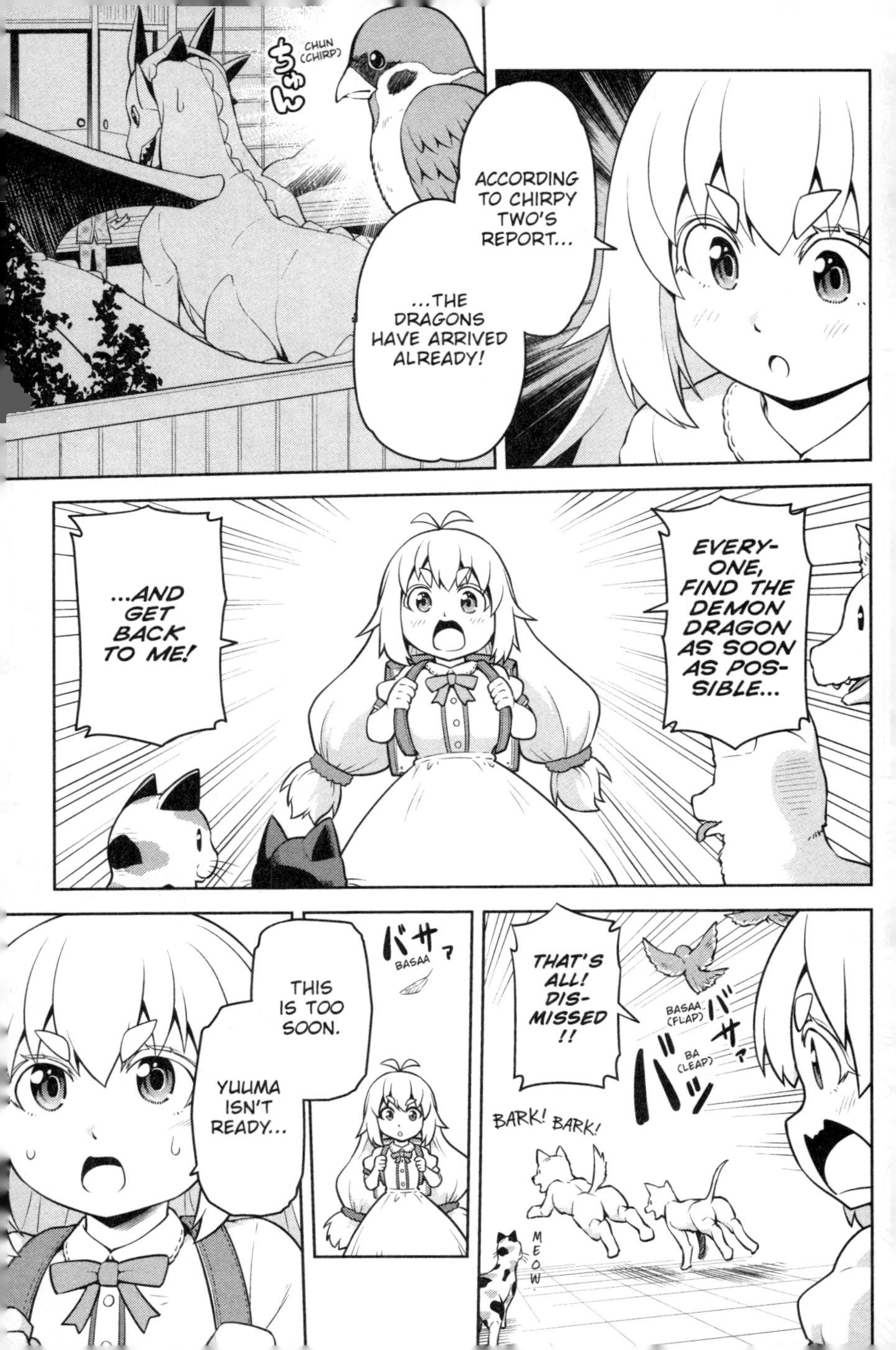

ACCORDING TO CHIRPY TWO'S REPORT...
...THE DRAGONS HAVE ARRIVED ALREADY!
ちゅん
CHUN (CHIRP)
EVERY-ONE, FIND THE DEMON DRAGON AS SOON AS POS-SIBLE...
...AND GET BACK TO ME!
THAT'S ALL! DIS-MISSED!!
バサァ
BASAA (FLAP)
バッ
BA (LEAP)
BARK! BARK!
MEOW
バサァ
BASAA
THIS IS TOO SOON.
YUUMA ISN'T READY...

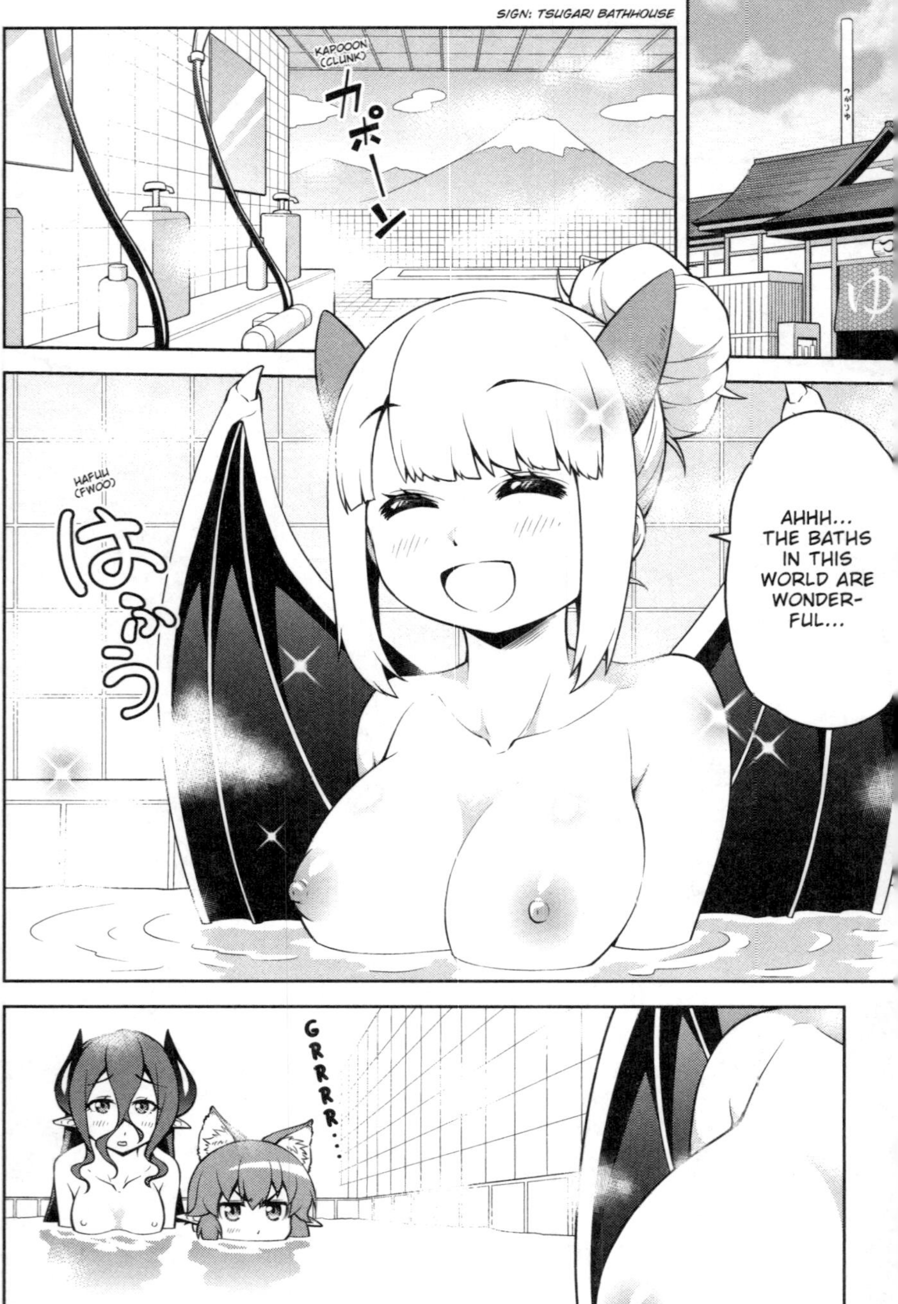
SIGN: TSUGARI BATHHOUSE
KAPOOON (CLUNK)
AHHH... THE BATHS IN THIS WORLD ARE WONDER-FUL...
HAFUU (FWOO)
GRRRR...

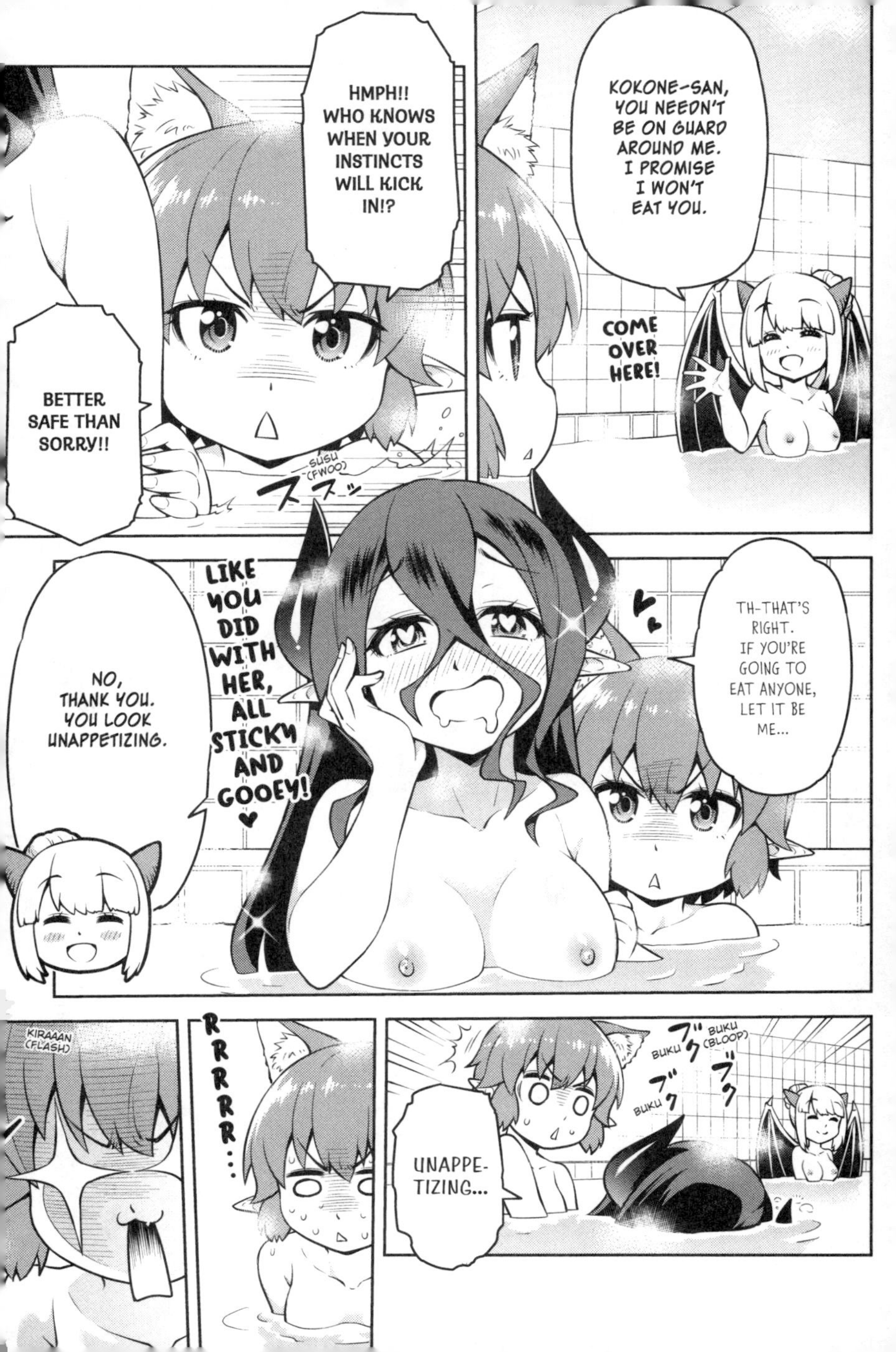
KOKONE-SAN, YOU NEEDN'T BE ON GUARD AROUND ME. I PROMISE I WON'T EAT YOU.
COME OVER HERE!
HMPH!! WHO KNOWS WHEN YOUR INSTINCTS WILL KICK IN!?
BETTER SAFE THAN SORRY!!
SUSU (FWOO)
TH-THAT'S RIGHT. IF YOU'RE GOING TO EAT ANYONE, LET IT BE ME...
LIKE YOU DID WITH HER, ALL STICKY AND GOOEY! ♥
NO, THANK YOU. YOU LOOK UNAPPETIZING.
BUKU BUKU (BLOOP)
BUKU
UNAPPE-TIZING...
RRRRR...
KIRAAAN (FLASH)

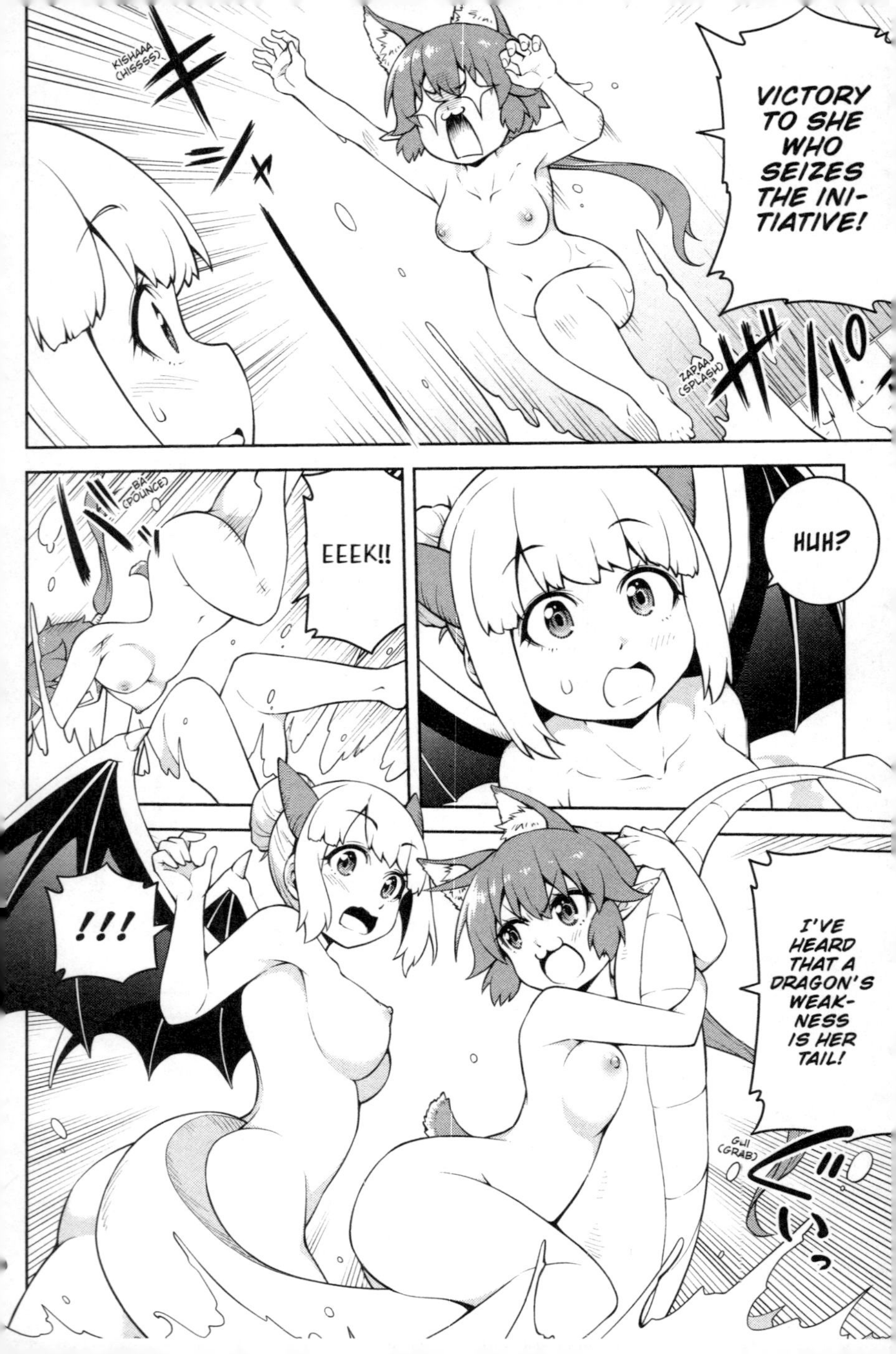
VICTORY TO SHE WHO SEIZES THE INITIATIVE!
KISHAAA (HISSSSS)
ZAPAA (SPLASH)
HUH?
BA (POUNCE)
EEEK!!
I'VE HEARD THAT A DRAGON'S WEAKNESS IS HER TAIL!
!!!
GUI (GRAB)

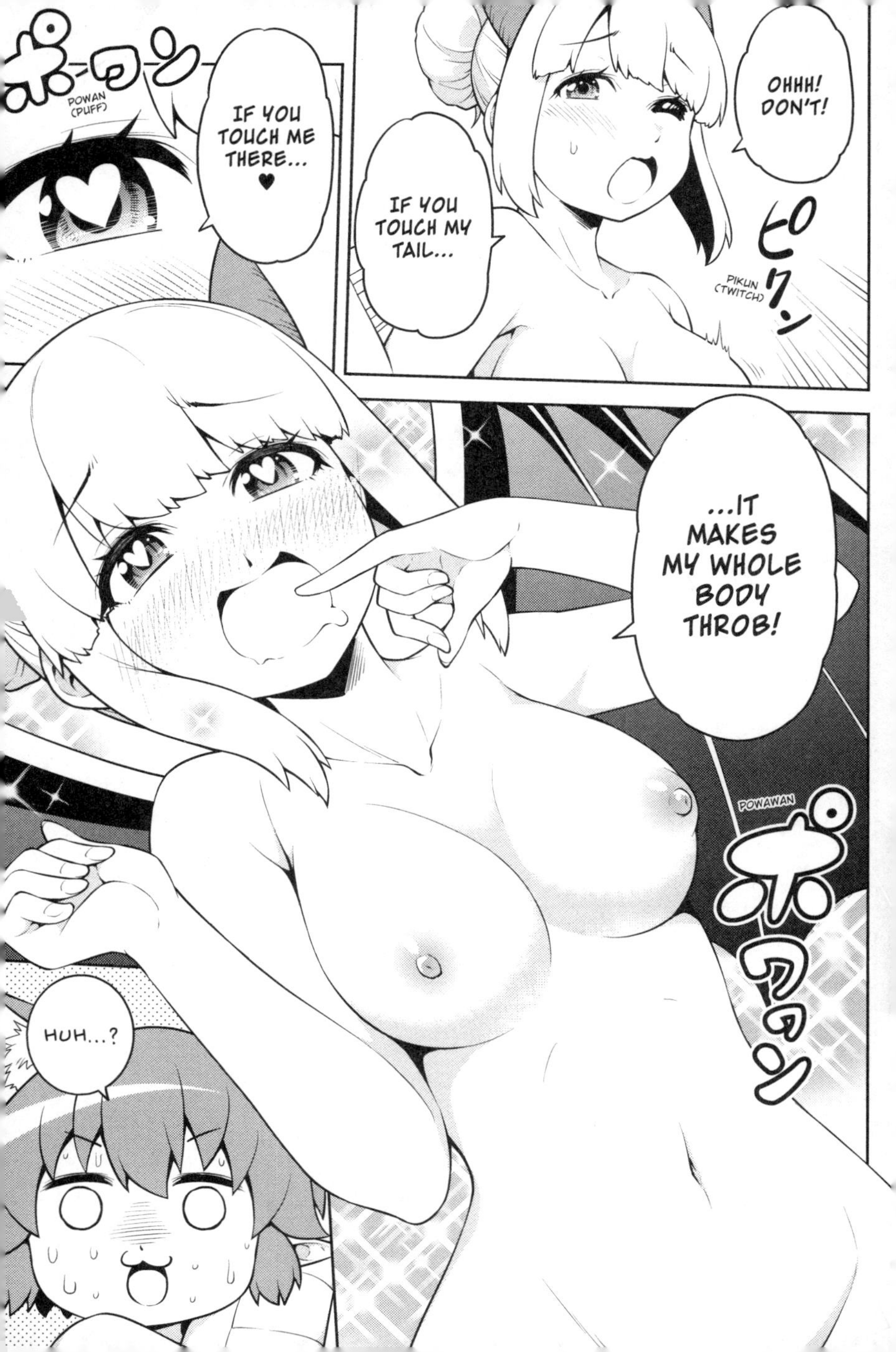
OHHH! DON'T!
IF YOU TOUCH MY TAIL...
ピクン
PIKUN (TWITCH)
IF YOU TOUCH ME THERE... ♥
ポワーン
POWAN (PUFF)
...IT MAKES MY WHOLE BODY THROB!
ポワワン
POWAWAN
HUH...?

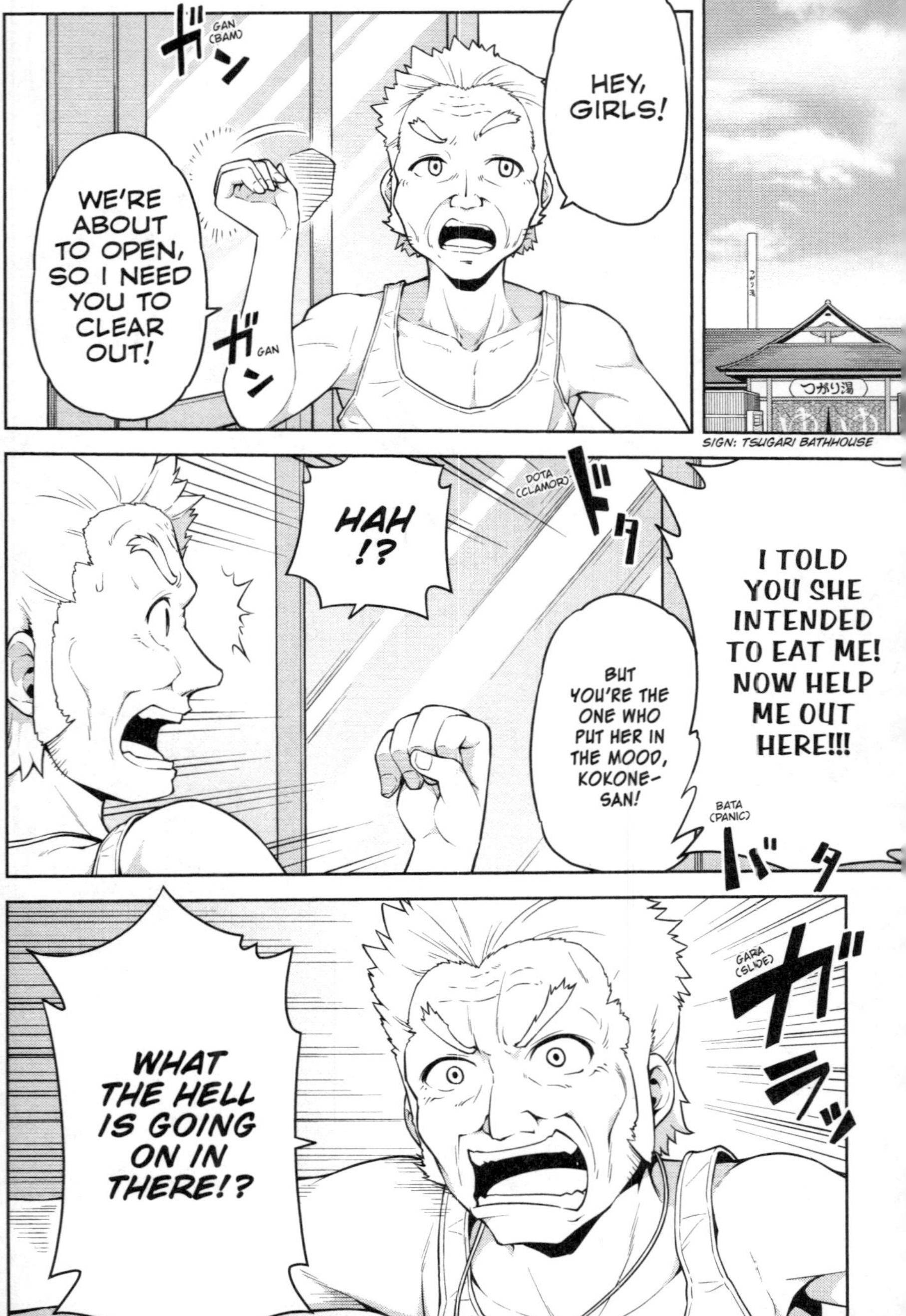
つがり湯
SIGN: TSUGARI BATHHOUSE
HEY, GIRLS!
GAN (BAM)
WE'RE ABOUT TO OPEN, SO I NEED YOU TO CLEAR OUT!
GAN
DOTA (CLAMOR)
I TOLD YOU SHE INTENDED TO EAT ME! NOW HELP ME OUT HERE!!!
BUT YOU'RE THE ONE WHO PUT HER IN THE MOOD, KOKONE-SAN!
HAH!?
BATA (PANIC)
GARA (SLIDE)
WHAT THE HELL IS GOING ON IN THERE!?

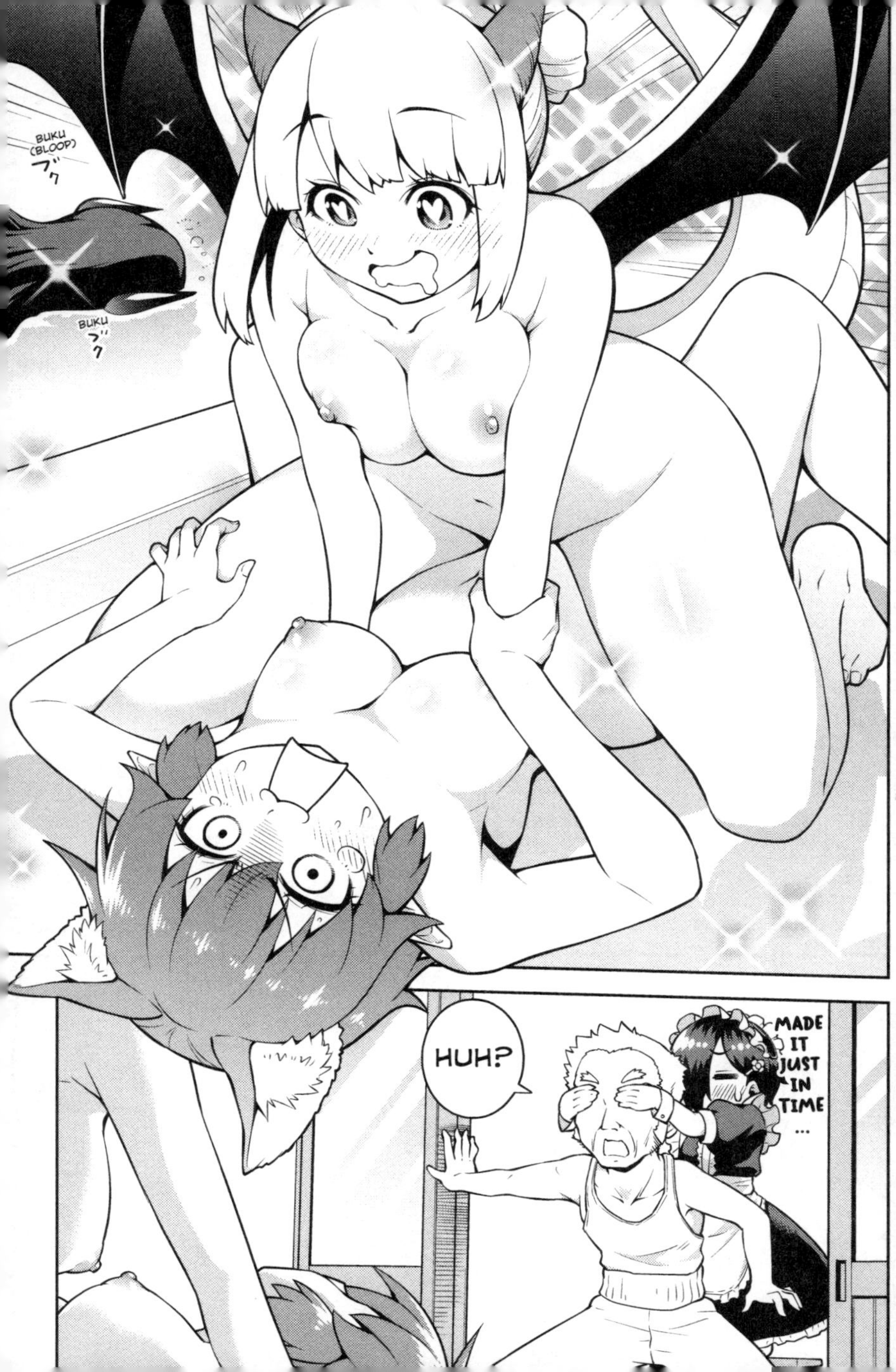
BUKU (BLOOP)
ブク
BUKU
ブク
MADE IT JUST IN TIME ...
HUH?

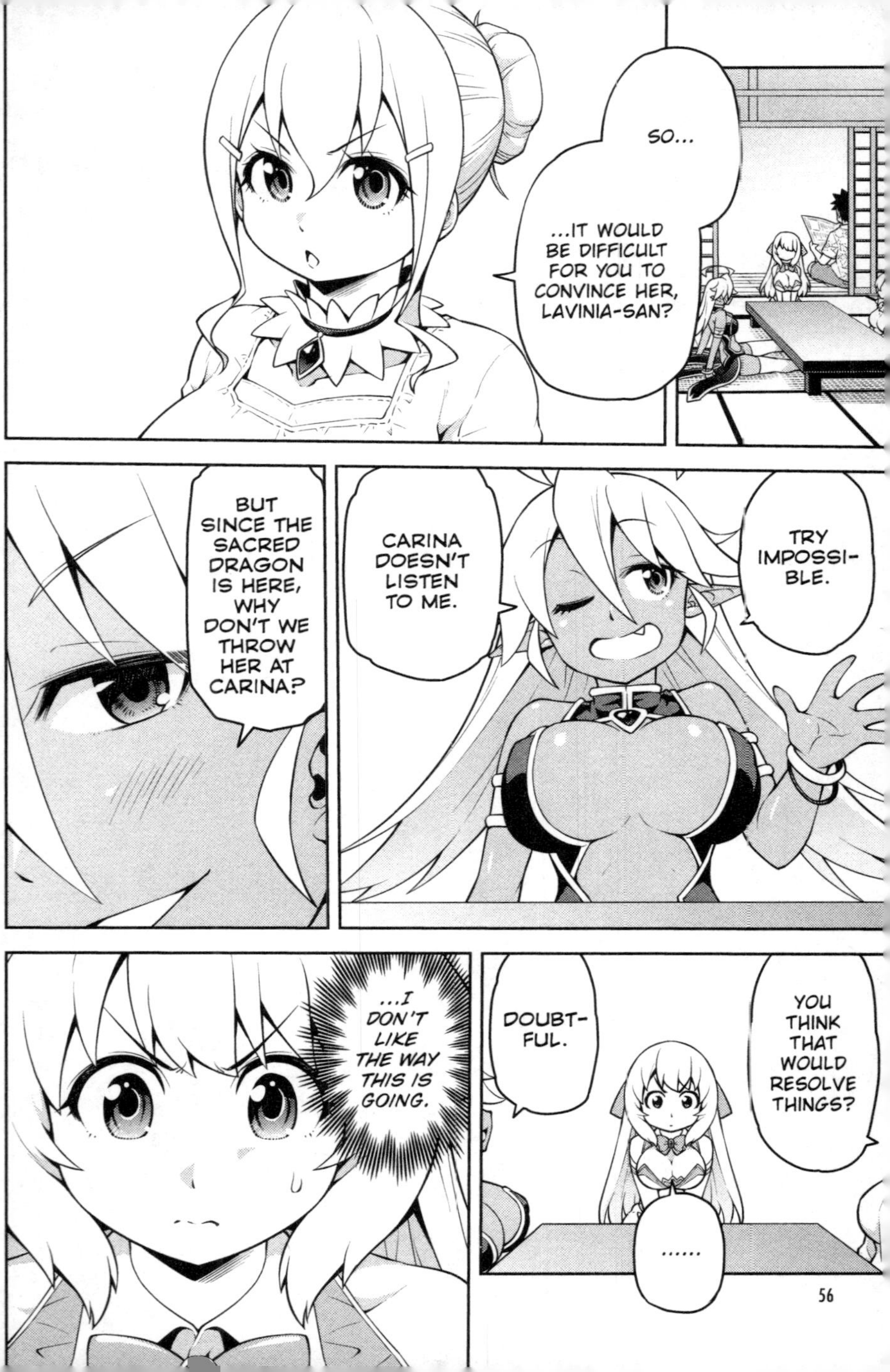
SO...
...IT WOULD BE DIFFICULT FOR YOU TO CONVINCE HER, LAVINIA-SAN?
TRY IMPOSSIBLE.
CARINA DOESN'T LISTEN TO ME.
BUT SINCE THE SACRED DRAGON IS HERE, WHY DON'T WE THROW HER AT CARINA?
YOU THINK THAT WOULD RESOLVE THINGS?
DOUBTFUL.
......
...I DON'T LIKE THE WAY THIS IS GOING.

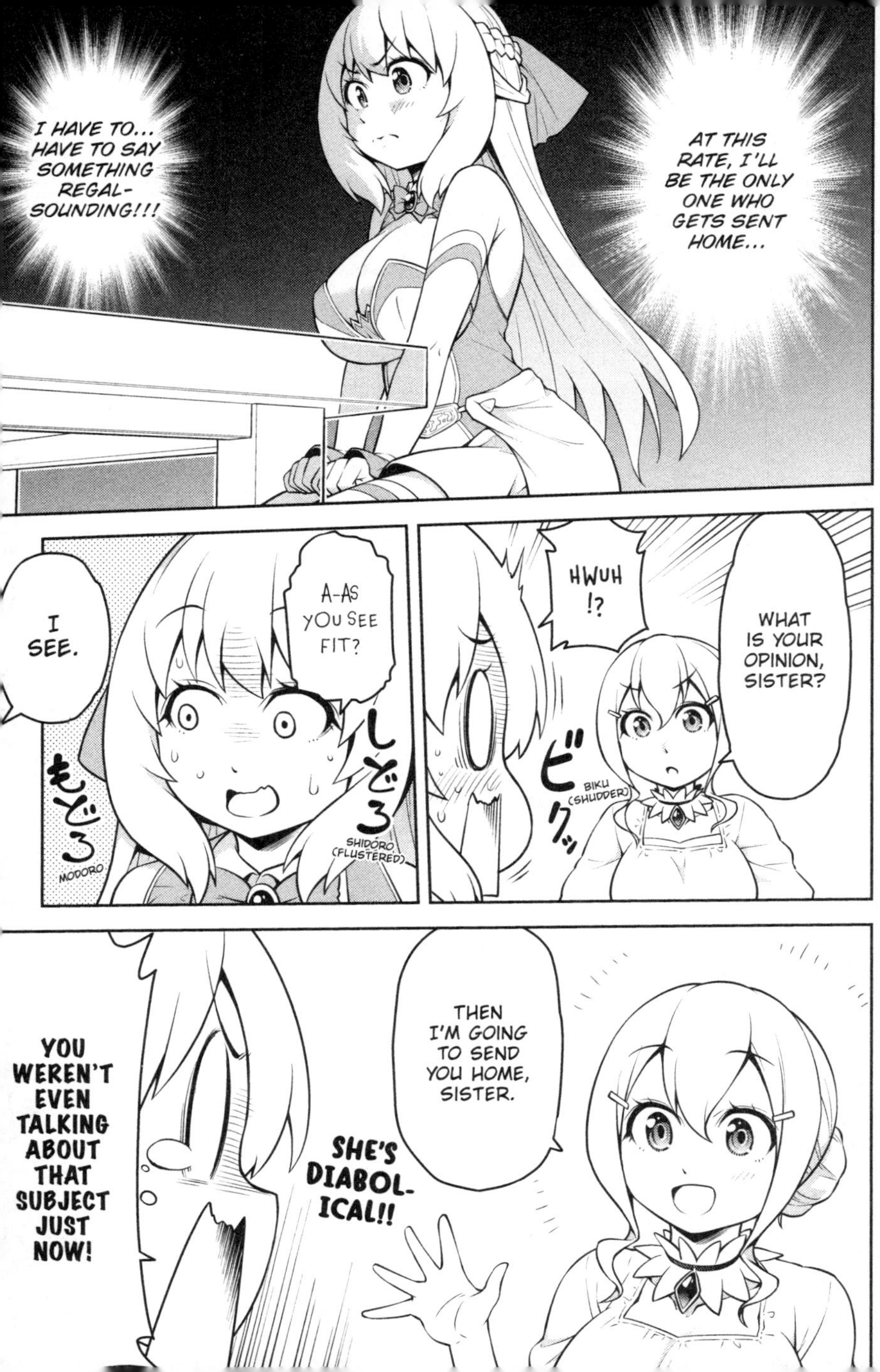
AT THIS RATE, I'LL BE THE ONLY ONE WHO GETS SENT HOME...
I HAVE TO... HAVE TO SAY SOMETHING REGAL-SOUNDING!!!
WHAT IS YOUR OPINION, SISTER?
HWUH !?
ビクッ
BIKU (SHUDDER)
A-AS YOU SEE FIT?
しどろ
SHIDORO (FLUSTERED)
I SEE.
もどろ
MODORO
THEN I'M GOING TO SEND YOU HOME, SISTER.
SHE'S DIABOL-ICAL!!
YOU WEREN'T EVEN TALKING ABOUT THAT SUBJECT JUST NOW!

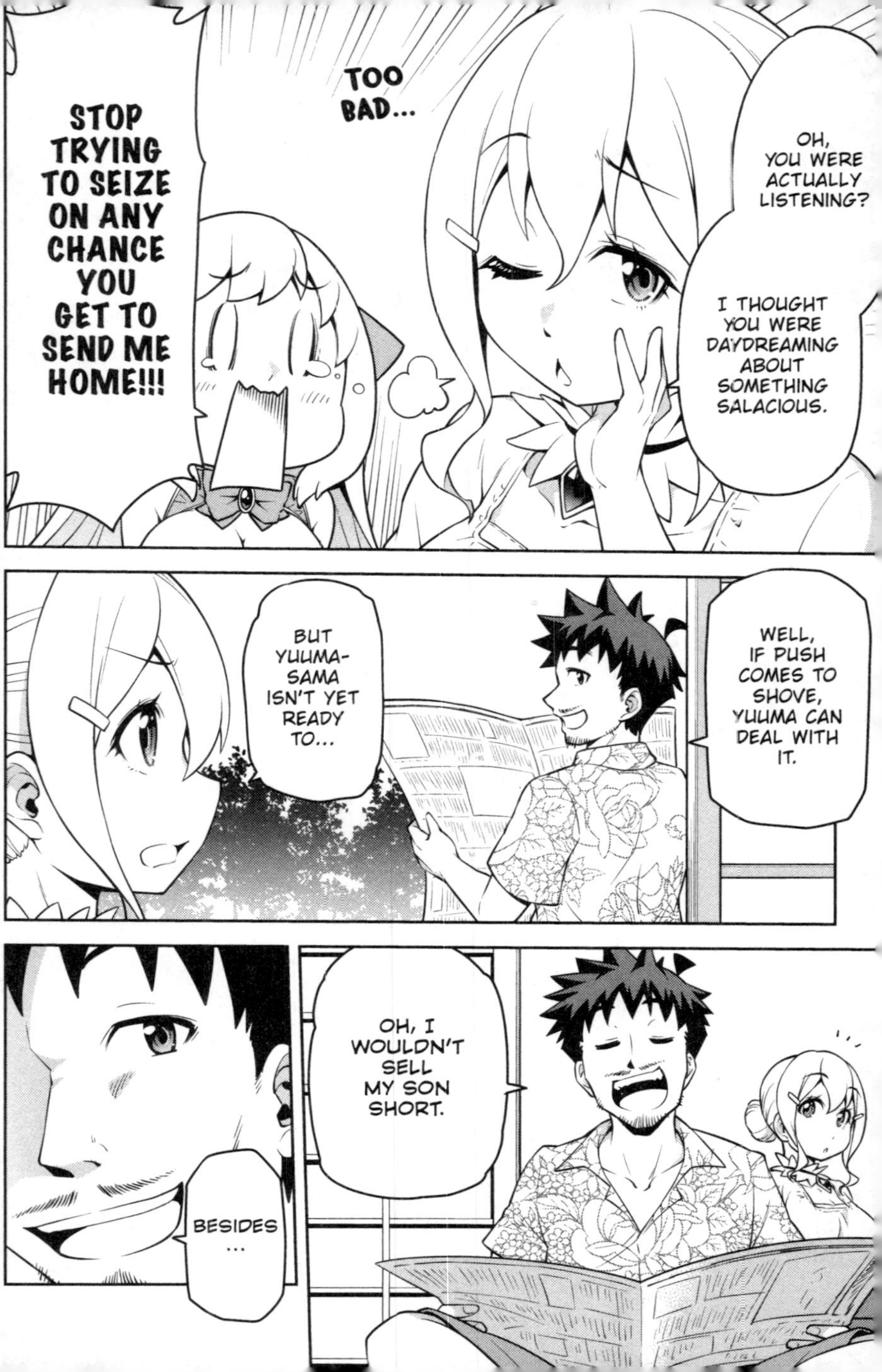
OH, YOU WERE ACTUALLY LISTENING?
I THOUGHT YOU WERE DAYDREAMING ABOUT SOMETHING SALACIOUS.
TOO BAD...
STOP TRYING TO SEIZE ON ANY CHANCE YOU GET TO SEND ME HOME!!!
WELL, IF PUSH COMES TO SHOVE, YUUMA CAN DEAL WITH IT.
BUT YUUMA-SAMA ISN'T YET READY TO...
OH, I WOULDN'T SELL MY SON SHORT.
BESIDES...

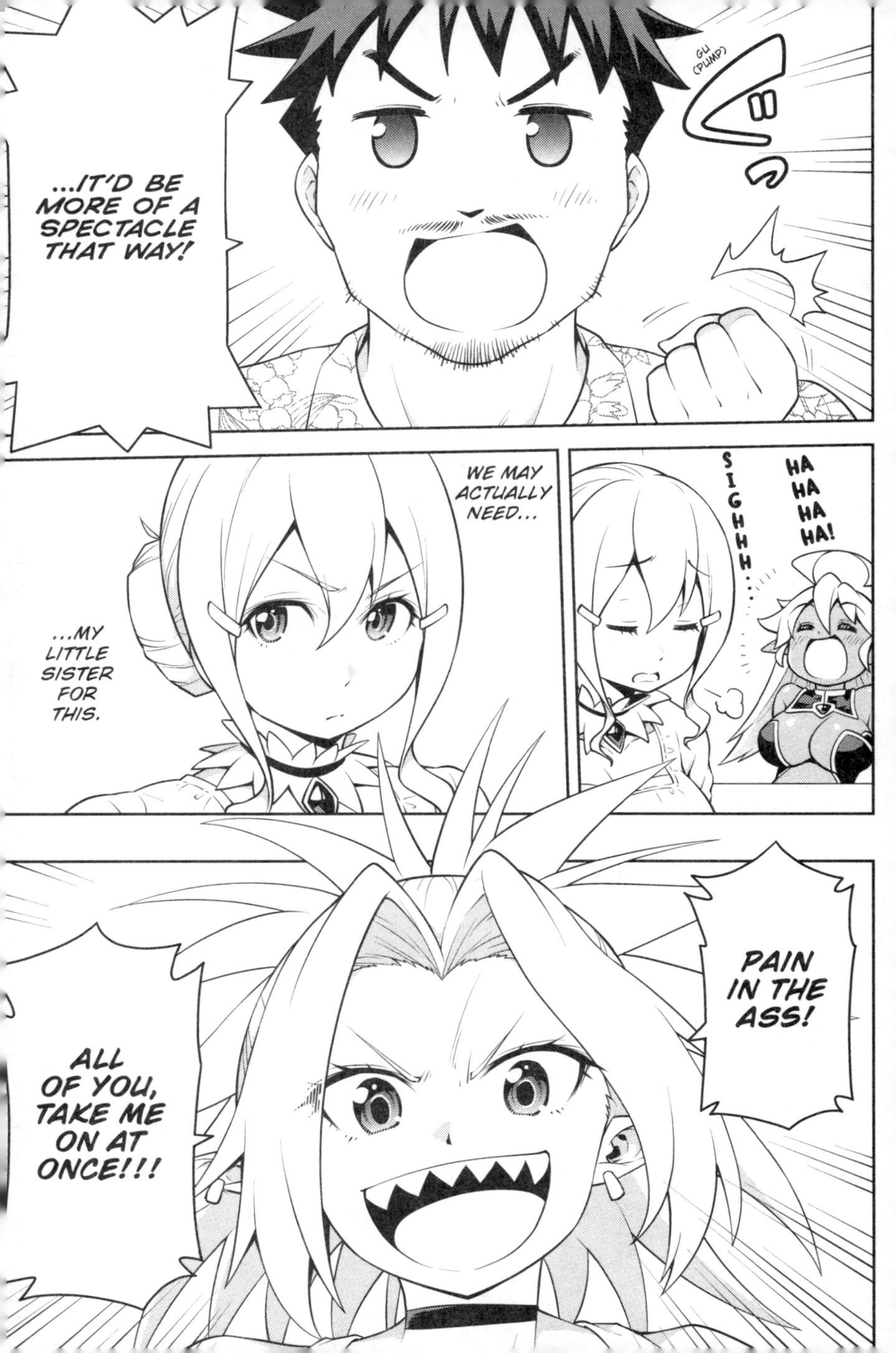
GU (PUMP)
...IT'D BE MORE OF A SPECTACLE THAT WAY!
HA HA HA HA!
SIGHHH...
WE MAY ACTUALLY NEED...
...MY LITTLE SISTER FOR THIS.
PAIN IN THE ASS!
ALL OF YOU, TAKE ME ON AT ONCE!!!

YAAAAAAAAY!

RAAAAAR!

THEN ME!

ME NEXT!

WHEEE!

APRONS: HANAMARU KINDERGARTEN

THE OTHER TEACHERS ARE SICK WITH THE SAME COLD...

WAAAA!

I'M SORRY TO BRING YOU IN ON SUCH SHORT NOTICE, CARINA-SAN.

WHEEE!

Hanamaru Kindergarten

← PRINCIPAL!

I'M UP HIGH!

WHEEE! PRINCIPAL!

EH, NO PROB! I COULD TAKE ON A PACK OF RUG RATS IN MY SLEEP!

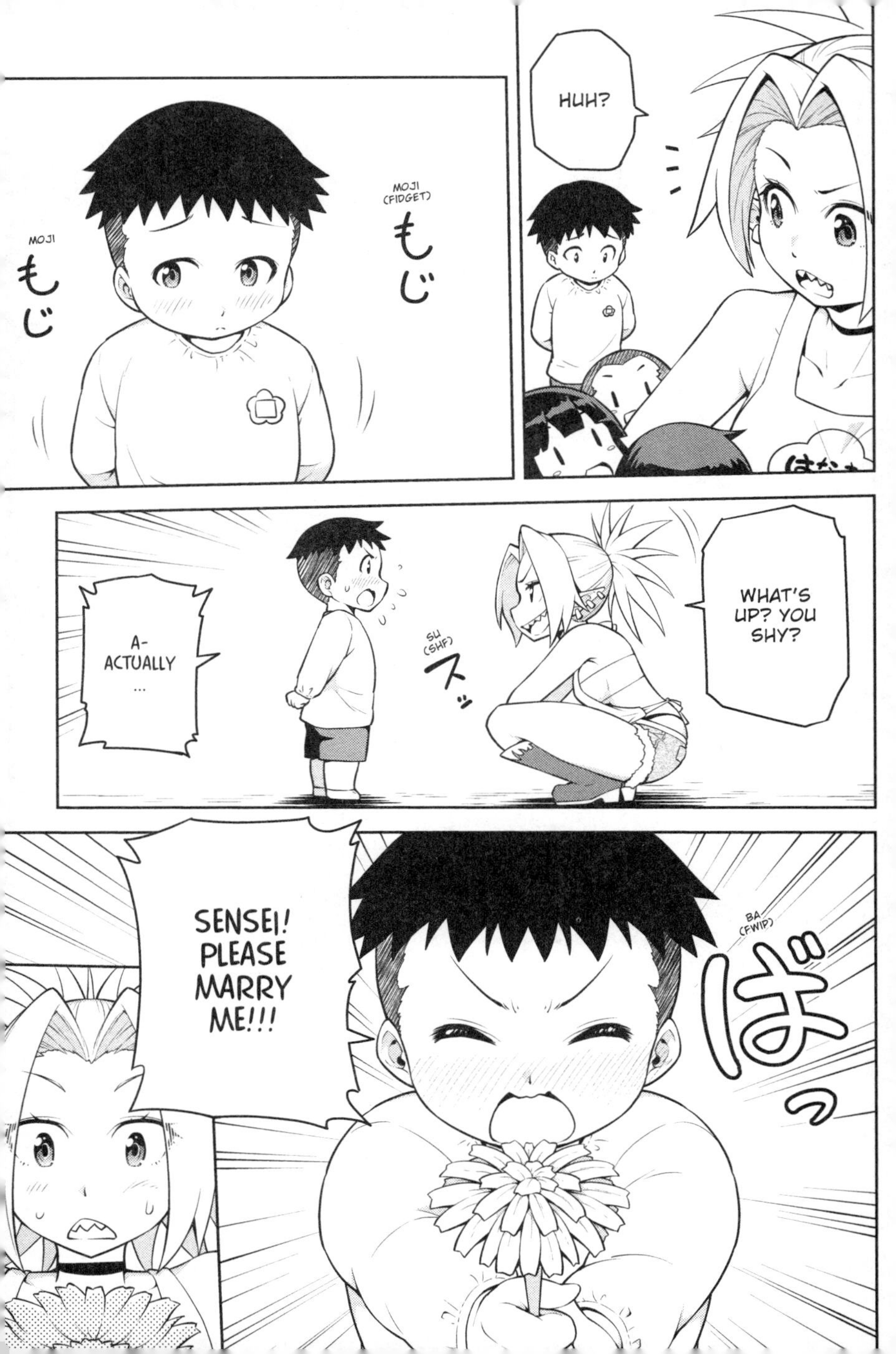
HUH?
MOJI (FIDGET)
もじ
MOJI
もじ
WHAT'S UP? YOU SHY?
SU (SHF)
スッ
A- ACTUALLY ...
BA (FWIP)
ばっ
SENSEI! PLEASE MARRY ME!!!

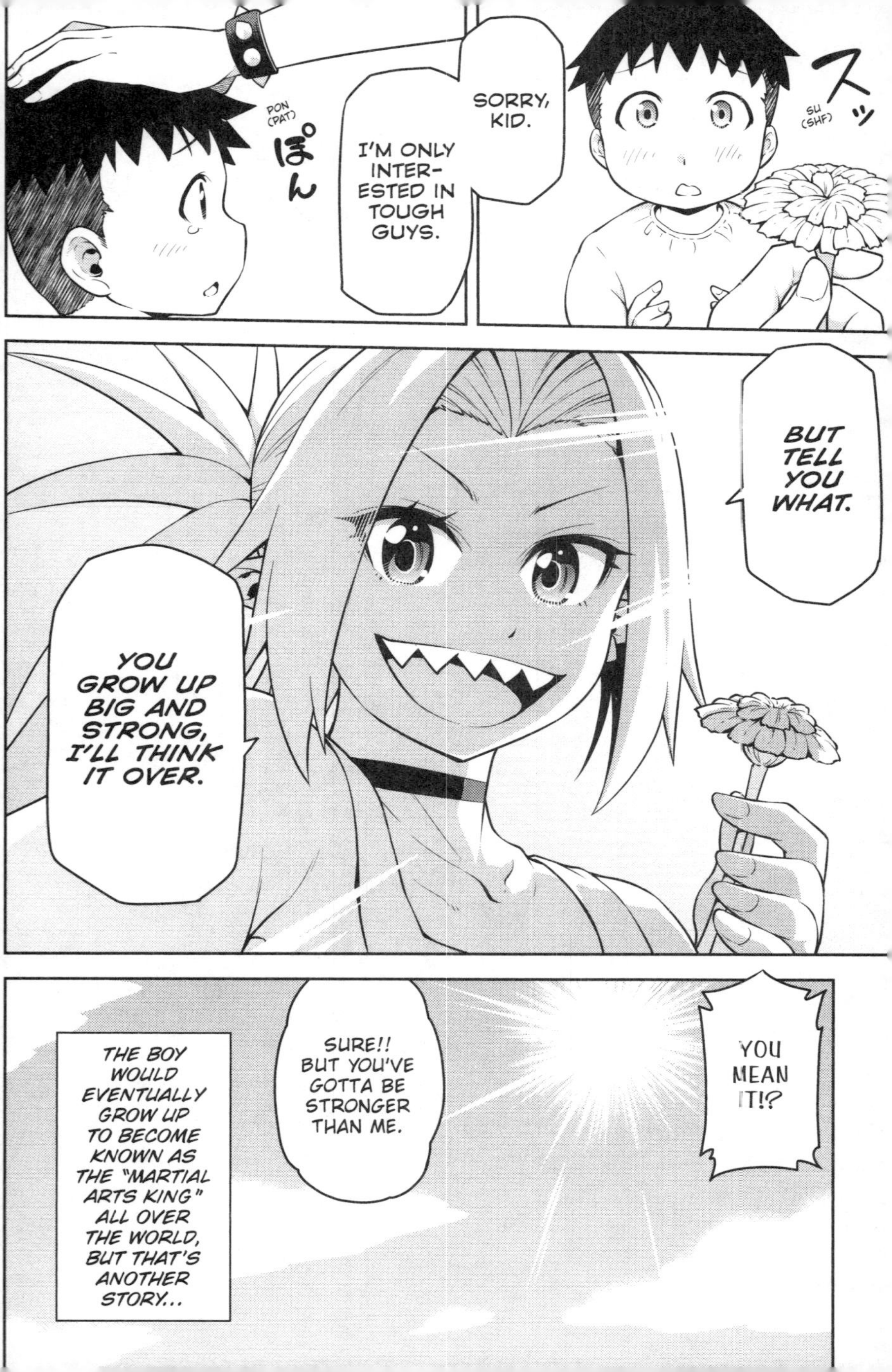
SU (SHF)
スッ
SORRY, KID.
I'M ONLY INTER-ESTED IN TOUGH GUYS.
PON (PAT)
ぽん
BUT TELL YOU WHAT.
YOU GROW UP BIG AND STRONG, I'LL THINK IT OVER.
YOU MEAN IT!?
SURE!! BUT YOU'VE GOTTA BE STRONGER THAN ME.
THE BOY WOULD EVENTUALLY GROW UP TO BECOME KNOWN AS THE "MARTIAL ARTS KING" ALL OVER THE WORLD, BUT THAT'S ANOTHER STORY...

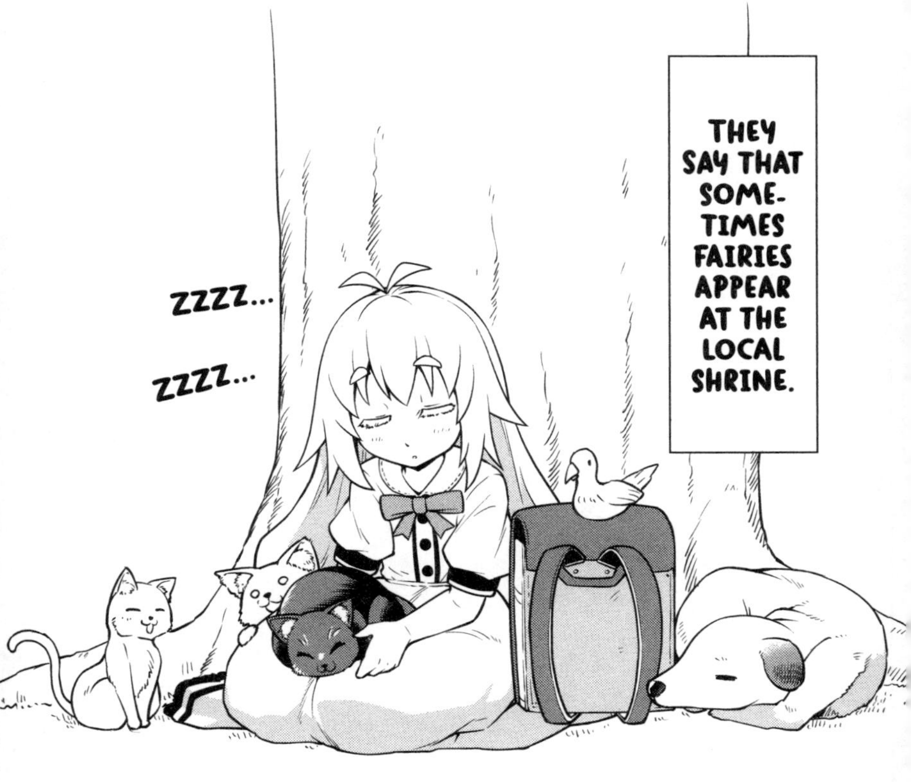
THEY SAY THAT SOME-TIMES FAIRIES APPEAR AT THE LOCAL SHRINE.
ZZZZ...
ZZZZ...

I'm the HERO, but the DEMON LORD's Also Me

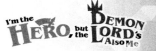

WRAPPER: YUMMY CROQUETTE

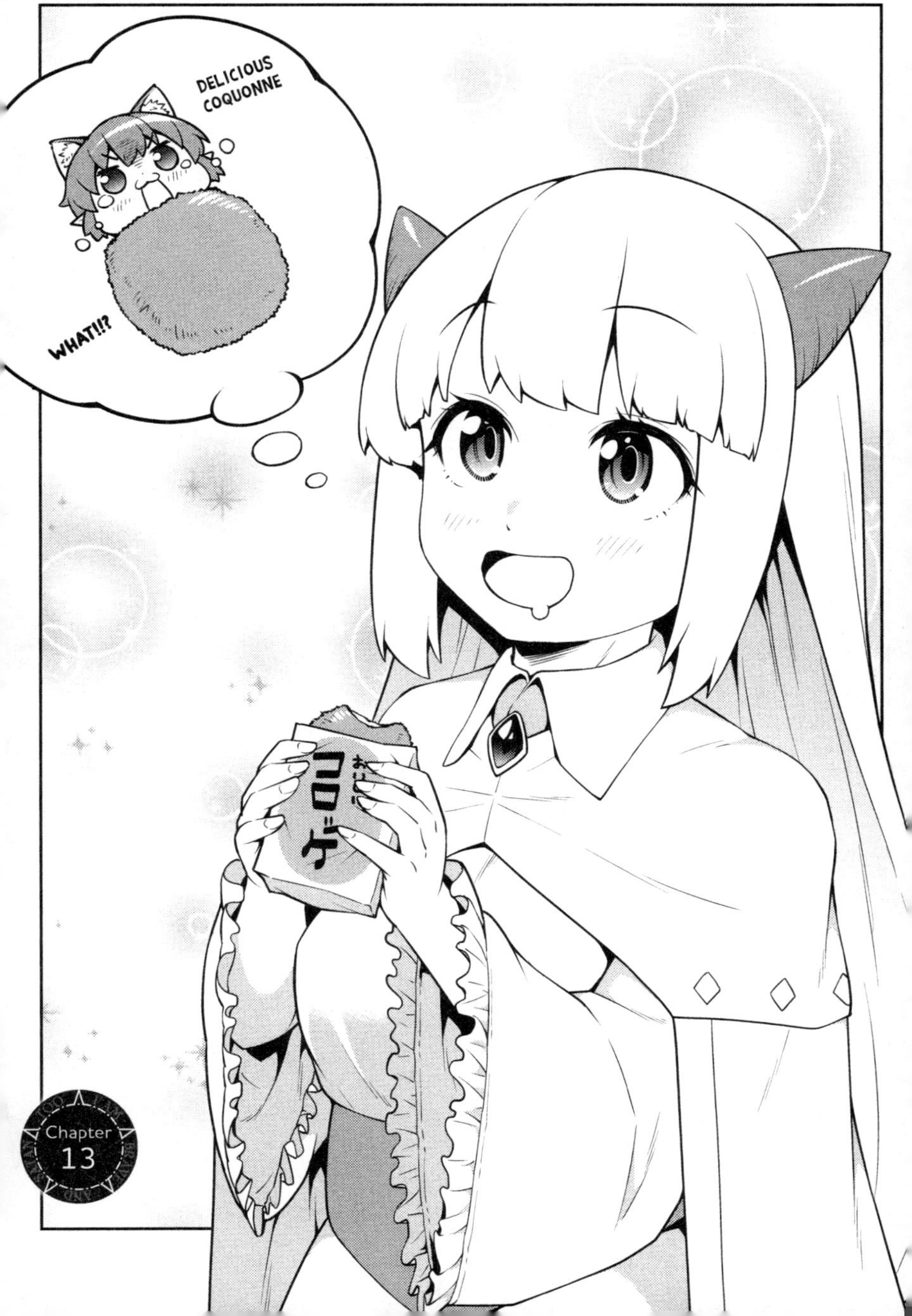

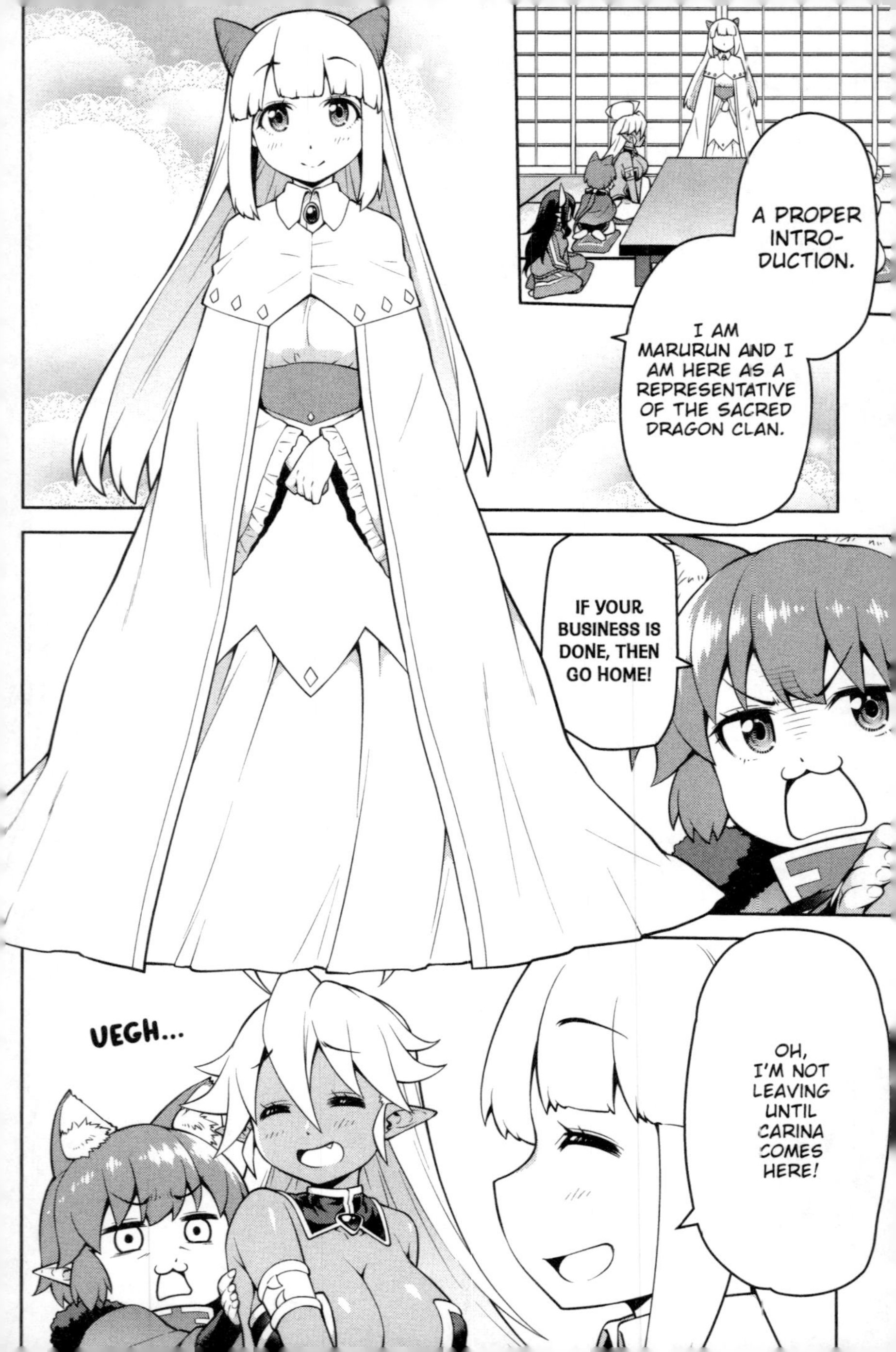
A PROPER INTRO-DUCTION.
I AM MARURUN AND I AM HERE AS A REPRESENTATIVE OF THE SACRED DRAGON CLAN.
IF YOUR BUSINESS IS DONE, THEN GO HOME!
OH, I'M NOT LEAVING UNTIL CARINA COMES HERE!
UEGH...

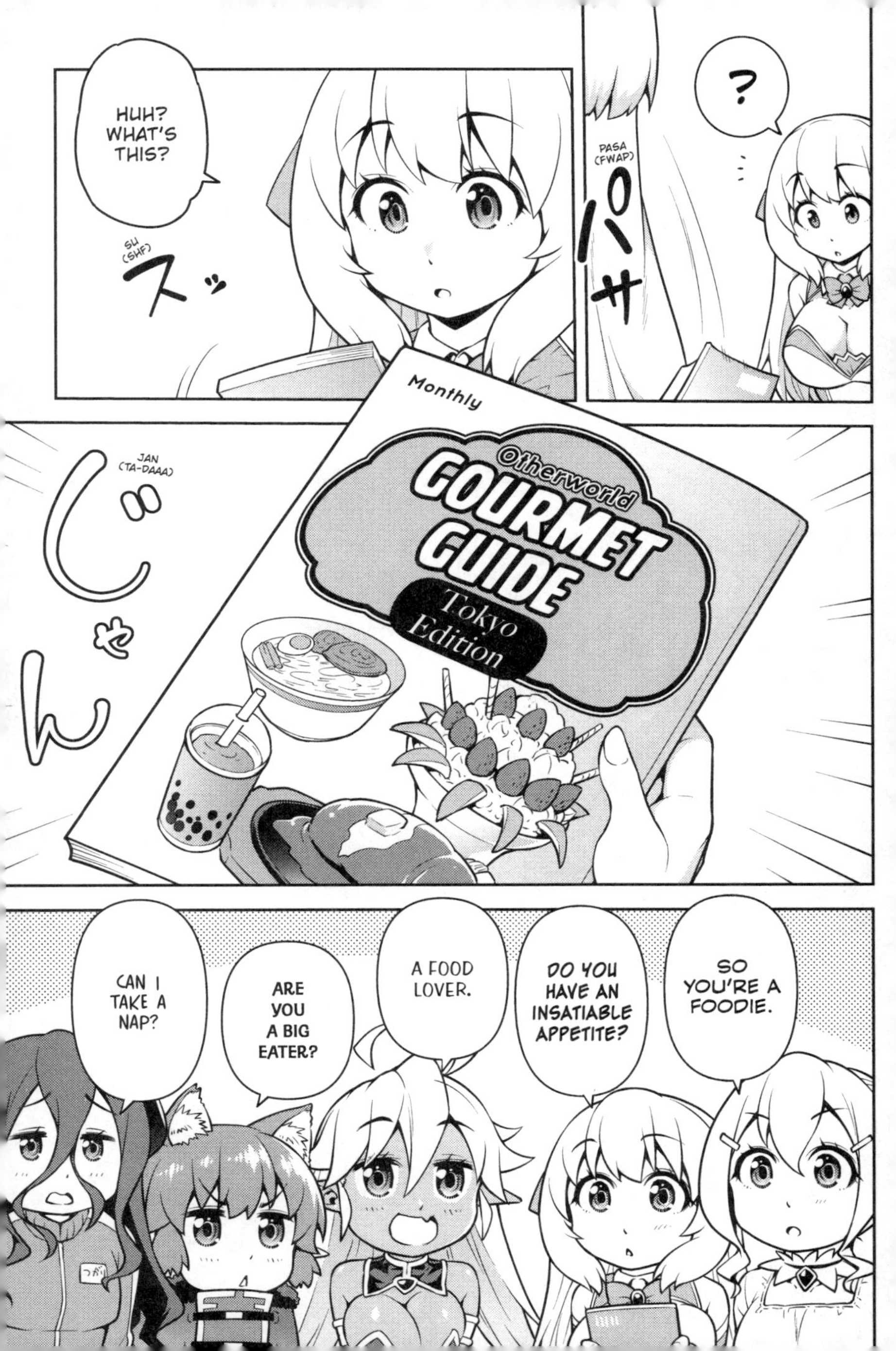
?
PASA (FWAP)
パサッ
HUH? WHAT'S THIS?
SU (SHF)
スッ
JAN (TA-DAAA)
じゃん
Monthly
Otherworld
GOURMET GUIDE
Tokyo Edition
SO YOU'RE A FOODIE.
DO YOU HAVE AN INSATIABLE APPETITE?
A FOOD LOVER.
ARE YOU A BIG EATER?
CAN I TAKE A NAP?

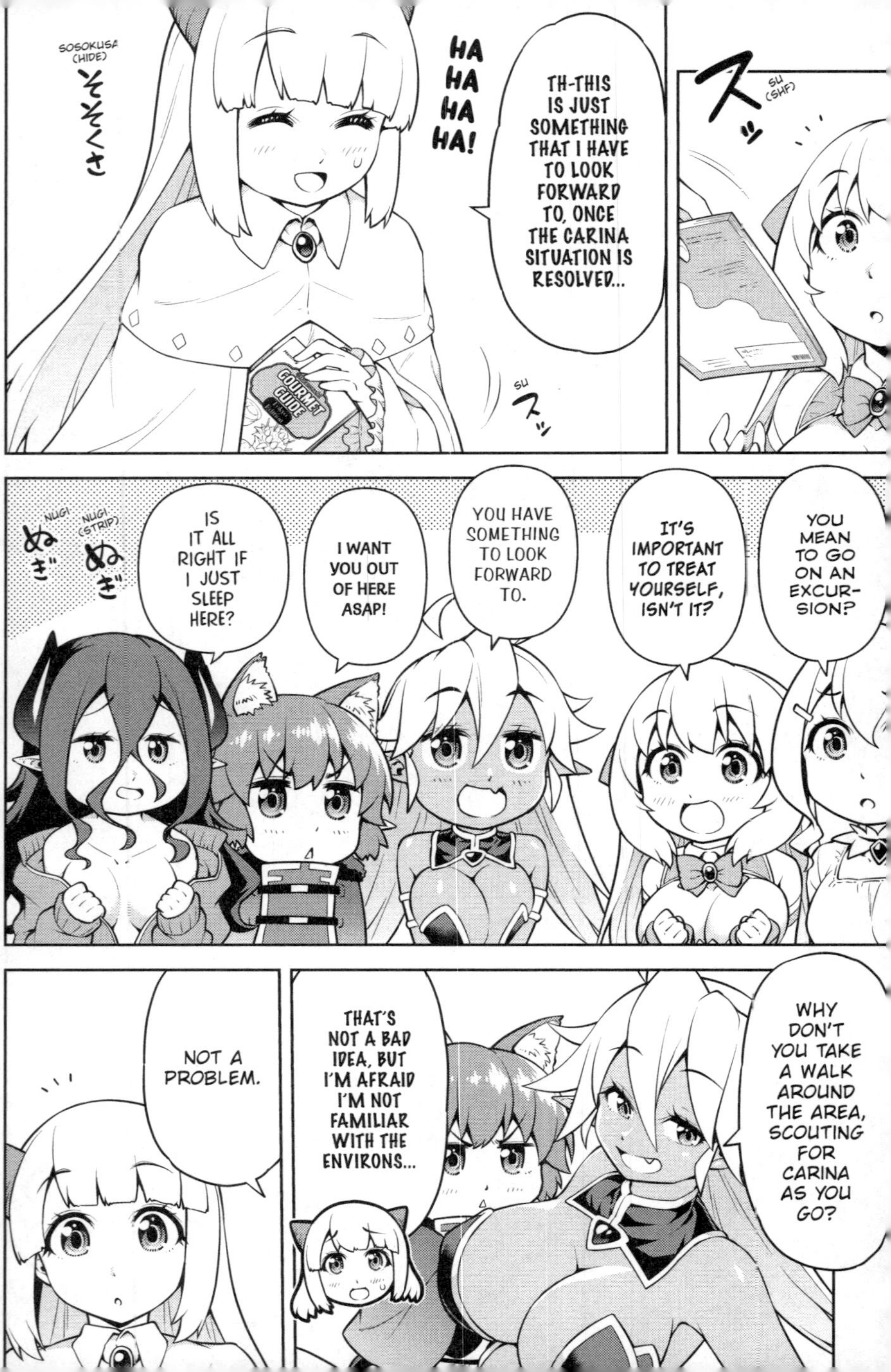
SU (SHF)
スッ
TH-THIS IS JUST SOMETHING THAT I HAVE TO LOOK FORWARD TO, ONCE THE CARINA SITUATION IS RESOLVED...
HA HA HA HA!
SOSOKUSA (HIDE)
そそくさ
SU
スッ
GOURMET GUIDE
YOU MEAN TO GO ON AN EXCUR-SION?
IT'S IMPORTANT TO TREAT YOURSELF, ISN'T IT?
YOU HAVE SOMETHING TO LOOK FORWARD TO.
I WANT YOU OUT OF HERE ASAP!
IS IT ALL RIGHT IF I JUST SLEEP HERE?
NUGI NUGI (STRIP)
ぬぎぬぎ
WHY DON'T YOU TAKE A WALK AROUND THE AREA, SCOUTING FOR CARINA AS YOU GO?
THAT'S NOT A BAD IDEA, BUT I'M AFRAID I'M NOT FAMILIAR WITH THE ENVIRONS...
NOT A PROBLEM.

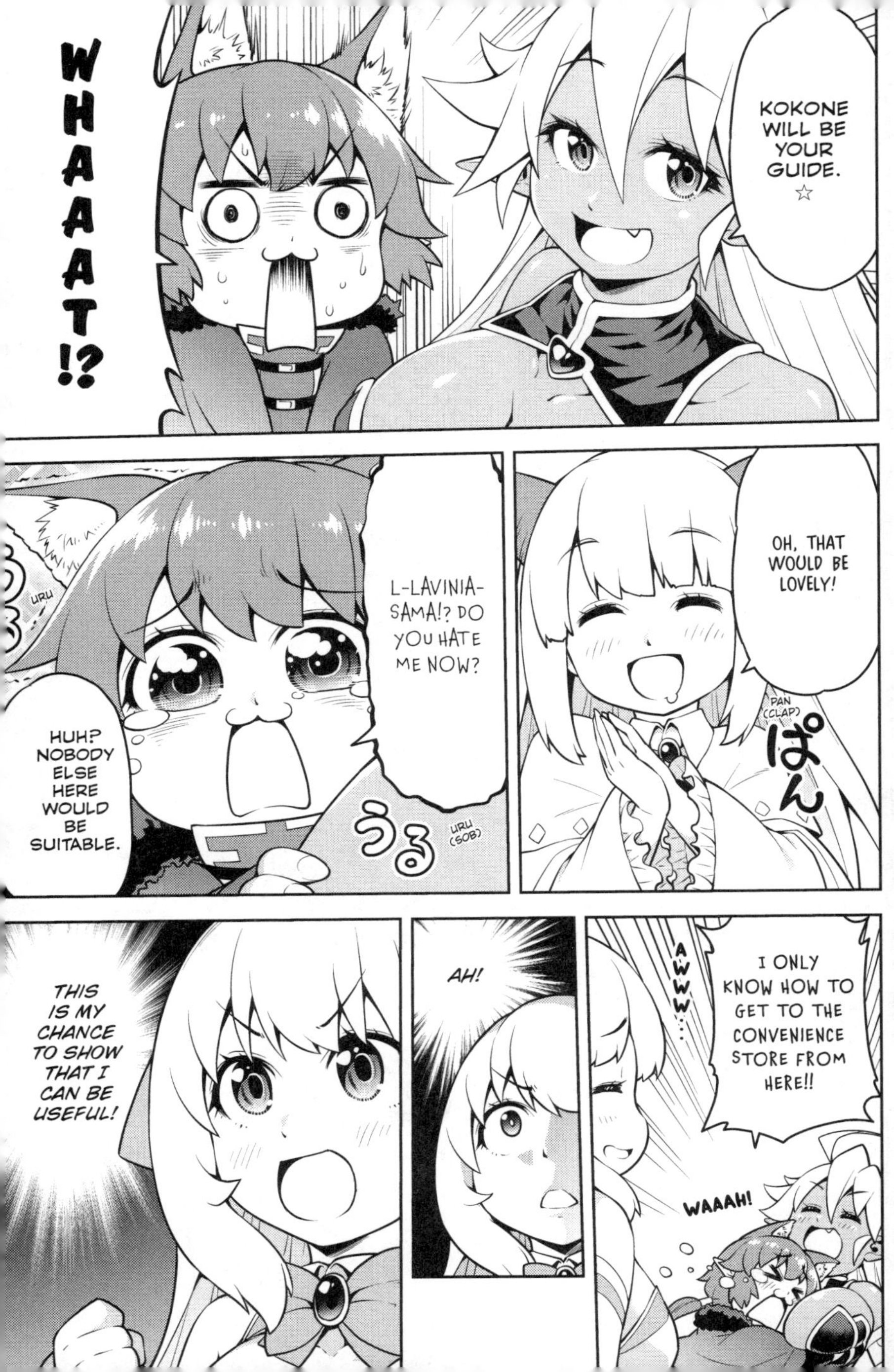
KOKONE WILL BE YOUR GUIDE. ☆
WHAAAAT!?
OH, THAT WOULD BE LOVELY!
PAN (CLAP)
ぱん
L-LAVINIA-SAMA!? DO YOU HATE ME NOW?
HUH? NOBODY ELSE HERE WOULD BE SUITABLE.
URU
うる
URU (SOB)
I ONLY KNOW HOW TO GET TO THE CONVENIENCE STORE FROM HERE!!
AWWW...
WAAAH!
AH!
THIS IS MY CHANCE TO SHOW THAT I CAN BE USEFUL!

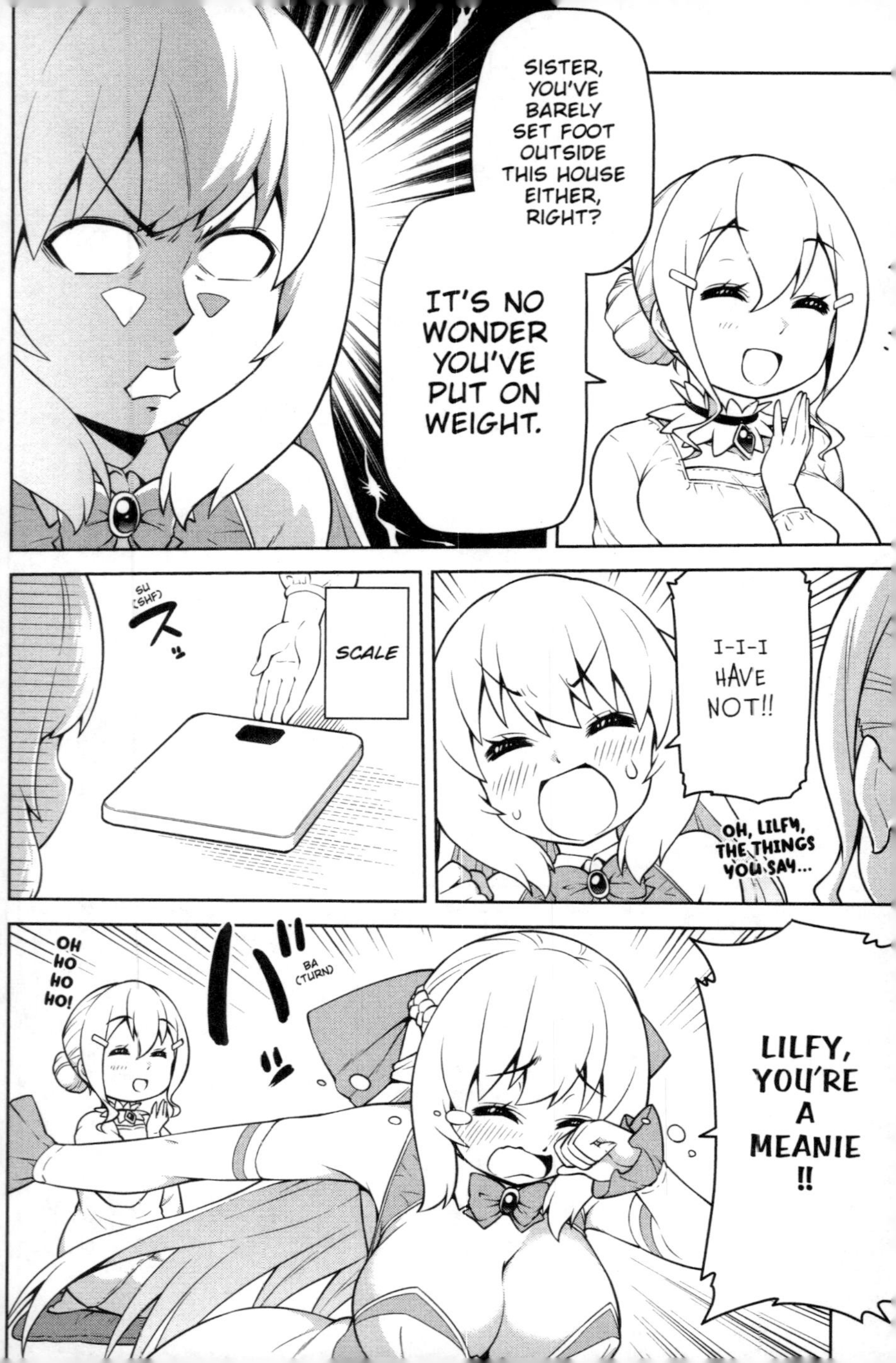
SISTER, YOU'VE BARELY SET FOOT OUTSIDE THIS HOUSE EITHER, RIGHT?
IT'S NO WONDER YOU'VE PUT ON WEIGHT.
I-I-I HAVE NOT!!
OH, LILFY, THE THINGS YOU SAY...
SCALE
SU (SHF)
LILFY, YOU'RE A MEANIE!!
BA (TURN)
OH HO HO HO!

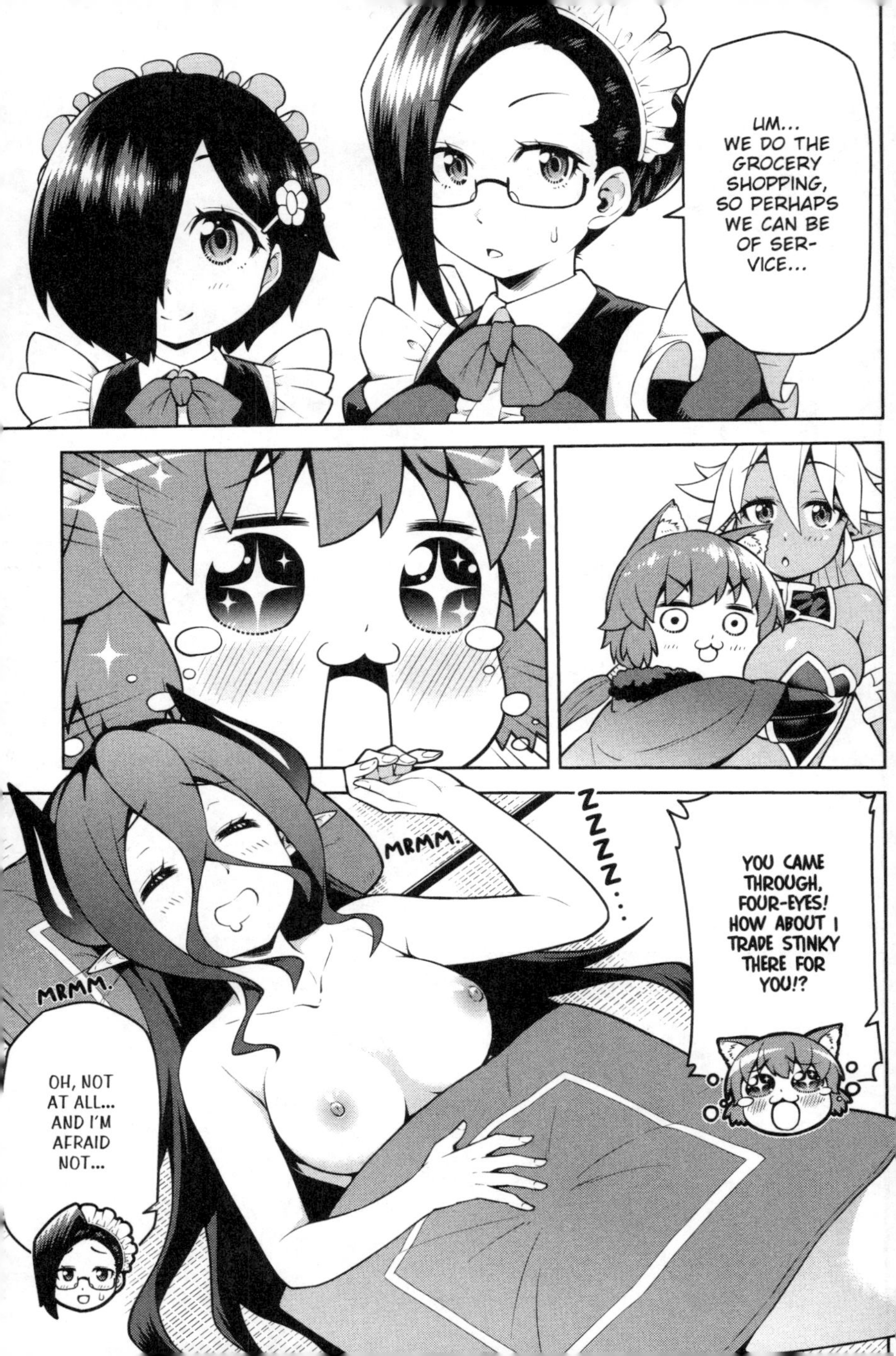
UM... WE DO THE GROCERY SHOPPING, SO PERHAPS WE CAN BE OF SER-VICE...
YOU CAME THROUGH, FOUR-EYES! HOW ABOUT I TRADE STINKY THERE FOR YOU!?
ZZZZ...
MRMM.
MRMM.
OH, NOT AT ALL... AND I'M AFRAID NOT...

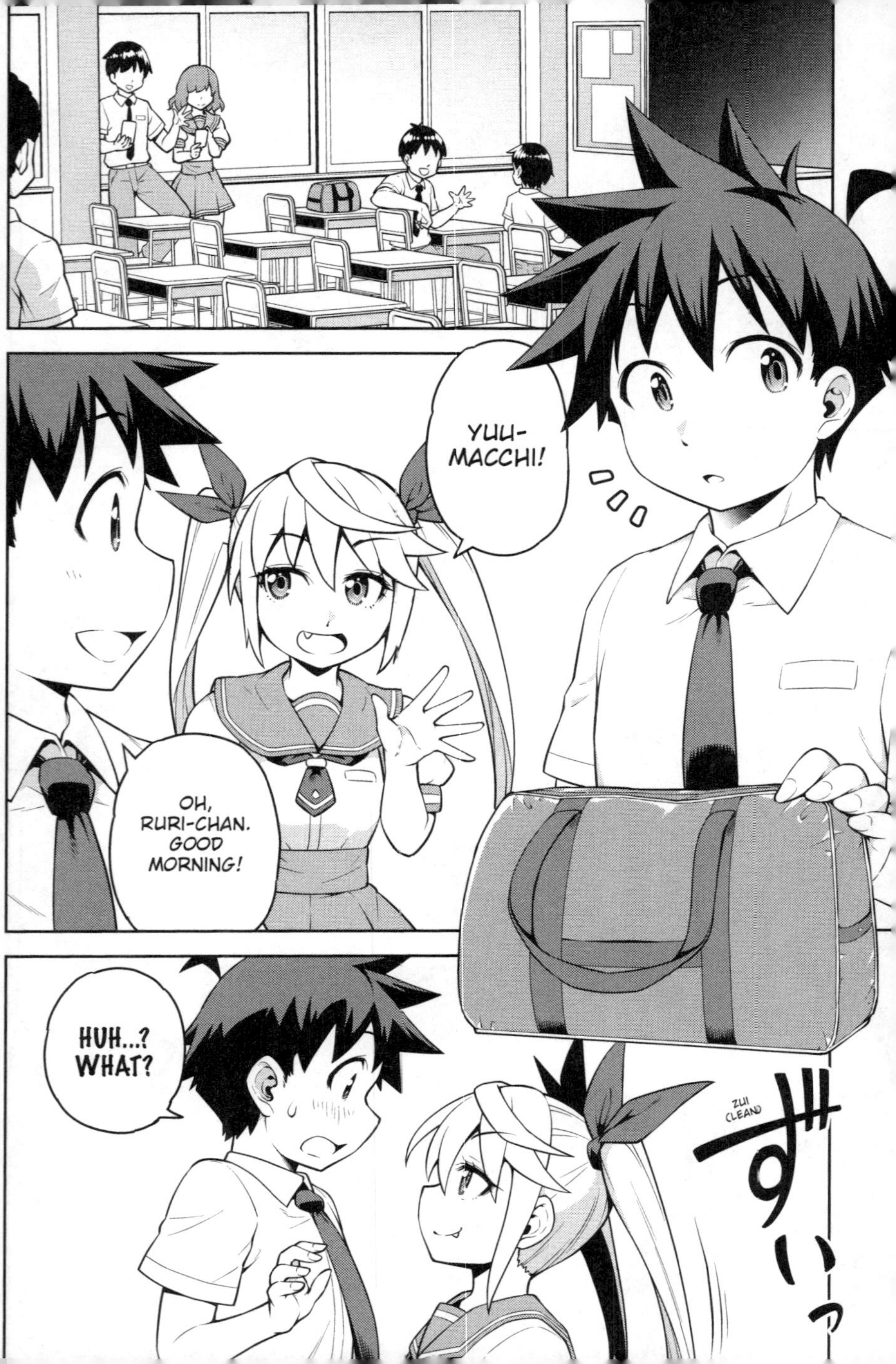
YUU-MACCHI!
OH, RURI-CHAN. GOOD MORNING!
ZUI (CLEAN)
HUH...? WHAT?

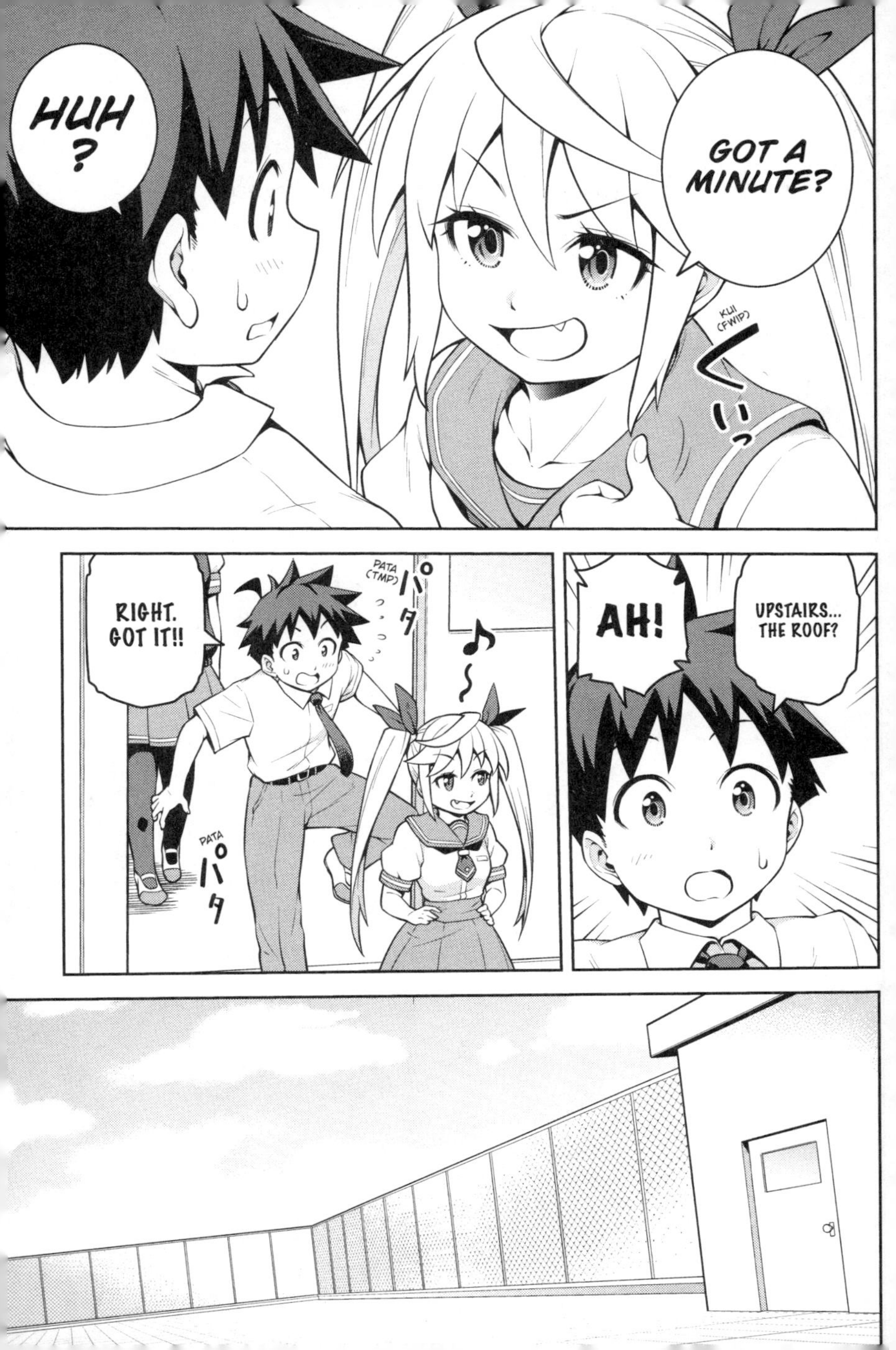

GOT A MINUTE?
KUI (FWIP)
HUH?
UPSTAIRS... THE ROOF?
AH!
RIGHT. GOT IT!!
PATA (TMP)
PATA

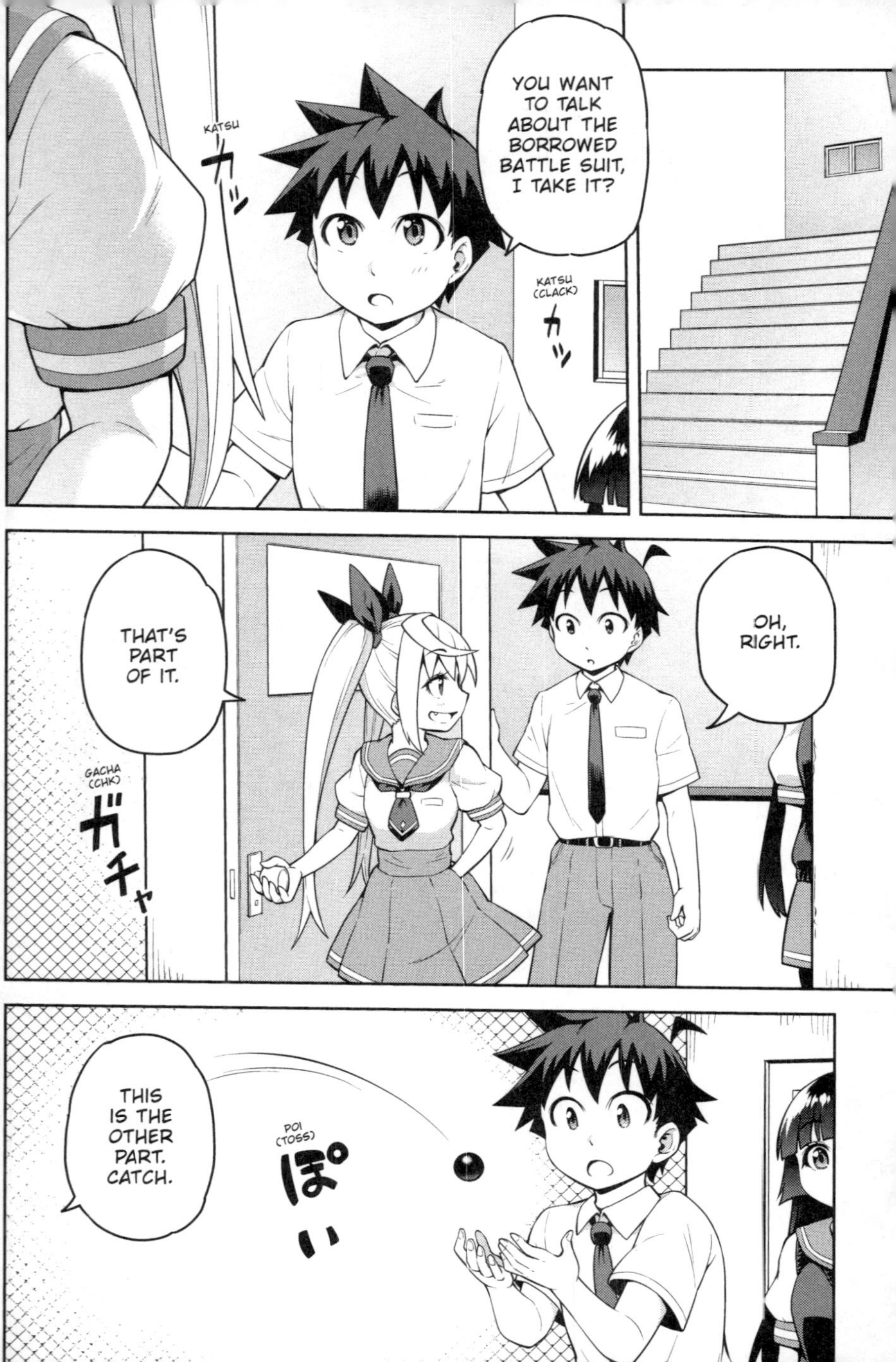
YOU WANT TO TALK ABOUT THE BORROWED BATTLE SUIT, I TAKE IT?
KATSU
カッ
KATSU (CLACK)
カッ
OH, RIGHT.
THAT'S PART OF IT.
GACHA (CHK)
ガチャ
THIS IS THE OTHER PART. CATCH.
POI (TOSS)
ぽい

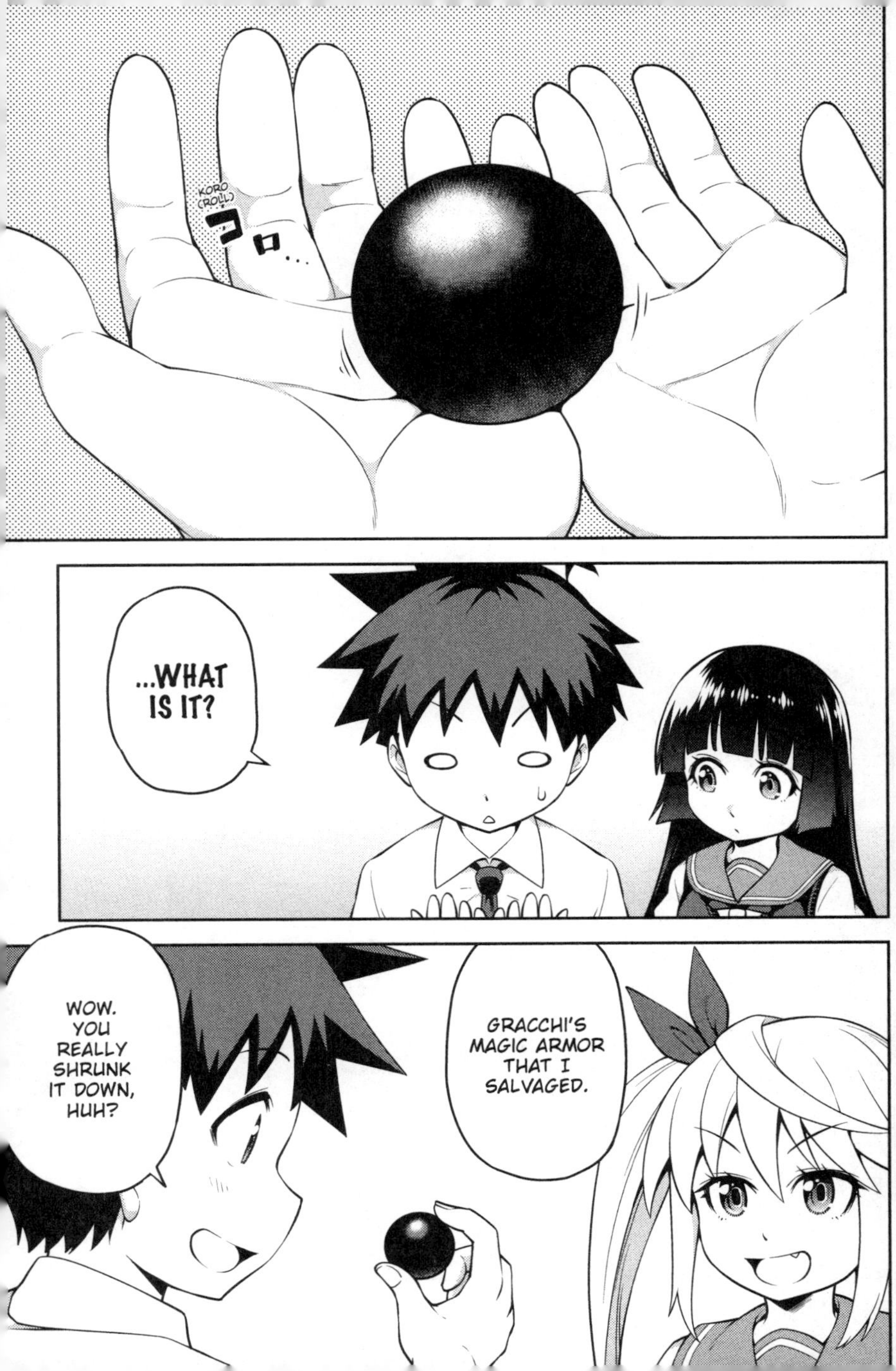
KORO (ROLL)
コロ…
...WHAT IS IT?
GRACCHI'S MAGIC ARMOR THAT I SALVAGED.
WOW. YOU REALLY SHRUNK IT DOWN, HUH?

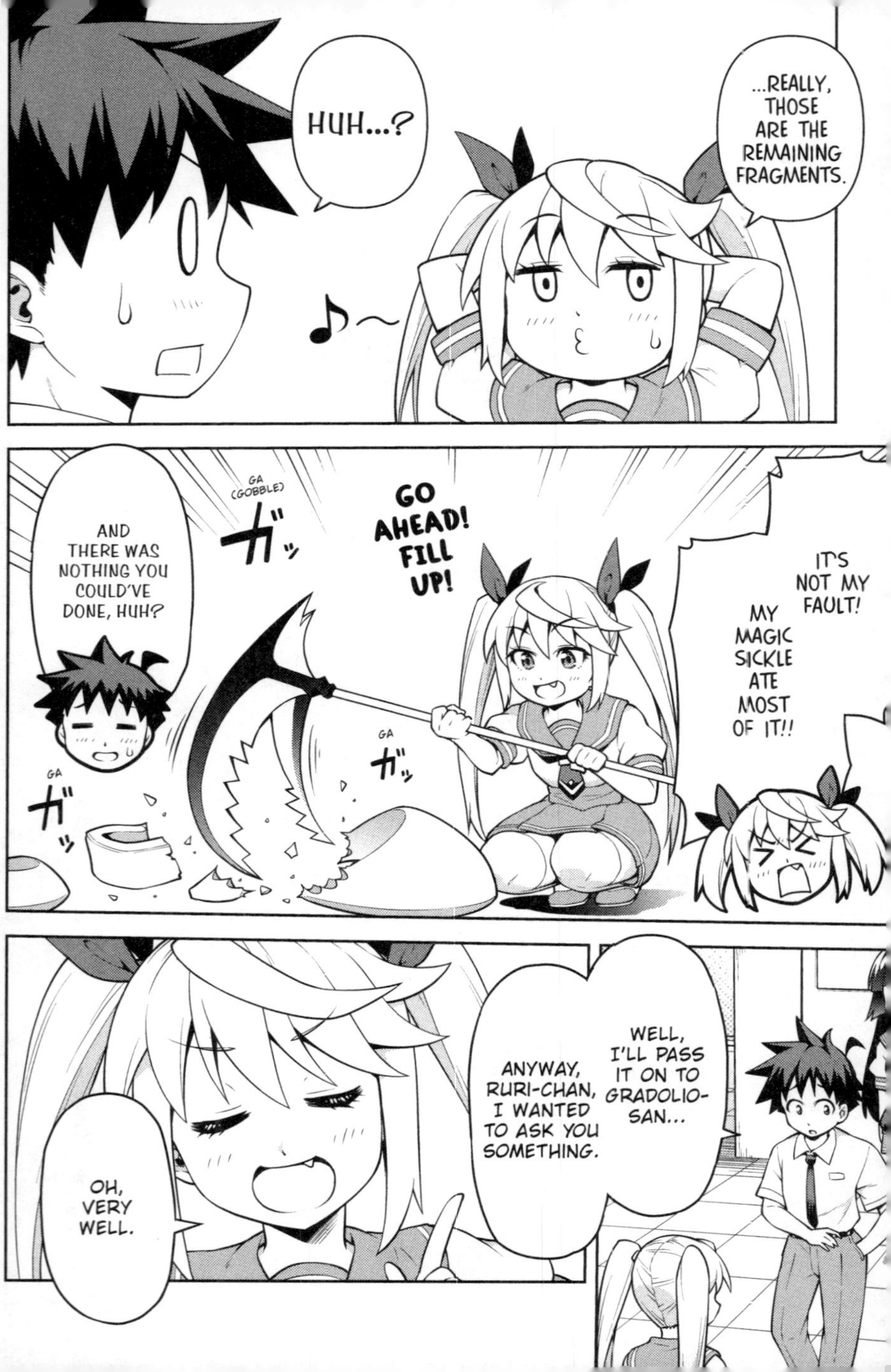
...REALLY, THOSE ARE THE REMAINING FRAGMENTS.
♪~
HUH...?
IT'S NOT MY FAULT!
MY MAGIC SICKLE ATE MOST OF IT!!
GO AHEAD! FILL UP!
GA (GOBBLE)
GA
GA
AND THERE WAS NOTHING YOU COULD'VE DONE, HUH?
WELL, I'LL PASS IT ON TO GRADOLIO-SAN...
ANYWAY, RURI-CHAN, I WANTED TO ASK YOU SOMETHING.
OH, VERY WELL.

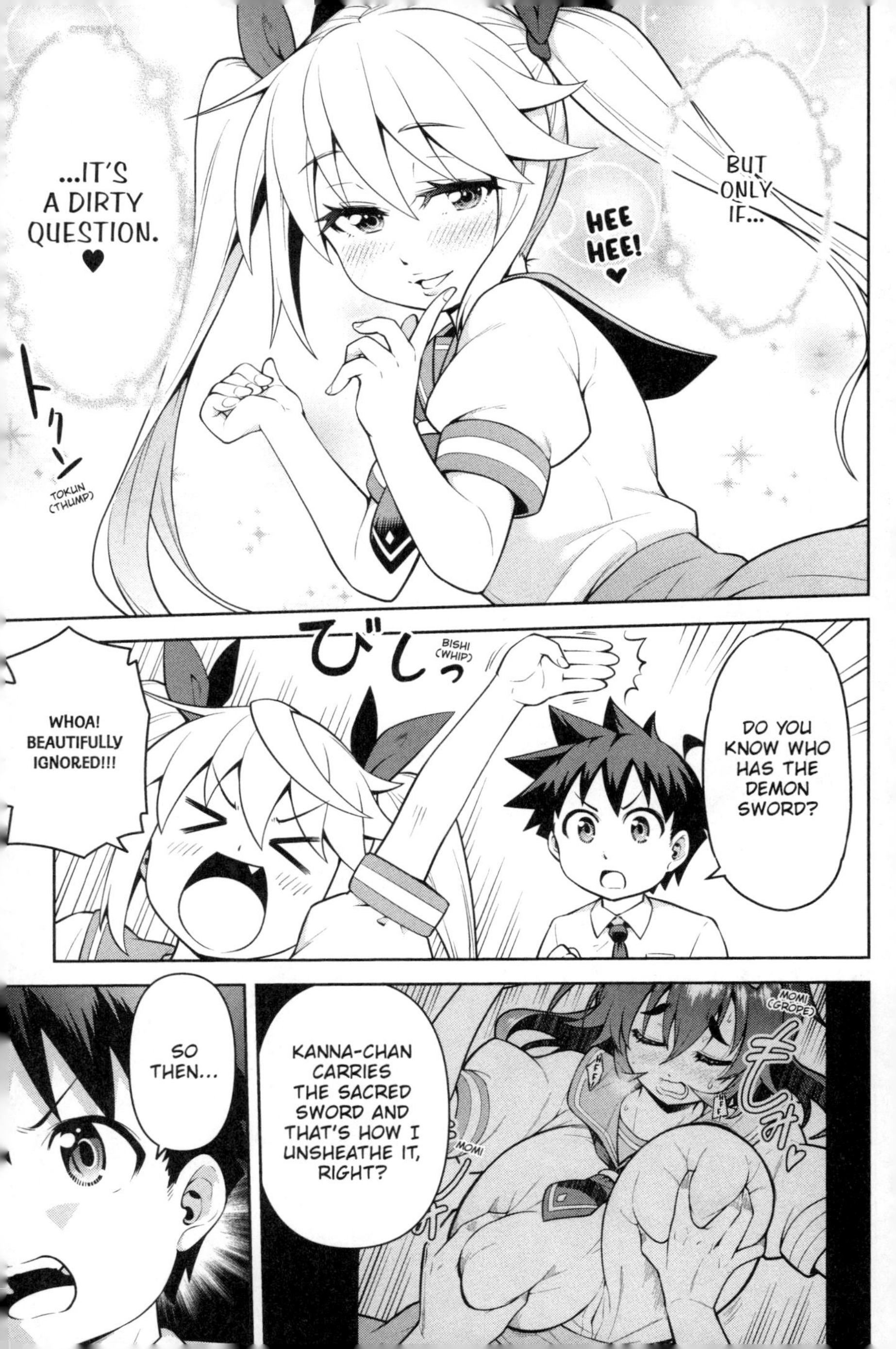
BUT ONLY IF...
HEE HEE! ♥
...IT'S A DIRTY QUESTION. ♥
TOKUN (THUMP)
DO YOU KNOW WHO HAS THE DEMON SWORD?
BISHI (WHIP)
WHOA! BEAUTIFULLY IGNORED!!!
MOMI (GROPE)
SO THEN...
KANNA-CHAN CARRIES THE SACRED SWORD AND THAT'S HOW I UNSHEATHE IT, RIGHT?
MOMI

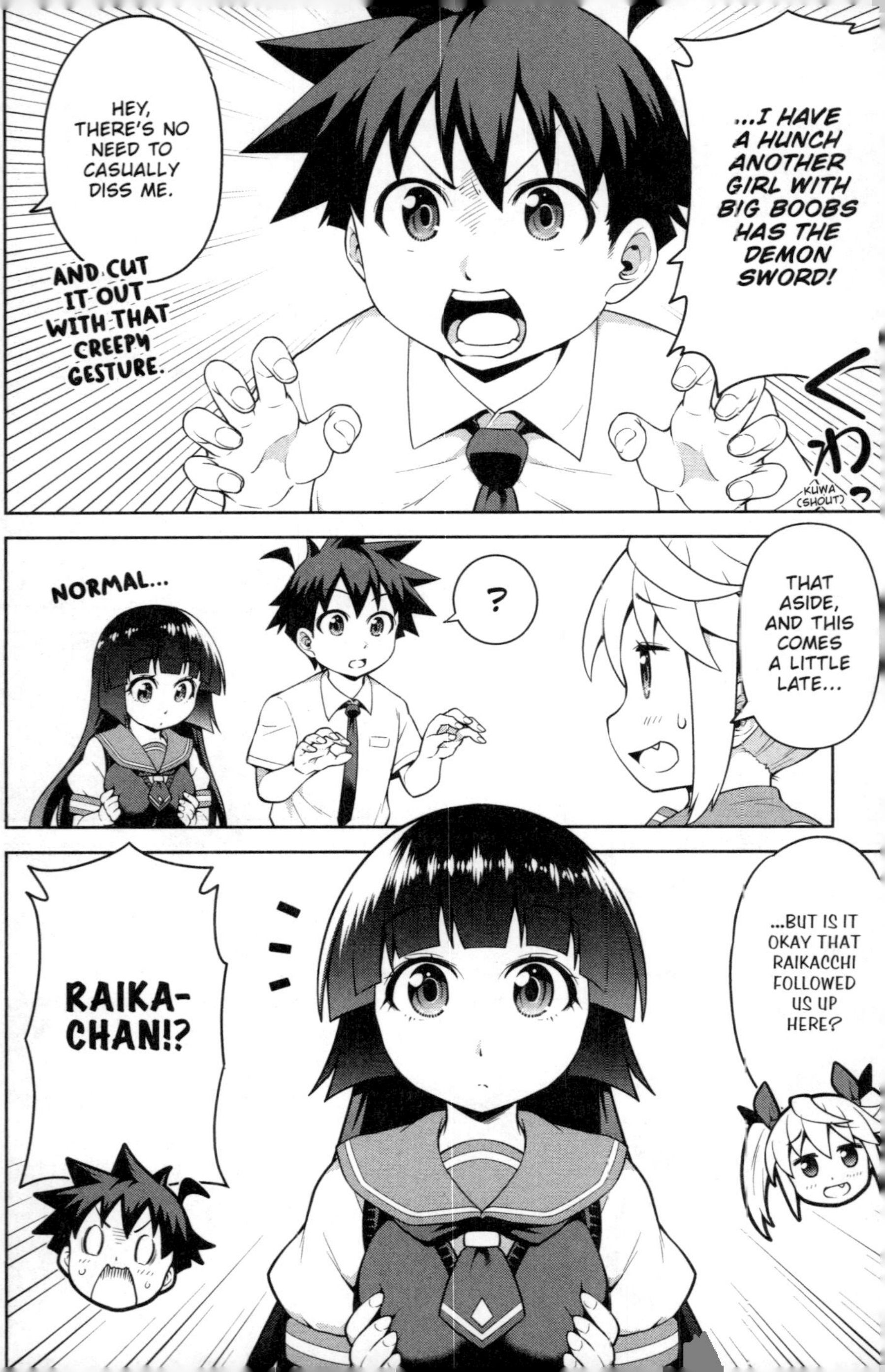
...I HAVE A HUNCH ANOTHER GIRL WITH BIG BOOBS HAS THE DEMON SWORD!
KUWA (SHOUT)
HEY, THERE'S NO NEED TO CASUALLY DISS ME.
AND CUT IT OUT WITH THAT CREEPY GESTURE.
THAT ASIDE, AND THIS COMES A LITTLE LATE...
?
NORMAL...
...BUT IS IT OKAY THAT RAIKACCHI FOLLOWED US UP HERE?
RAIKA-CHAN!?

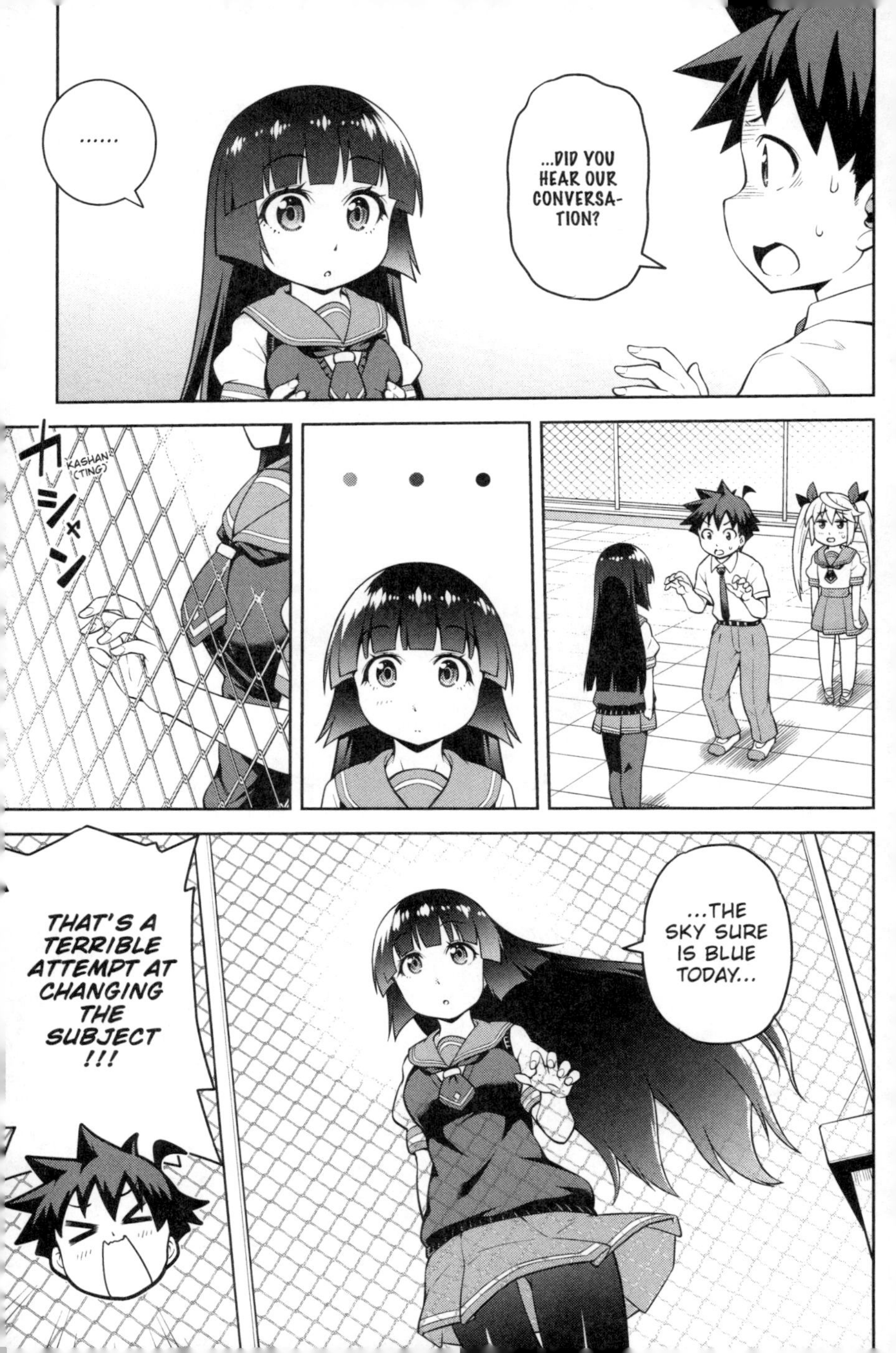
...DID YOU HEAR OUR CONVERSATION?
......
• • •
カシャン
KASHAN (TING)
...THE SKY SURE IS BLUE TODAY...
THAT'S A TERRIBLE ATTEMPT AT CHANGING THE SUBJECT!!!

GOOD-BYE, SENSEI!

BYE-BYE!

BYE! CAREFUL GOIN' HOME!!

YOU'RE GOOD WITH THE KIDS.

SORRY, BUT I KIND OF GOT A PRIOR ENGAGEMENT.

HEH HEH...

FEEL LIKE GOING OUT FOR A PINT? MY TREAT.

KUI (FWIP)

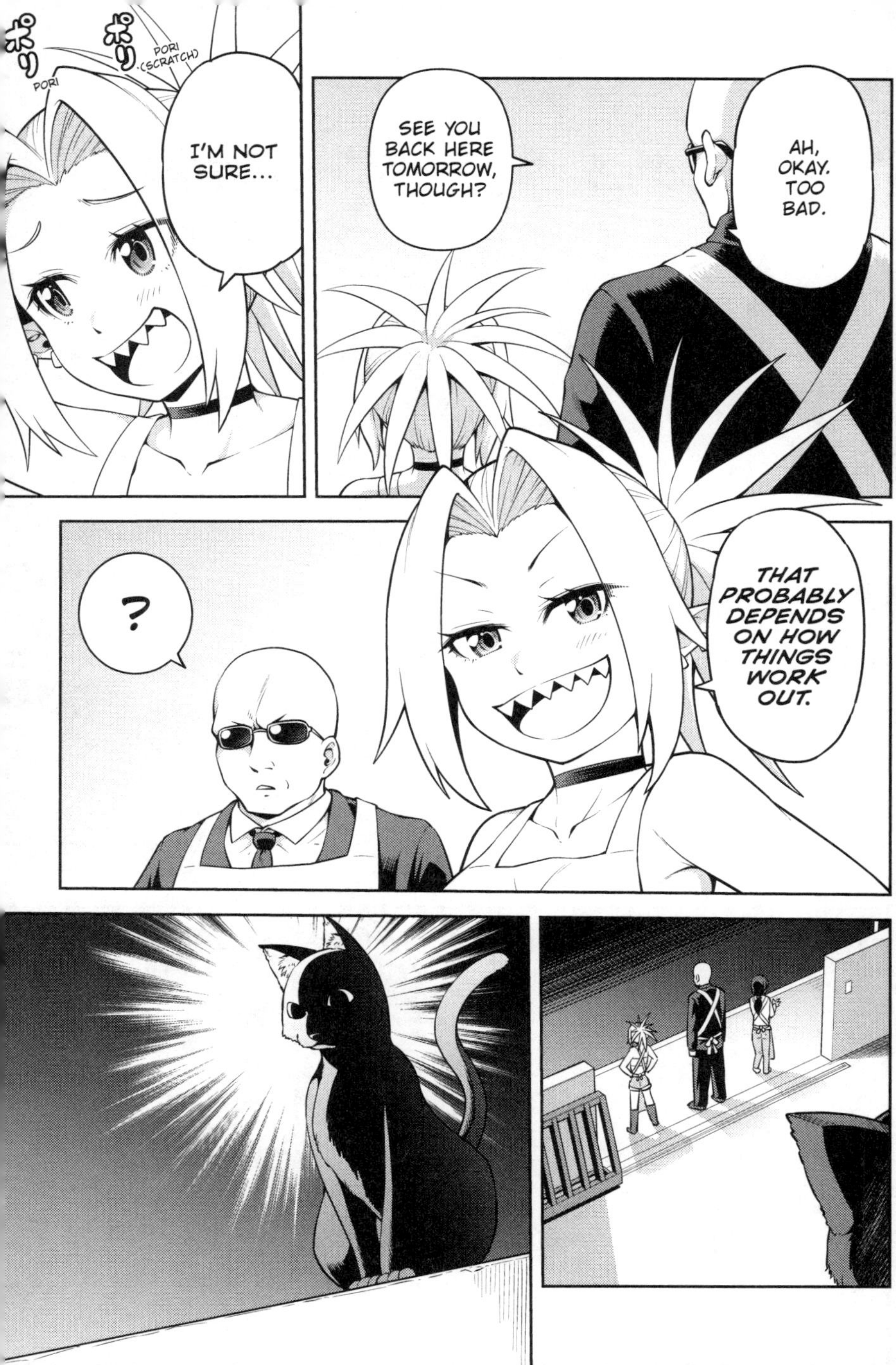
AH, OKAY. TOO BAD.
SEE YOU BACK HERE TOMORROW, THOUGH?
ポリ
PORI (SCRATCH)
ポリ
PORI
I'M NOT SURE...
THAT PROBABLY DEPENDS ON HOW THINGS WORK OUT.
?

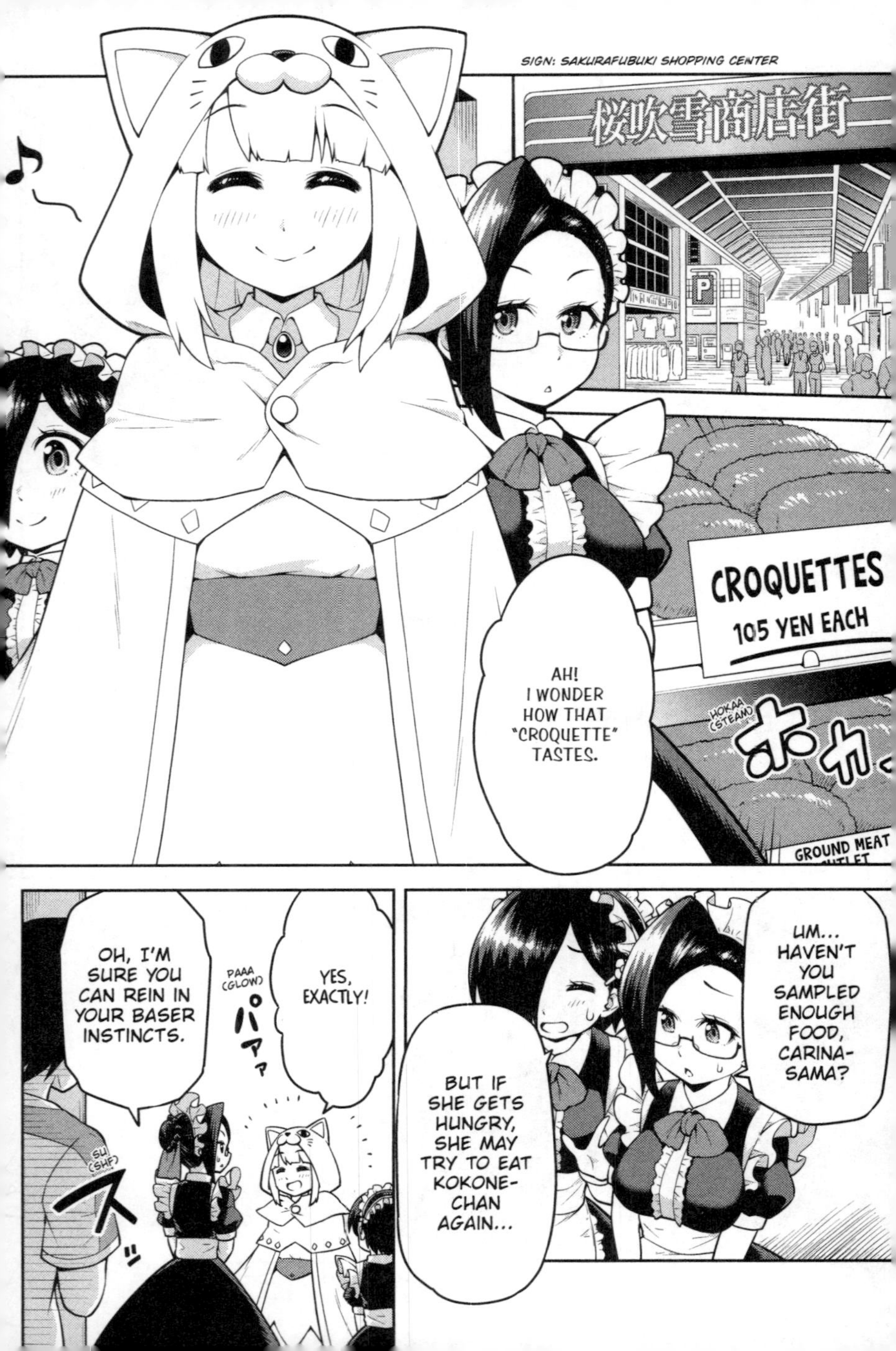
SIGN: SAKURAFUBUKI SHOPPING CENTER
桜吹雪商店街
♪
CROQUETTES
105 YEN EACH
GROUND MEAT
HOKAA (STEAM)
ホカ
AH! I WONDER HOW THAT "CROQUETTE" TASTES.
UM... HAVEN'T YOU SAMPLED ENOUGH FOOD, CARINA-SAMA?
BUT IF SHE GETS HUNGRY, SHE MAY TRY TO EAT KOKONE-CHAN AGAIN...
YES, EXACTLY!
PAAA (GLOW)
パアァ
OH, I'M SURE YOU CAN REIN IN YOUR BASER INSTINCTS.
SU (SHF)

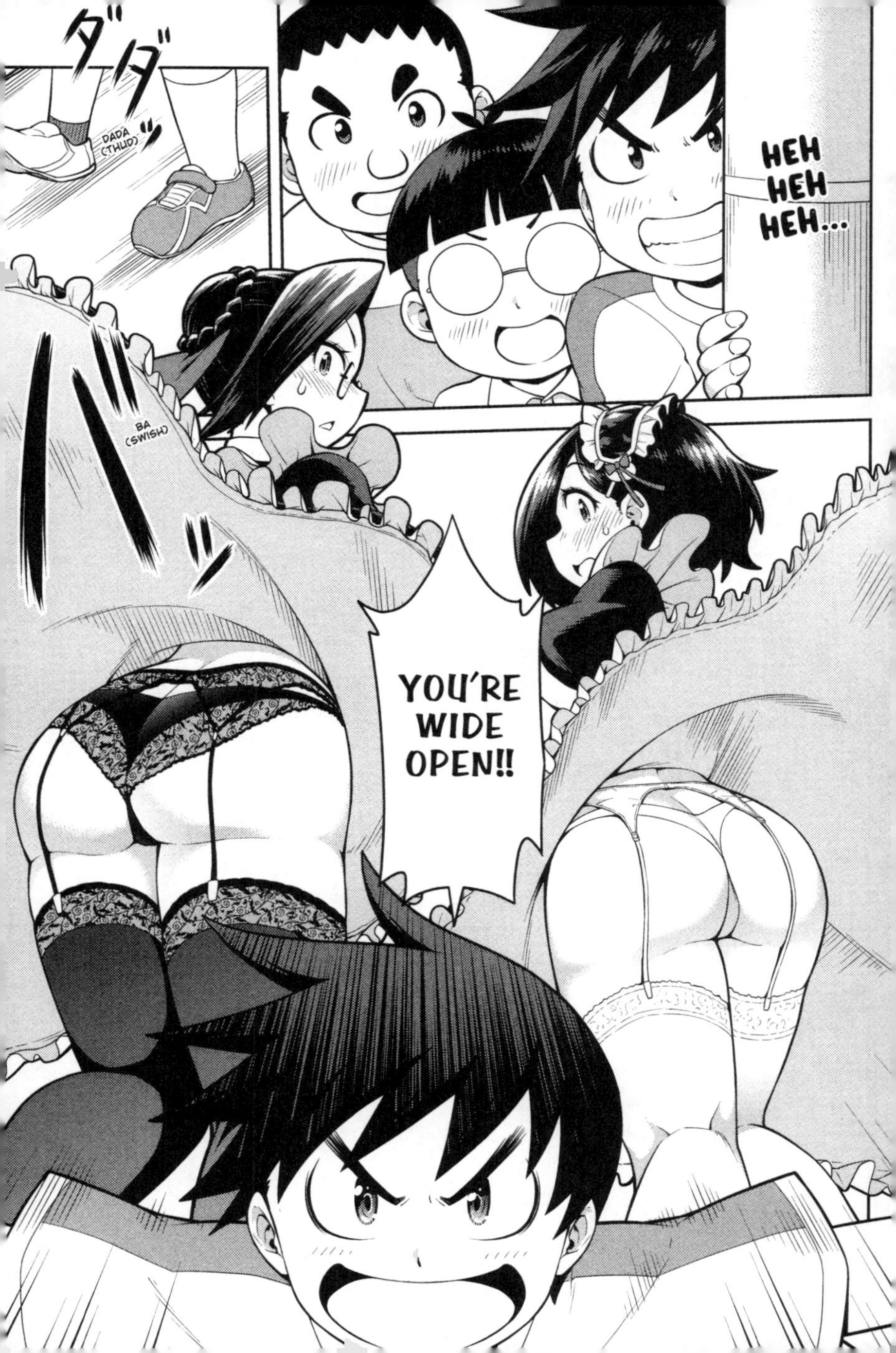
HEH HEH HEH...
ダダ
DADA (THUD)
バッ
BA (SWISH)
YOU'RE WIDE OPEN!!

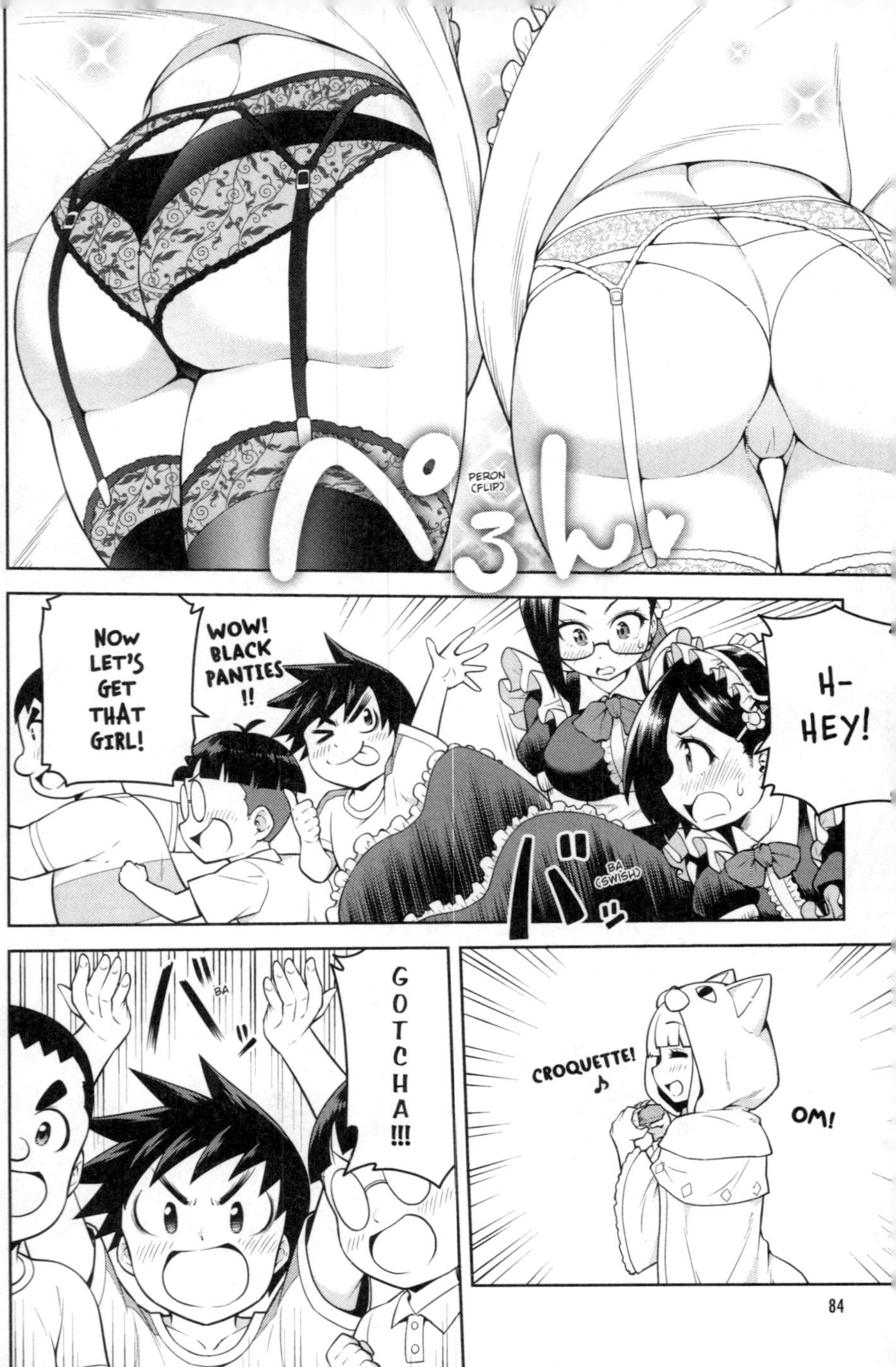
ぺろん♥
PERON (FLIP)
H-HEY!
BA (SWISH)
WOW! BLACK PANTIES!!
NOW LET'S GET THAT GIRL!
CROQUETTE! ♪
OM!
GOTCHA!!!
BA

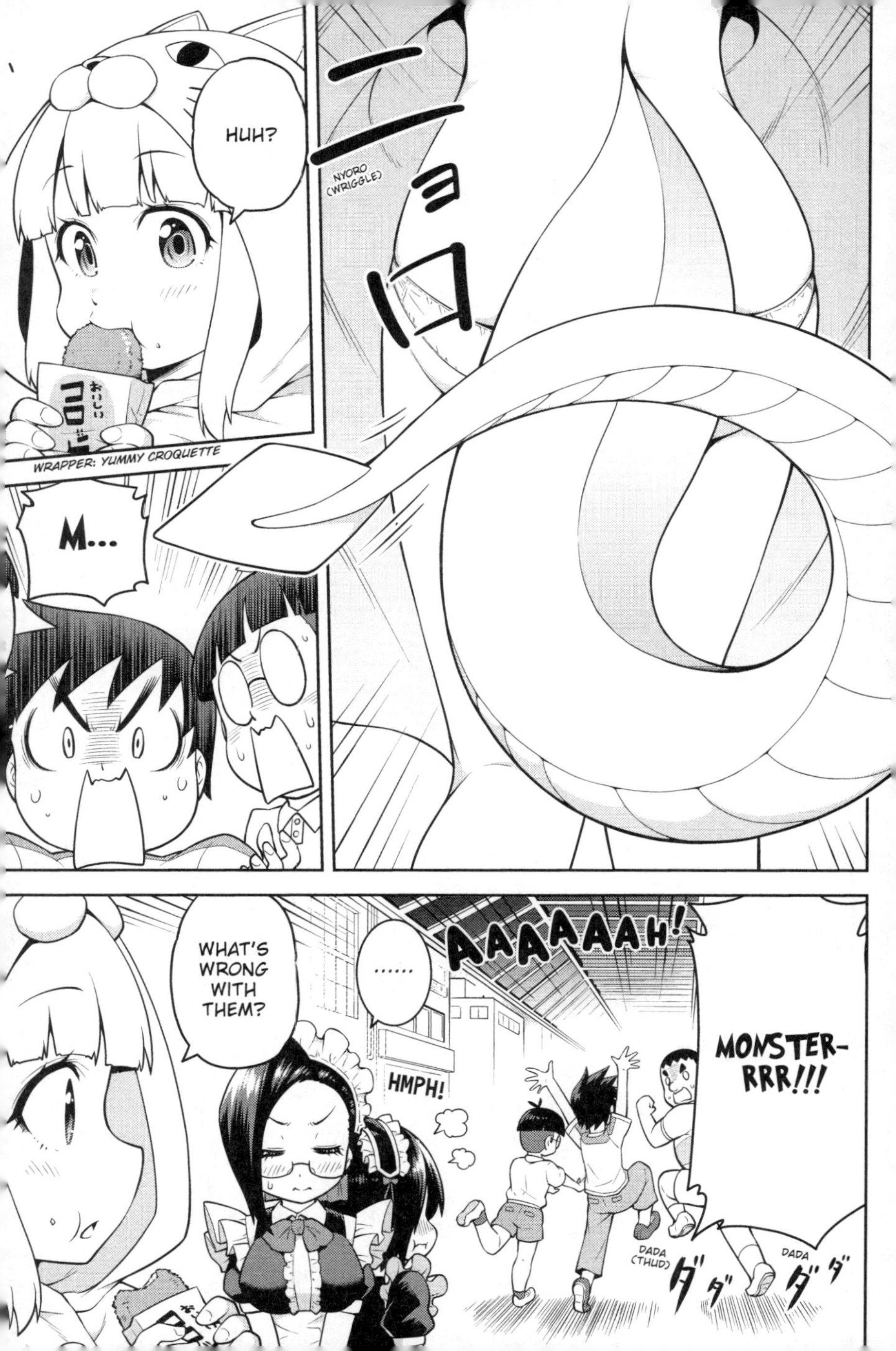
NYORO (WRIGGLE)
HUH?
WRAPPER: YUMMY CROQUETTE
M...
MONSTER-RRR!!!
AAAAAAH!
DADA
DADA (THUD)
......
WHAT'S WRONG WITH THEM?
HMPH!

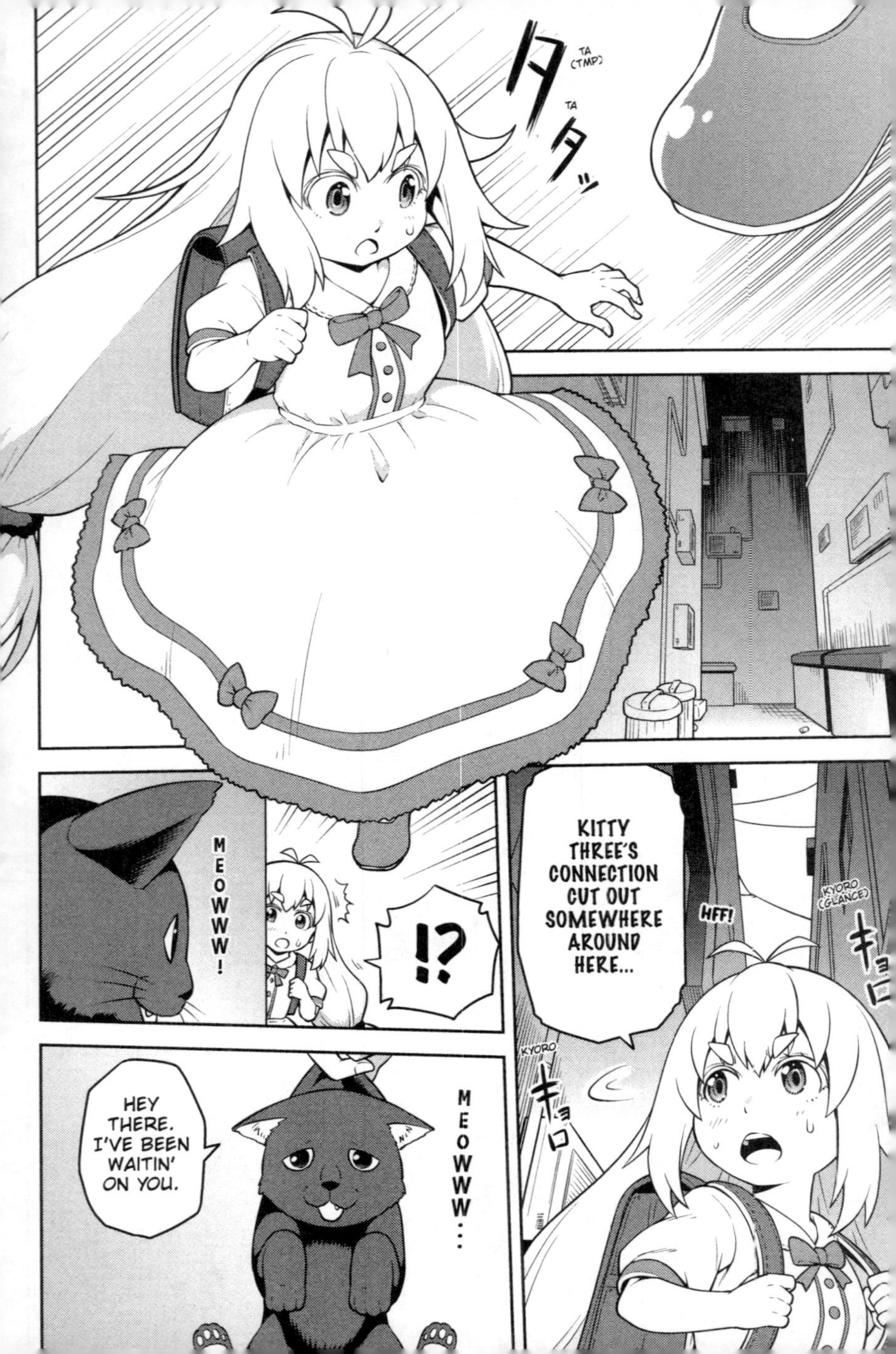
TA (TMP)
TA
KYORO (GLANCE)
HFF!
KITTY THREE'S CONNECTION CUT OUT SOMEWHERE AROUND HERE...
KYORO
!?
MEOWWW!
MEOWWW...
HEY THERE. I'VE BEEN WAITIN' ON YOU.

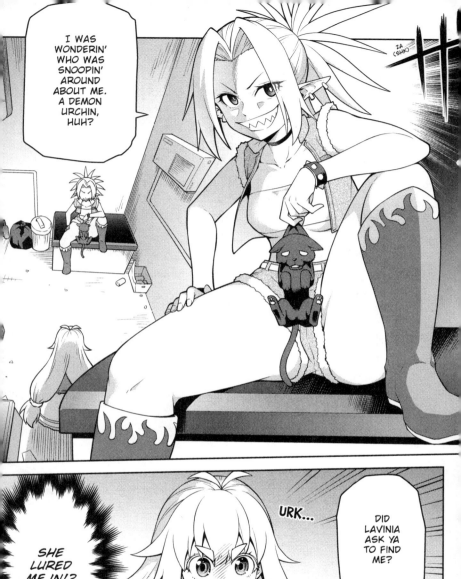

I WAS WONDERIN' WHO WAS SNOOPIN' AROUND ABOUT ME. A DEMON URCHIN, HUH?

ZA (SHK)

URK...

DID LAVINIA ASK YA TO FIND ME?

SHE LURED ME IN!?

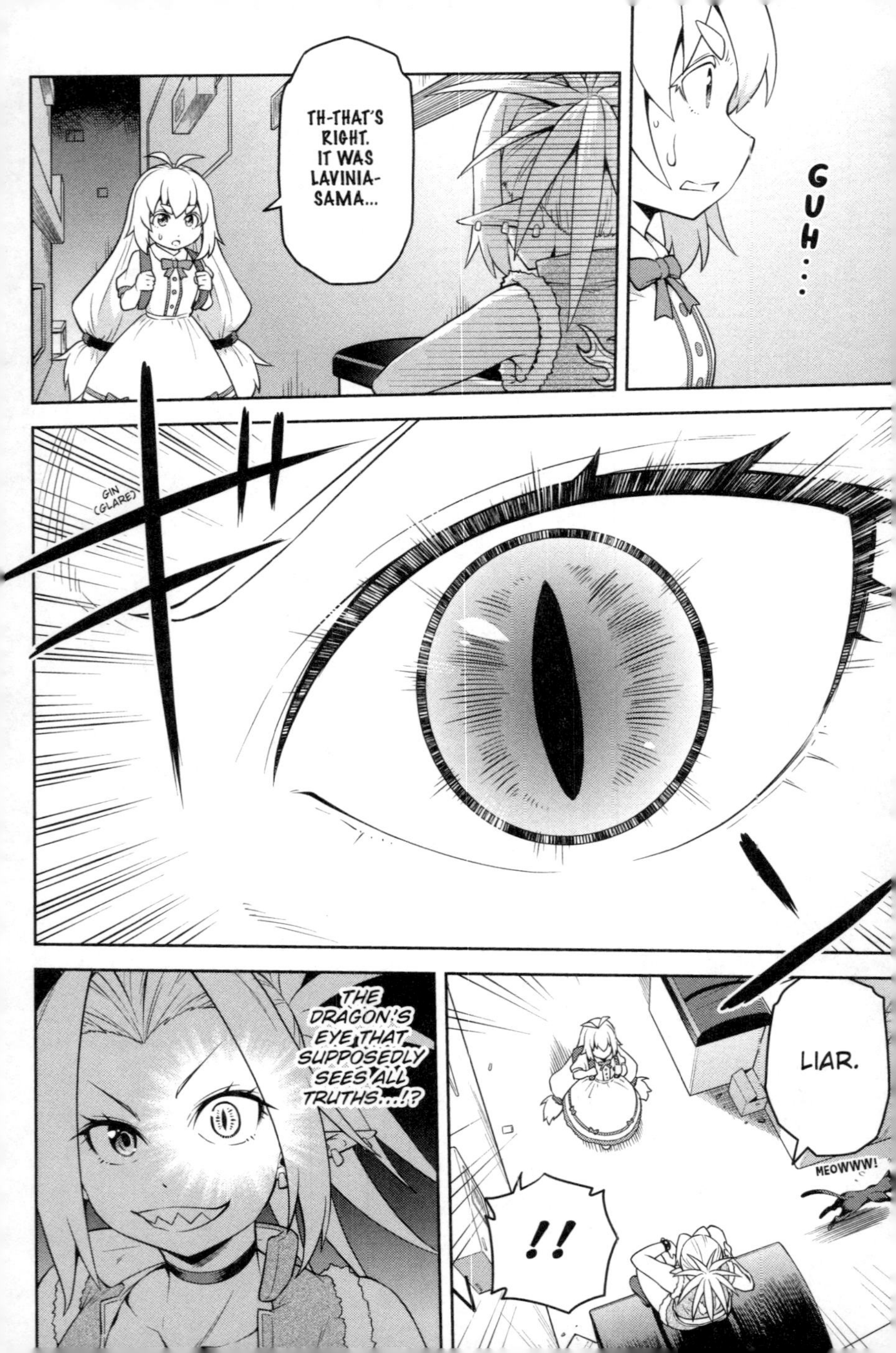
GUH...
TH-THAT'S RIGHT. IT WAS LAVINIA-SAMA...
GIN (GLARE)
LIAR.
MEOWWW!
!!
THE DRAGON'S EYE THAT SUPPOSEDLY SEES ALL TRUTHS...!?

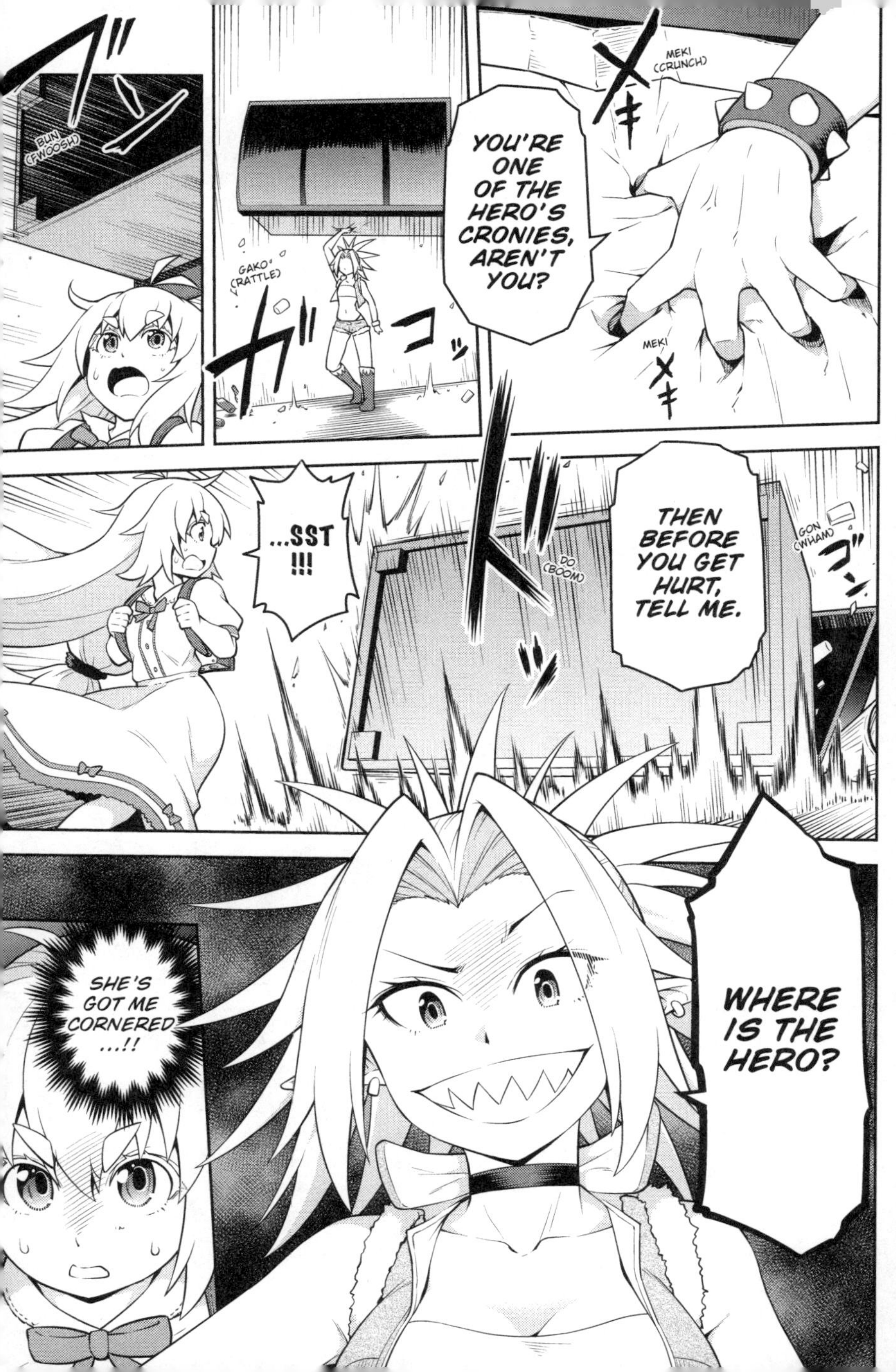
MEKI (CRUNCH)
YOU'RE ONE OF THE HERO'S CRONIES, AREN'T YOU?
MEKI
GAKO (RATTLE)
BUN (FWOOSH)
GON (WHAM)
THEN BEFORE YOU GET HURT, TELL ME.
DO (BOOM)
...SST!!!
WHERE IS THE HERO?
SHE'S GOT ME CORNERED...!!

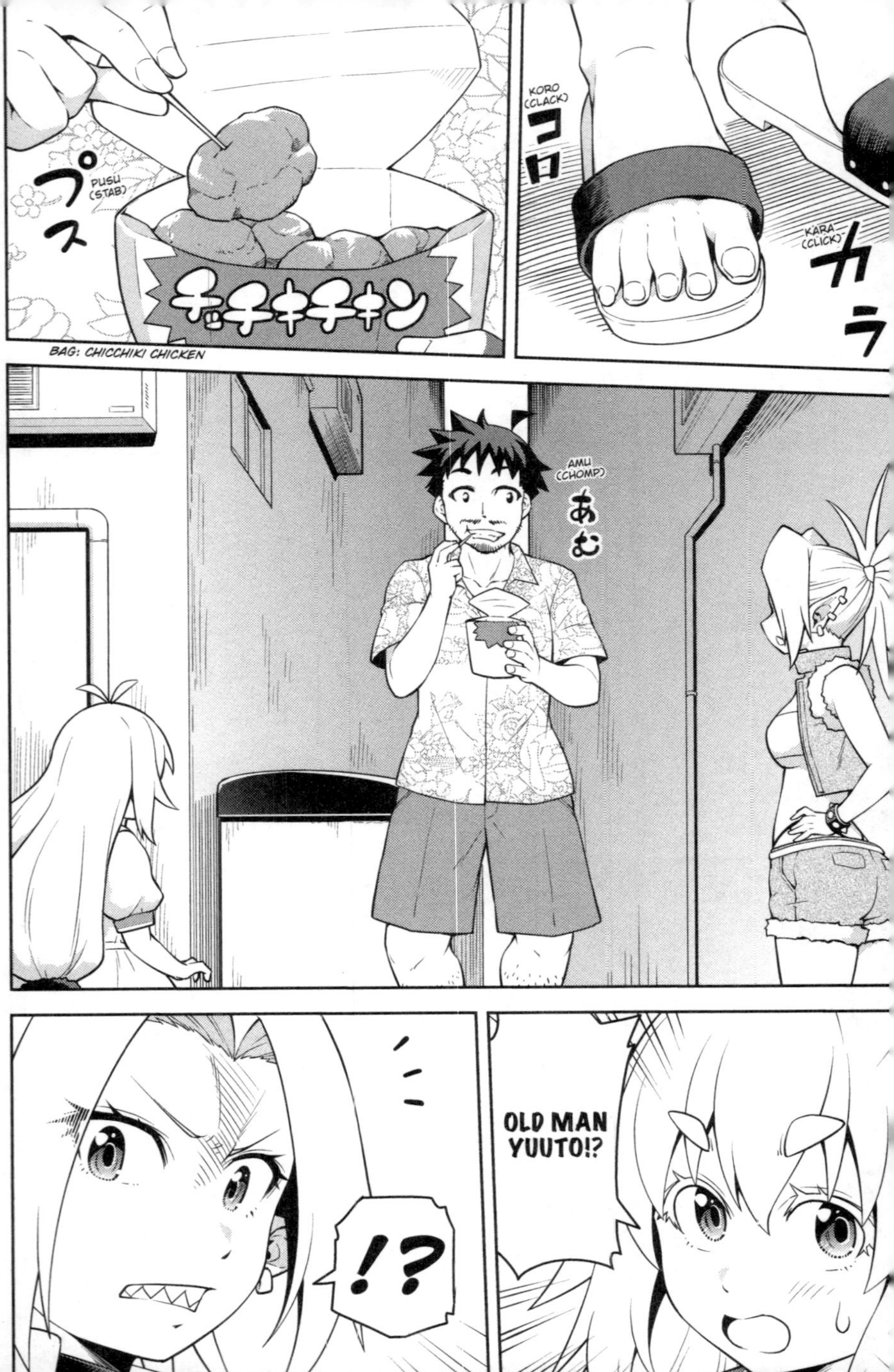
KORO (CLACK)
コロ
KARA (CLICK)
カラ
PUSU (STAB)
プス
チッチキチキン
BAG: CHICCHIKI CHICKEN
AMU (CHOMP)
あむ
OLD MAN YUUTO!?
...
!?

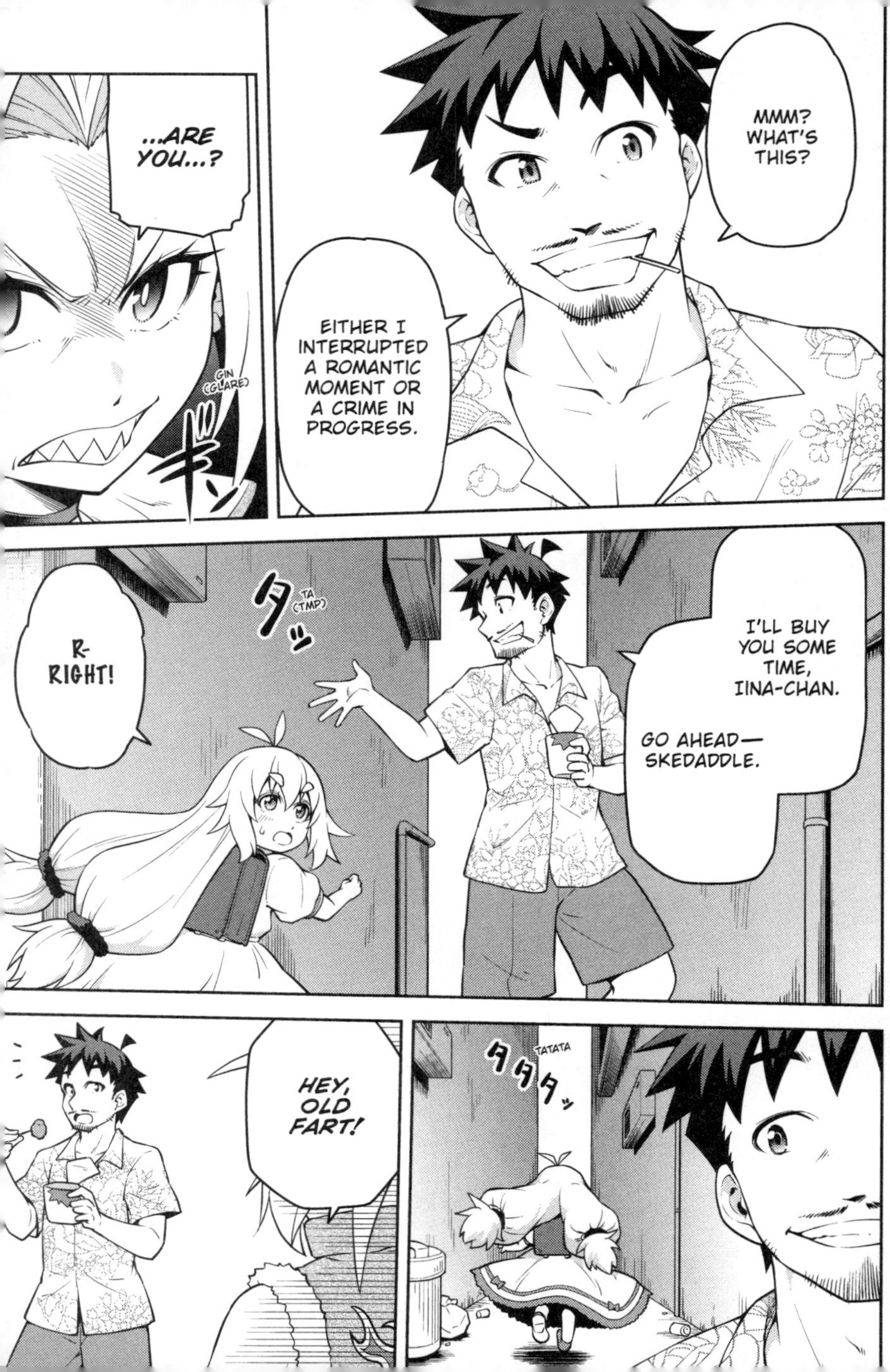
MMM? WHAT'S THIS?
EITHER I INTERRUPTED A ROMANTIC MOMENT OR A CRIME IN PROGRESS.
...ARE YOU...?
GIN (GLARE)
I'LL BUY YOU SOME TIME, IINA-CHAN.
GO AHEAD— SKEDADDLE.
TA (TMP)
R-RIGHT!
TATATA
HEY, OLD FART!

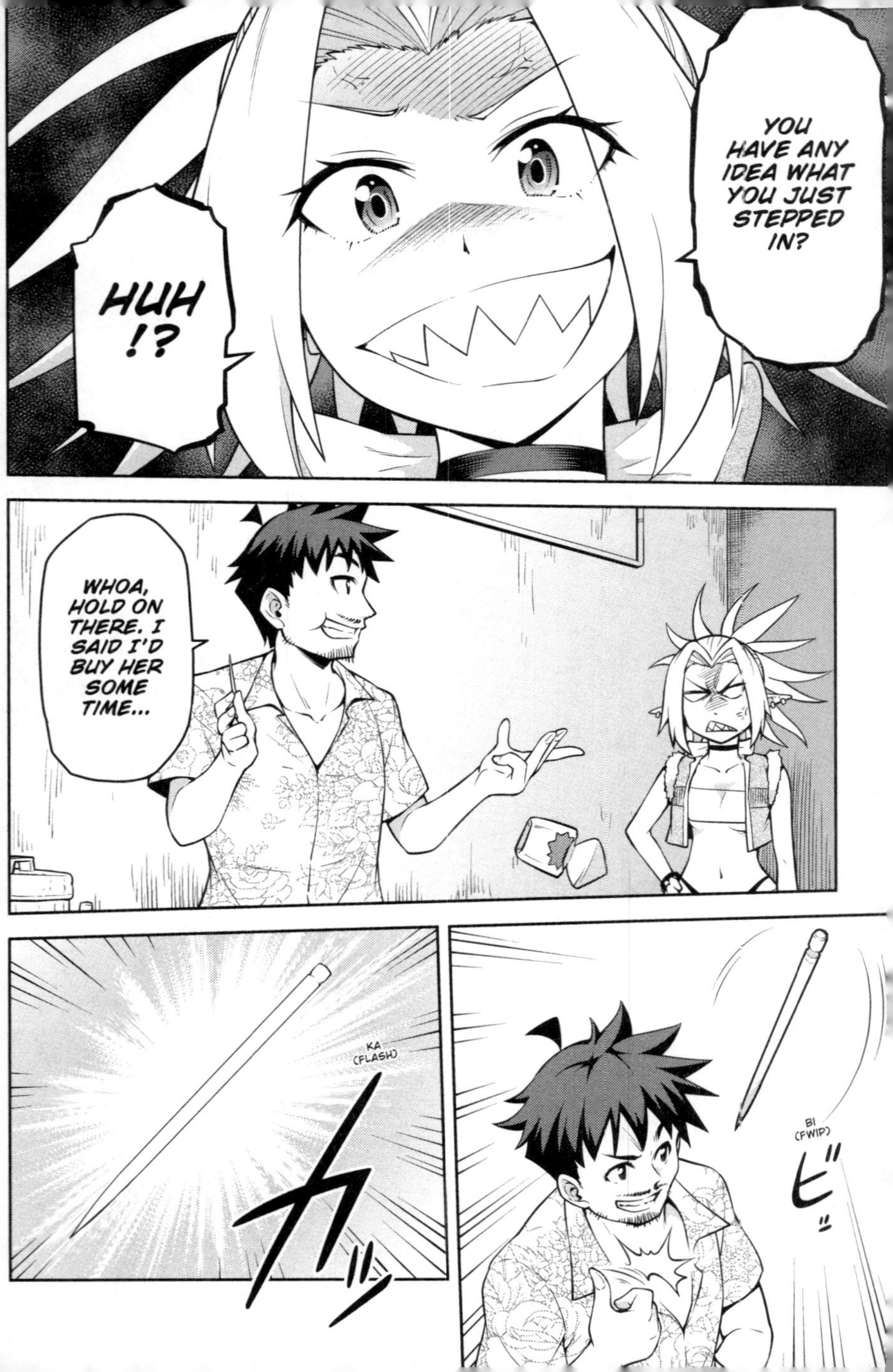
YOU HAVE ANY IDEA WHAT YOU JUST STEPPED IN?
HUH!?
WHOA, HOLD ON THERE. I SAID I'D BUY HER SOME TIME...
BI (FWIP)
KA (FLASH)

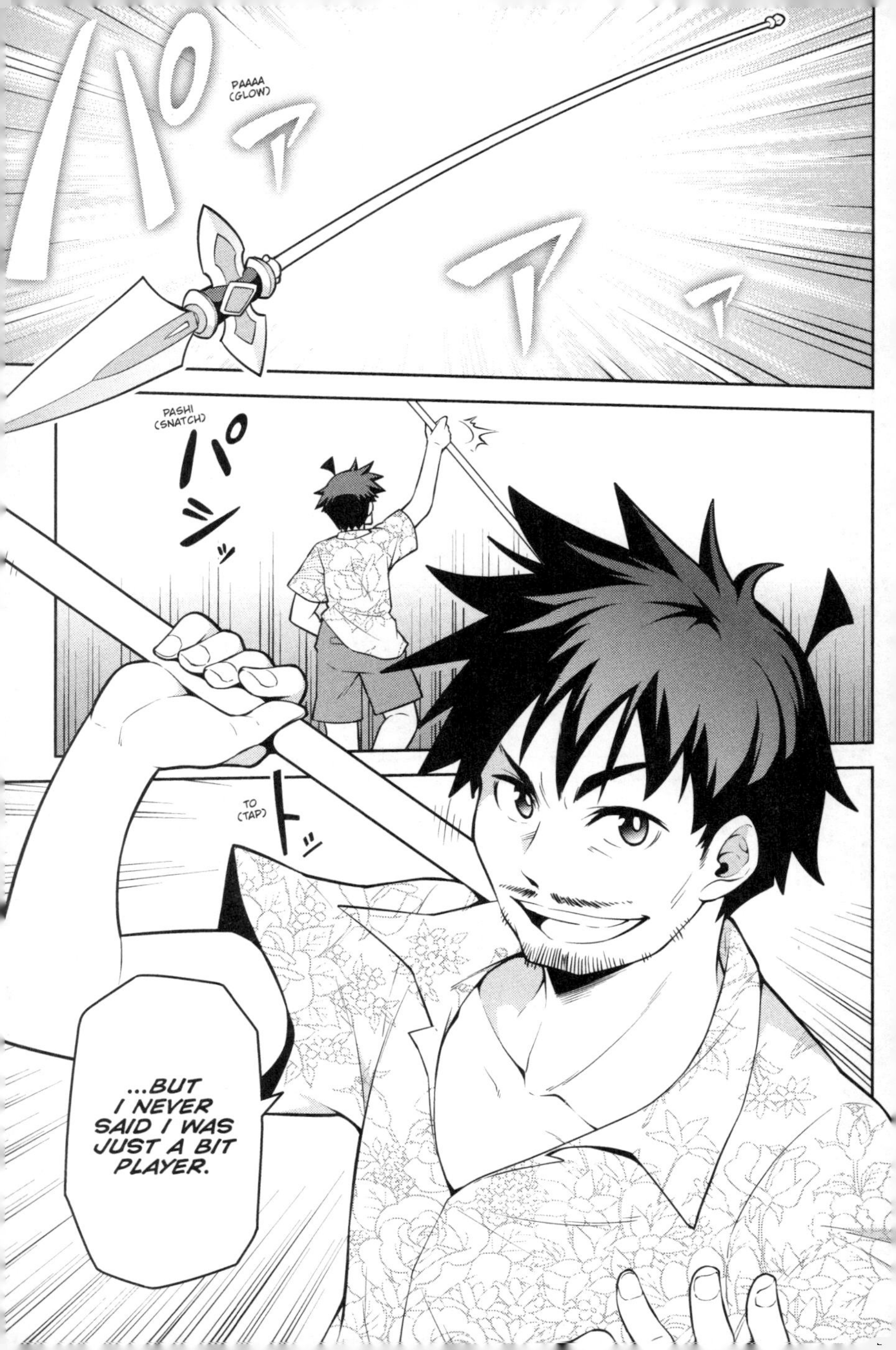
PAAAA (GLOW)
PASHI (SNATCH)
TO (TAP)
...BUT I NEVER SAID I WAS JUST A BIT PLAYER.

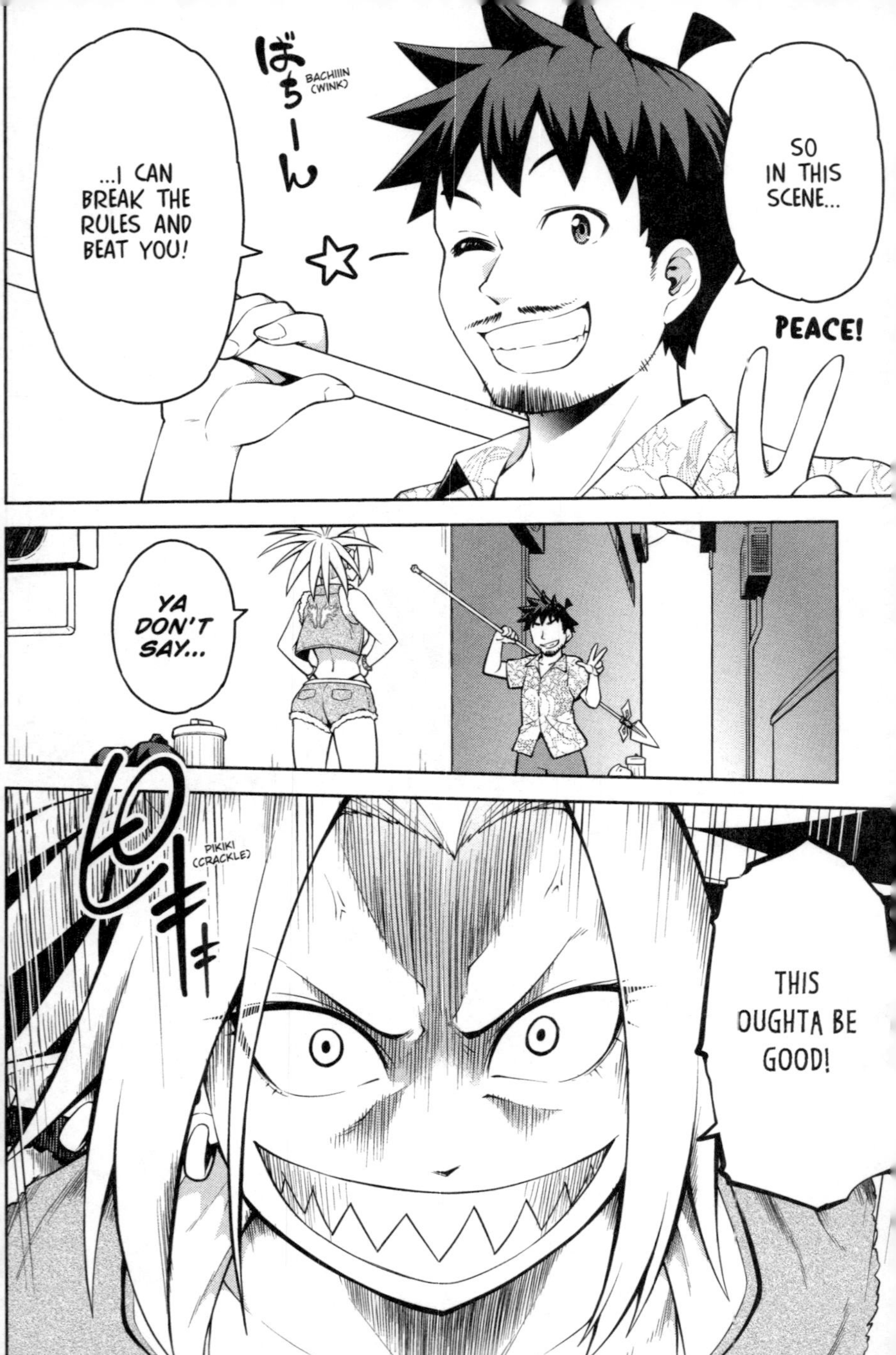
SO IN THIS SCENE...
PEACE!
ばちーん
BACHIIIN (WINK)
...I CAN BREAK THE RULES AND BEAT YOU!
YA DON'T SAY...
THIS OUGHTA BE GOOD!
ピキキ
PIKIKI (CRACKLE)

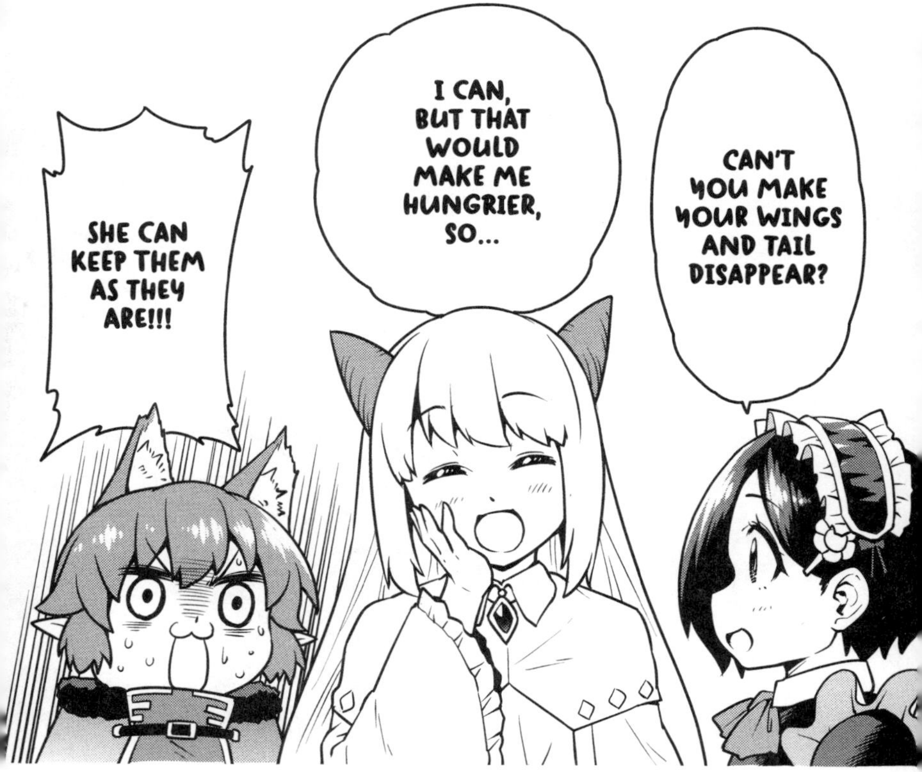
CAN'T YOU MAKE YOUR WINGS AND TAIL DISAPPEAR?
I CAN, BUT THAT WOULD MAKE ME HUNGRIER, SO...
SHE CAN KEEP THEM AS THEY ARE!!!

I'm the HERO, but the DEMON LORD's Also Me

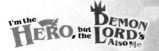

# Chapter 14

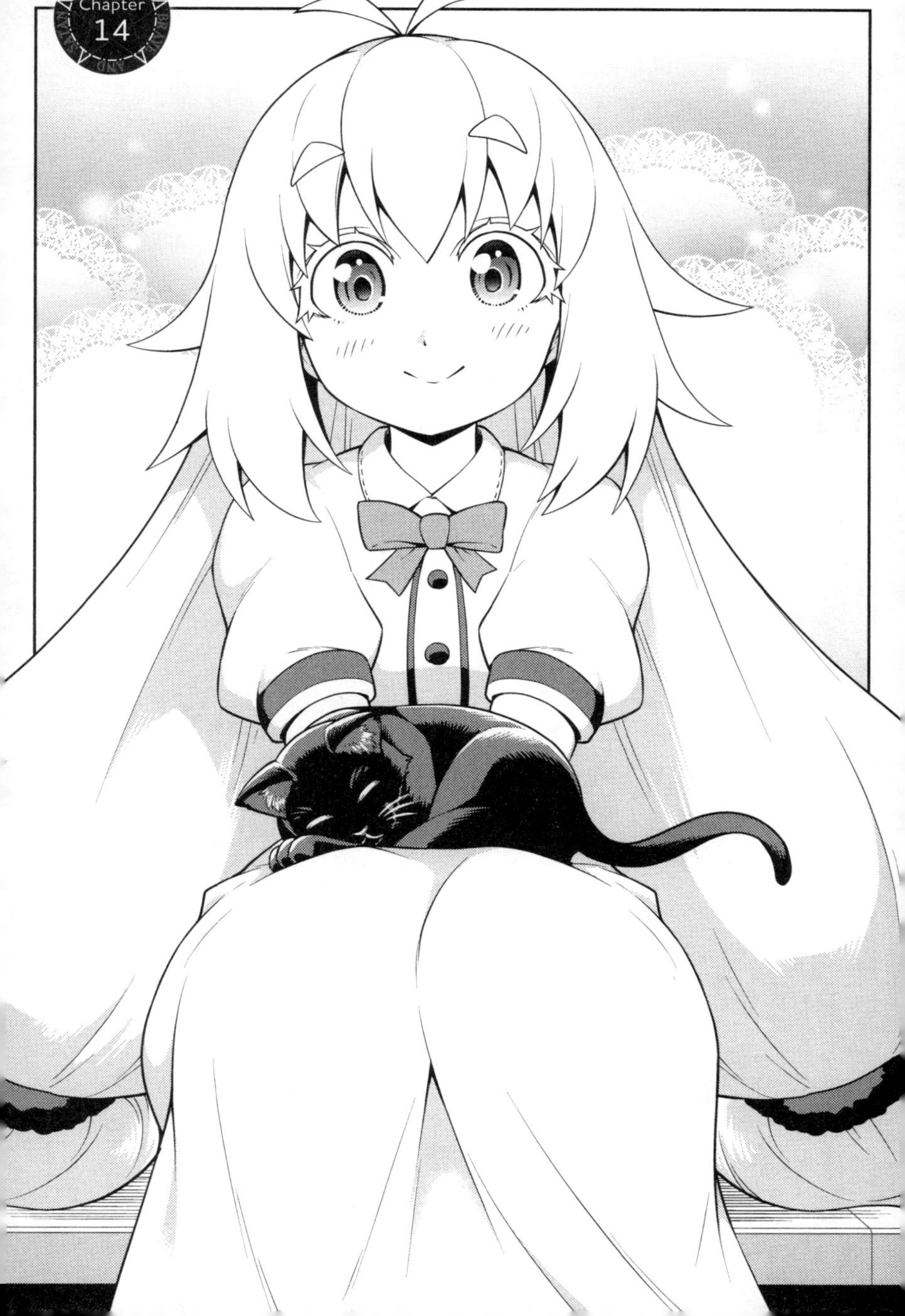

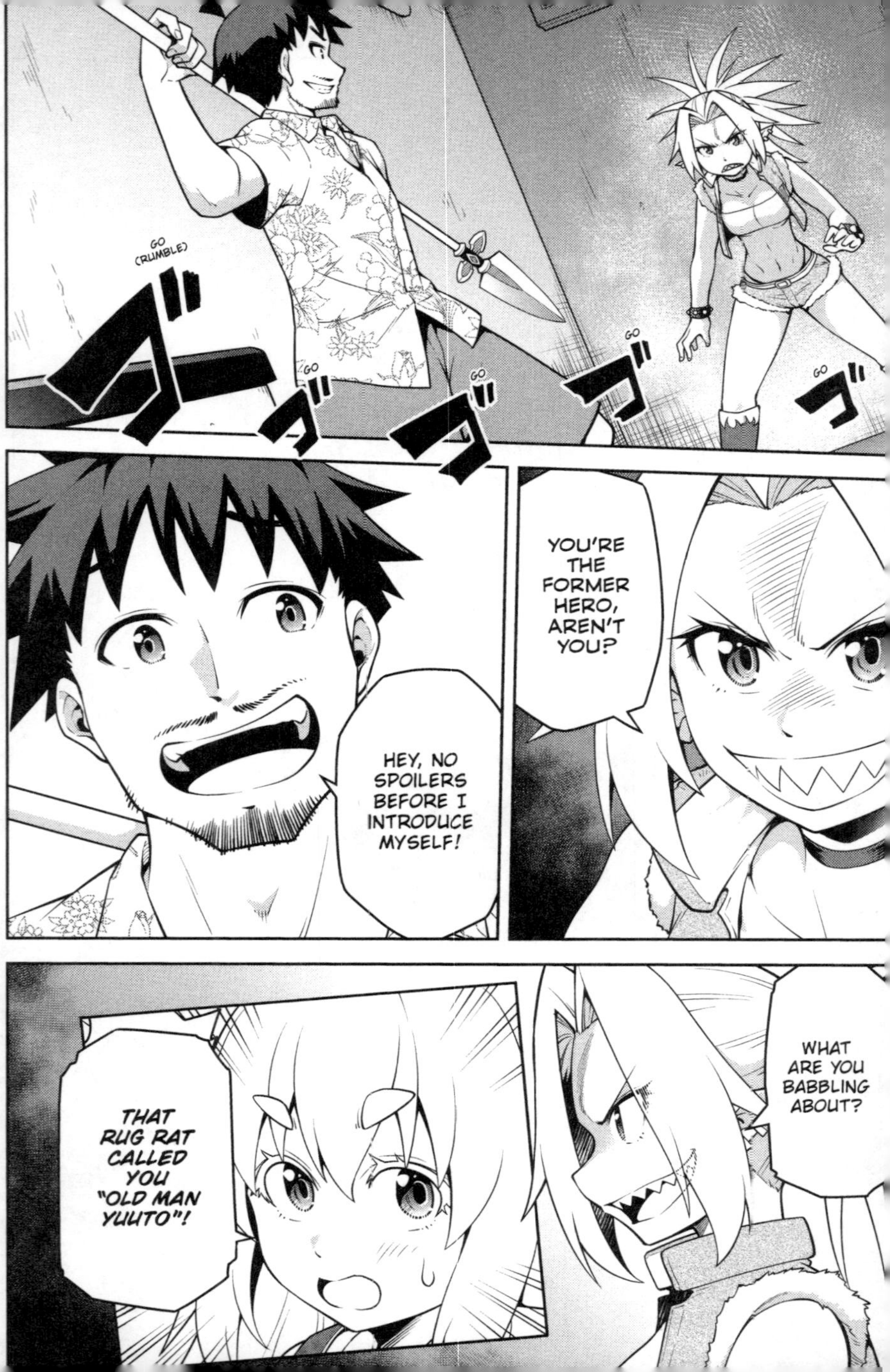
GO
GO
GO
GO
GO (RUMBLE)
YOU'RE THE FORMER HERO, AREN'T YOU?
HEY, NO SPOILERS BEFORE I INTRODUCE MYSELF!
WHAT ARE YOU BABBLING ABOUT?
THAT RUG RAT CALLED YOU "OLD MAN YUUTO"!

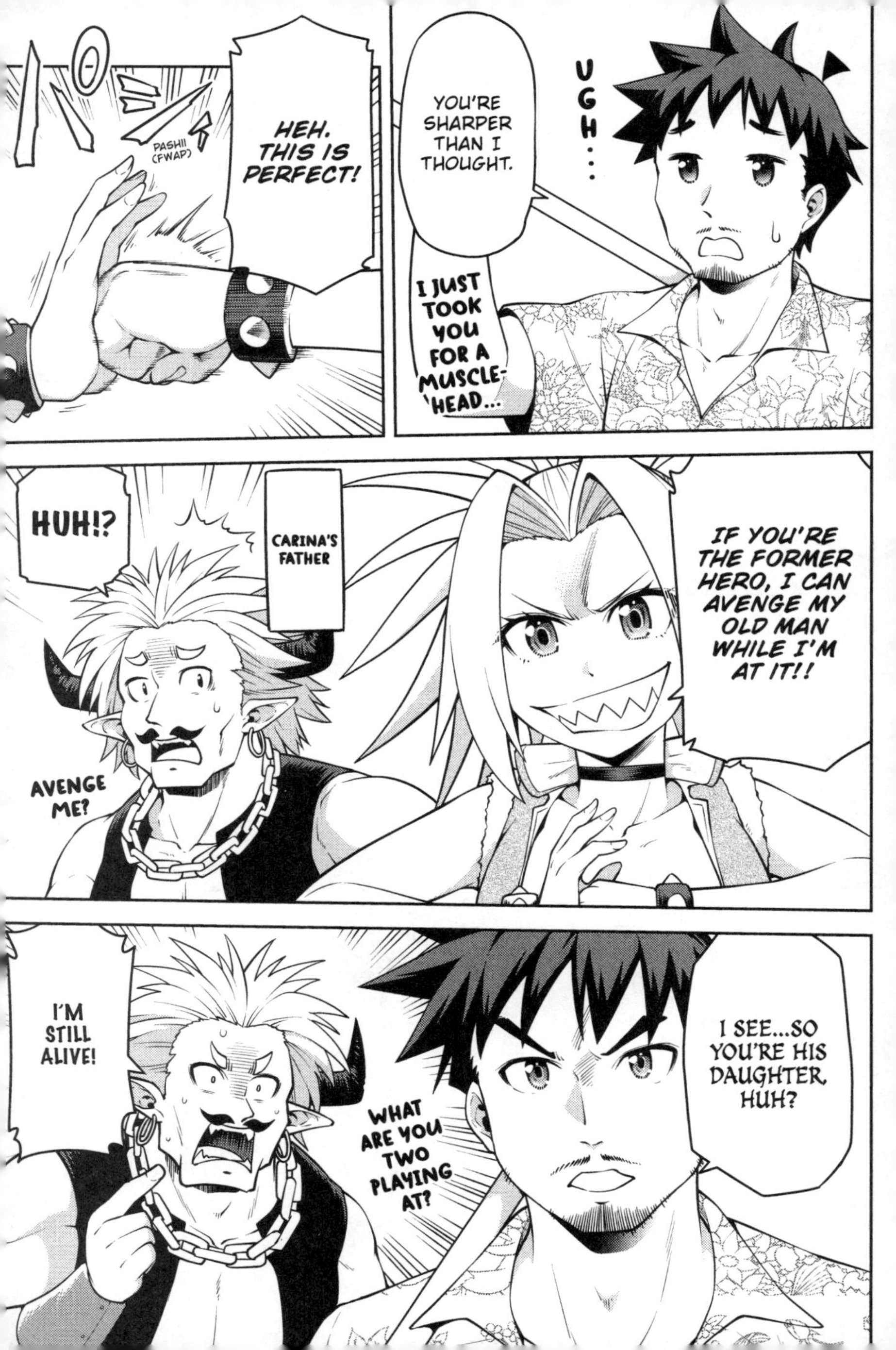
UGH...
YOU'RE SHARPER THAN I THOUGHT.
I JUST TOOK YOU FOR A MUSCLE-HEAD...
HEH. THIS IS PERFECT!
PASHII (FWAP)
IF YOU'RE THE FORMER HERO, I CAN AVENGE MY OLD MAN WHILE I'M AT IT!!
CARINA'S FATHER
HUH!?
AVENGE ME?
I SEE...SO YOU'RE HIS DAUGHTER, HUH?
WHAT ARE YOU TWO PLAYING AT?
I'M STILL ALIVE!

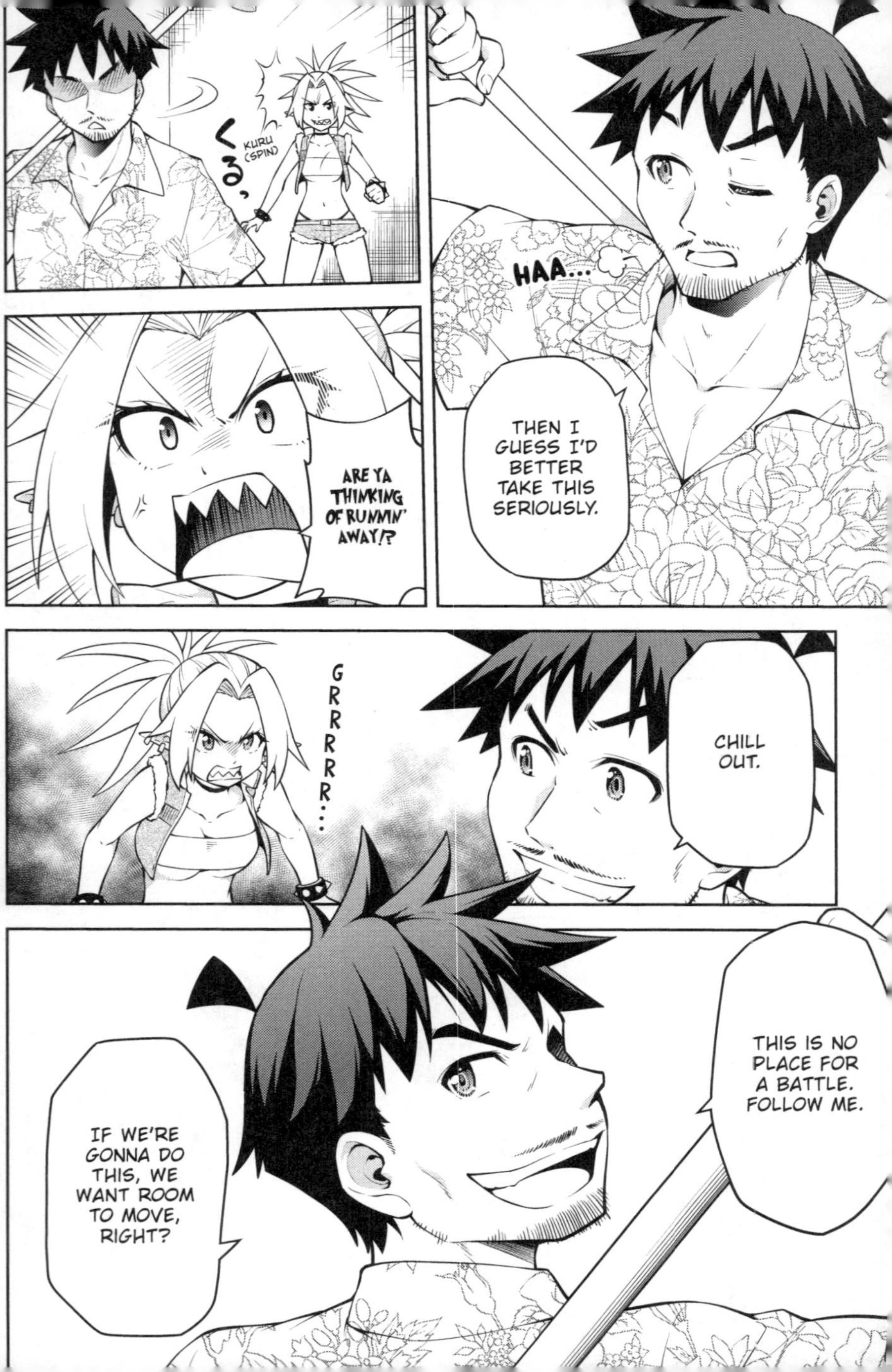
HAA...
THEN I GUESS I'D BETTER TAKE THIS SERIOUSLY.
くる,
KURU (SPIN)
ARE YA THINKING OF RUNNIN' AWAY!?
CHILL OUT.
GRRRRR...
THIS IS NO PLACE FOR A BATTLE. FOLLOW ME.
IF WE'RE GONNA DO THIS, WE WANT ROOM TO MOVE, RIGHT?

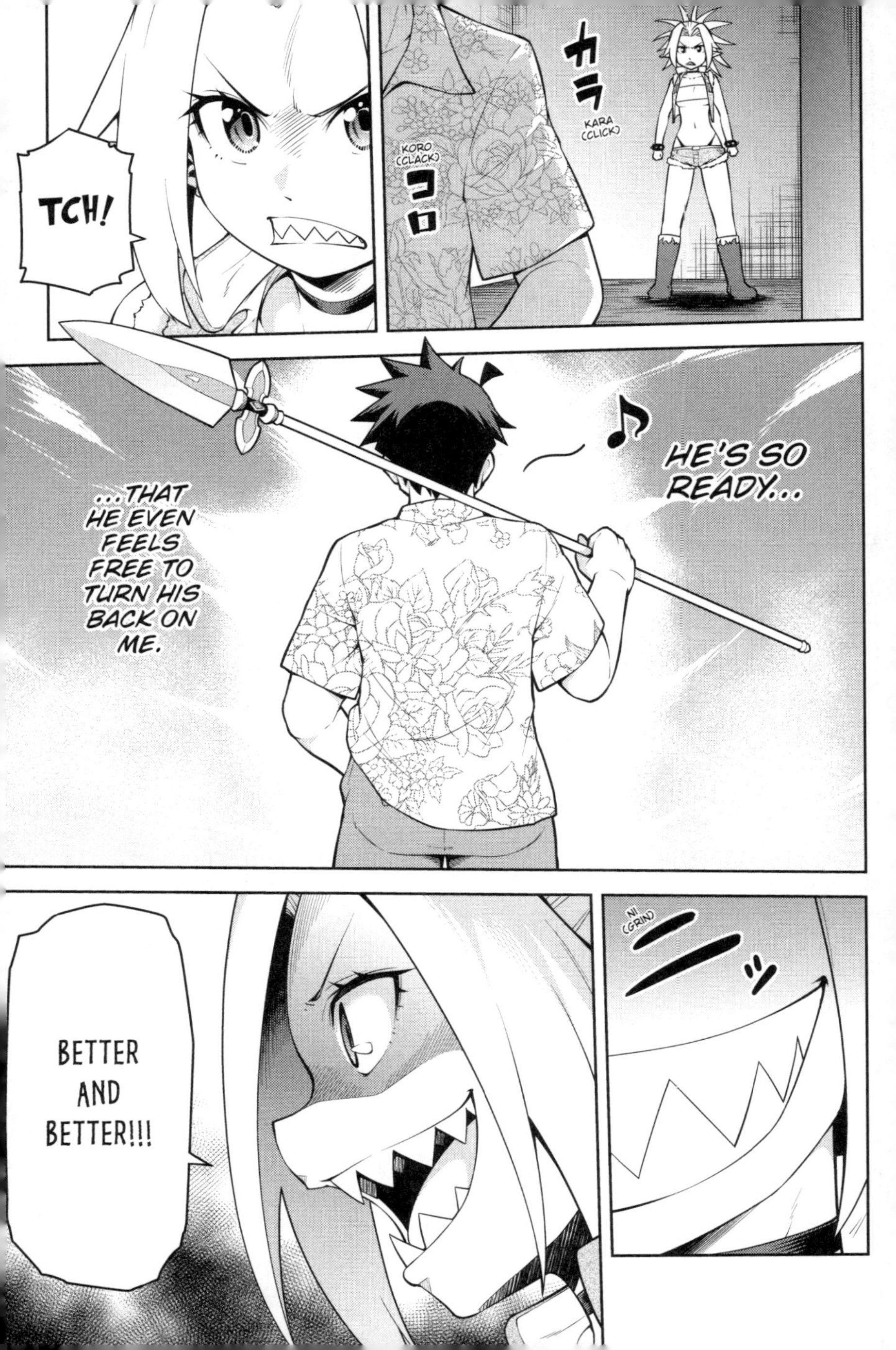

カラ
KARA (CLICK)
KORO (CLACK)
コロ
TCH!
HE'S SO READY...
...THAT HE EVEN FEELS FREE TO TURN HIS BACK ON ME.
NI (GRIN)
ニッ
BETTER AND BETTER!!!

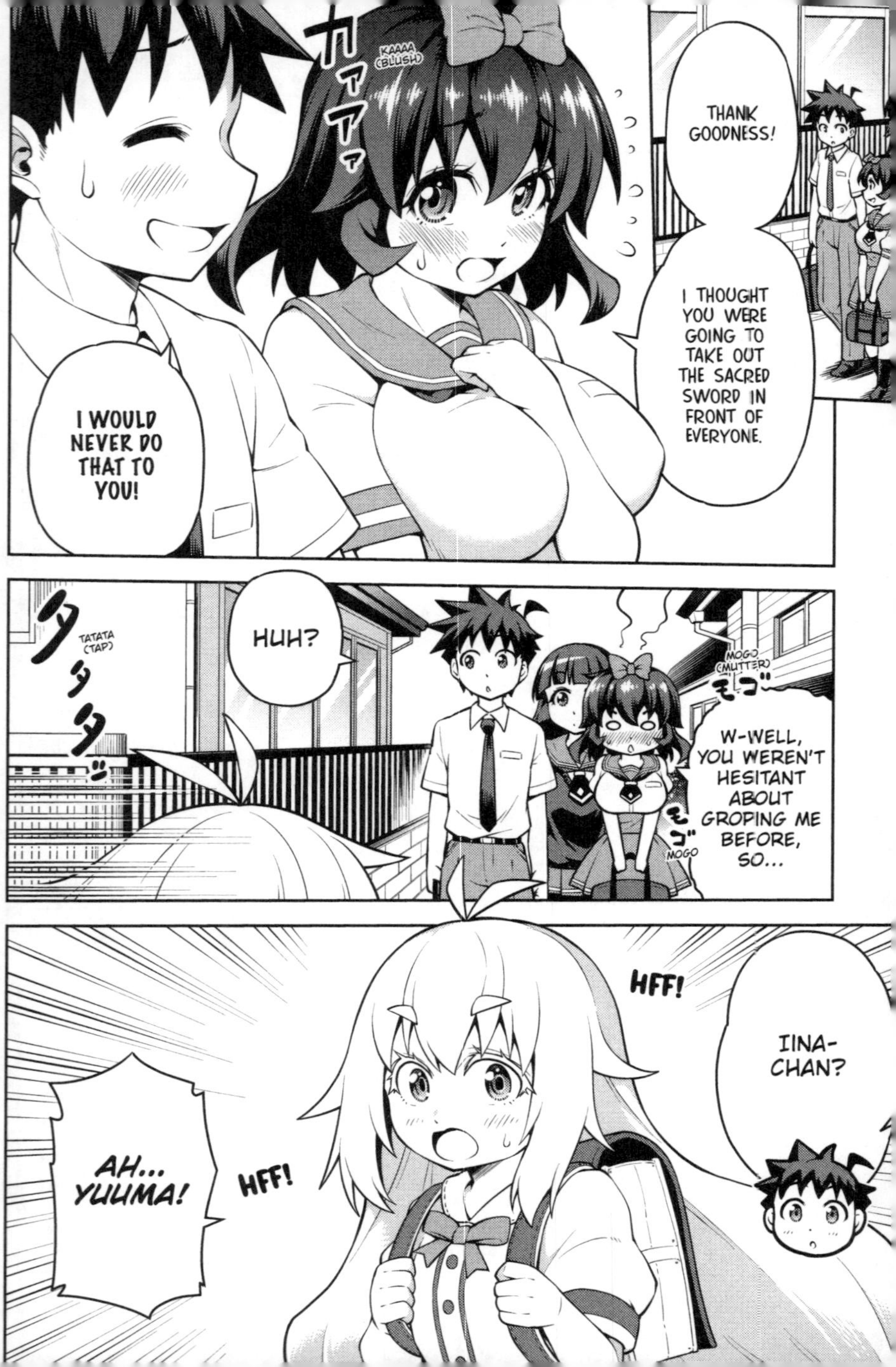
THANK GOODNESS!
I THOUGHT YOU WERE GOING TO TAKE OUT THE SACRED SWORD IN FRONT OF EVERYONE.
KAAAA (BLUSH)
I WOULD NEVER DO THAT TO YOU!
MOGO (MUTTER)
W-WELL, YOU WEREN'T HESITANT ABOUT GROPING ME BEFORE, SO...
MOGO
HUH?
TATATA (TAP)
INA-CHAN?
HFF!
HFF!
AH... YUUMA!

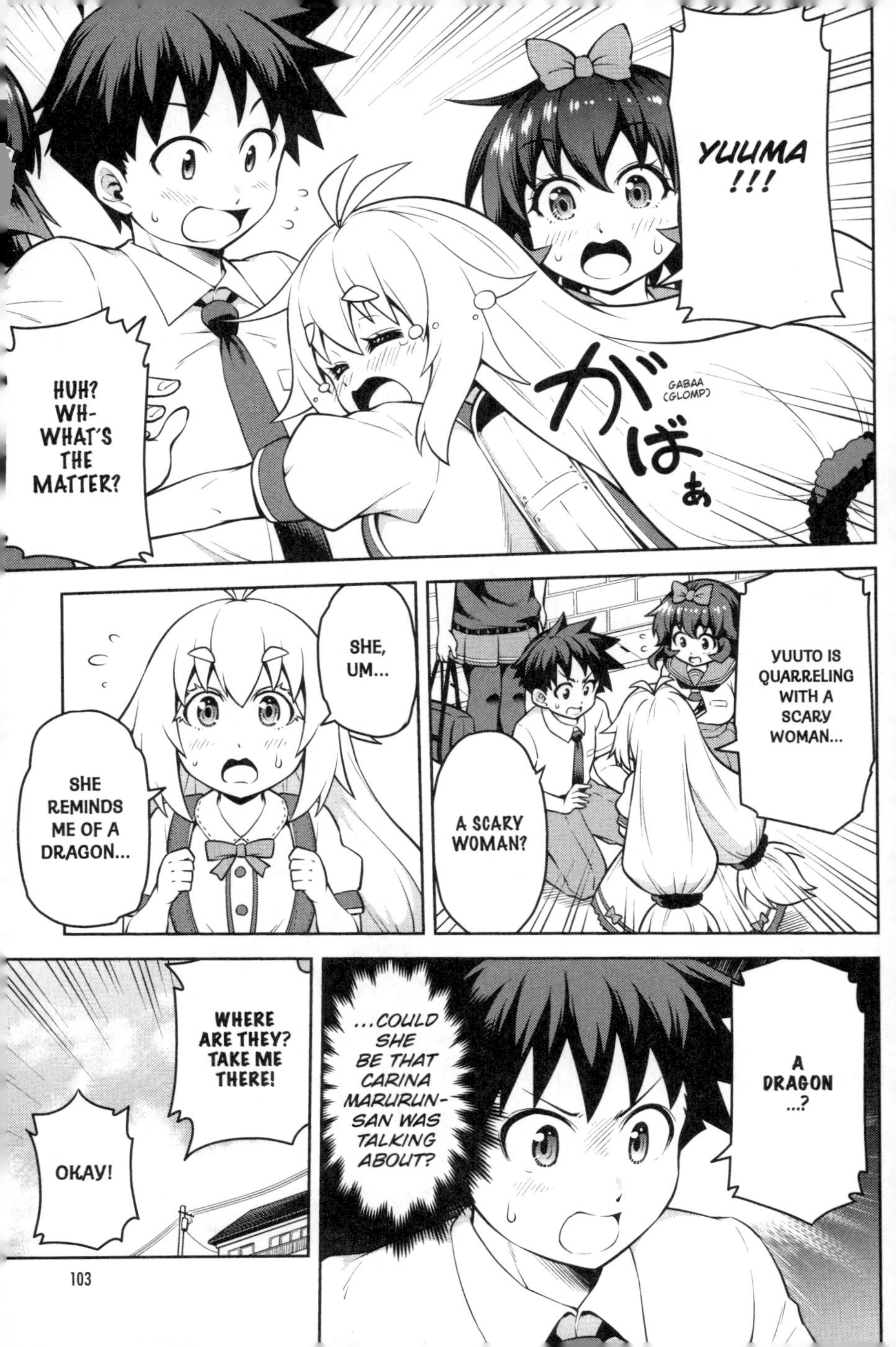
YUUMA!!!
がばぁ
GABAA (GLOMP)
HUH? WH-WHAT'S THE MATTER?
YUUTO IS QUARRELING WITH A SCARY WOMAN...
A SCARY WOMAN?
SHE, UM...
SHE REMINDS ME OF A DRAGON...
A DRAGON...?
...COULD SHE BE THAT CARINA MARURUN-SAN WAS TALKING ABOUT?
WHERE ARE THEY? TAKE ME THERE!
OKAY!

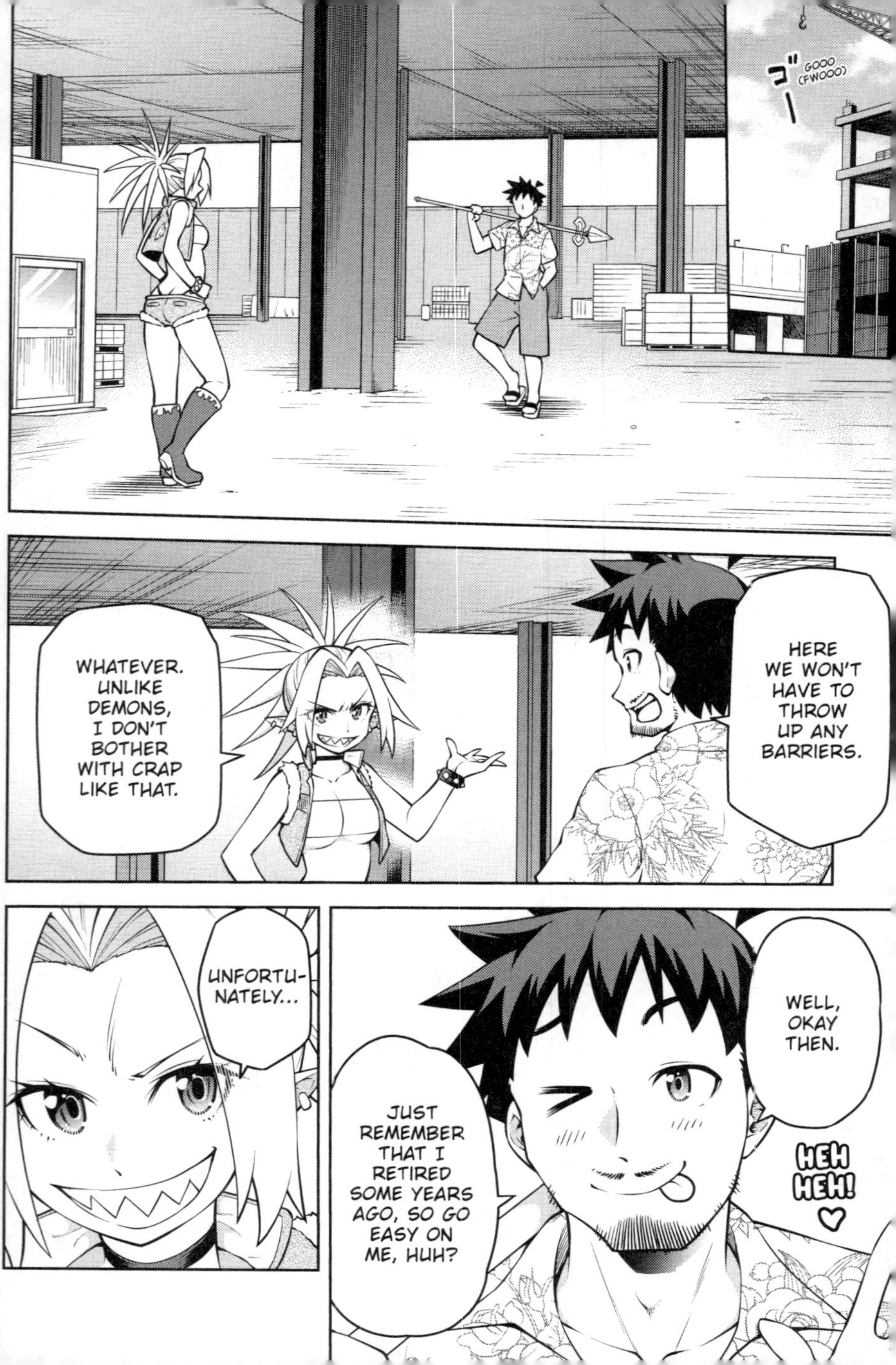
GOOO (FWOOO)
HERE WE WON'T HAVE TO THROW UP ANY BARRIERS.
WHATEVER. UNLIKE DEMONS, I DON'T BOTHER WITH CRAP LIKE THAT.
WELL, OKAY THEN.
JUST REMEMBER THAT I RETIRED SOME YEARS AGO, SO GO EASY ON ME, HUH?
HEH HEH! ♥
UNFORTU-NATELY...

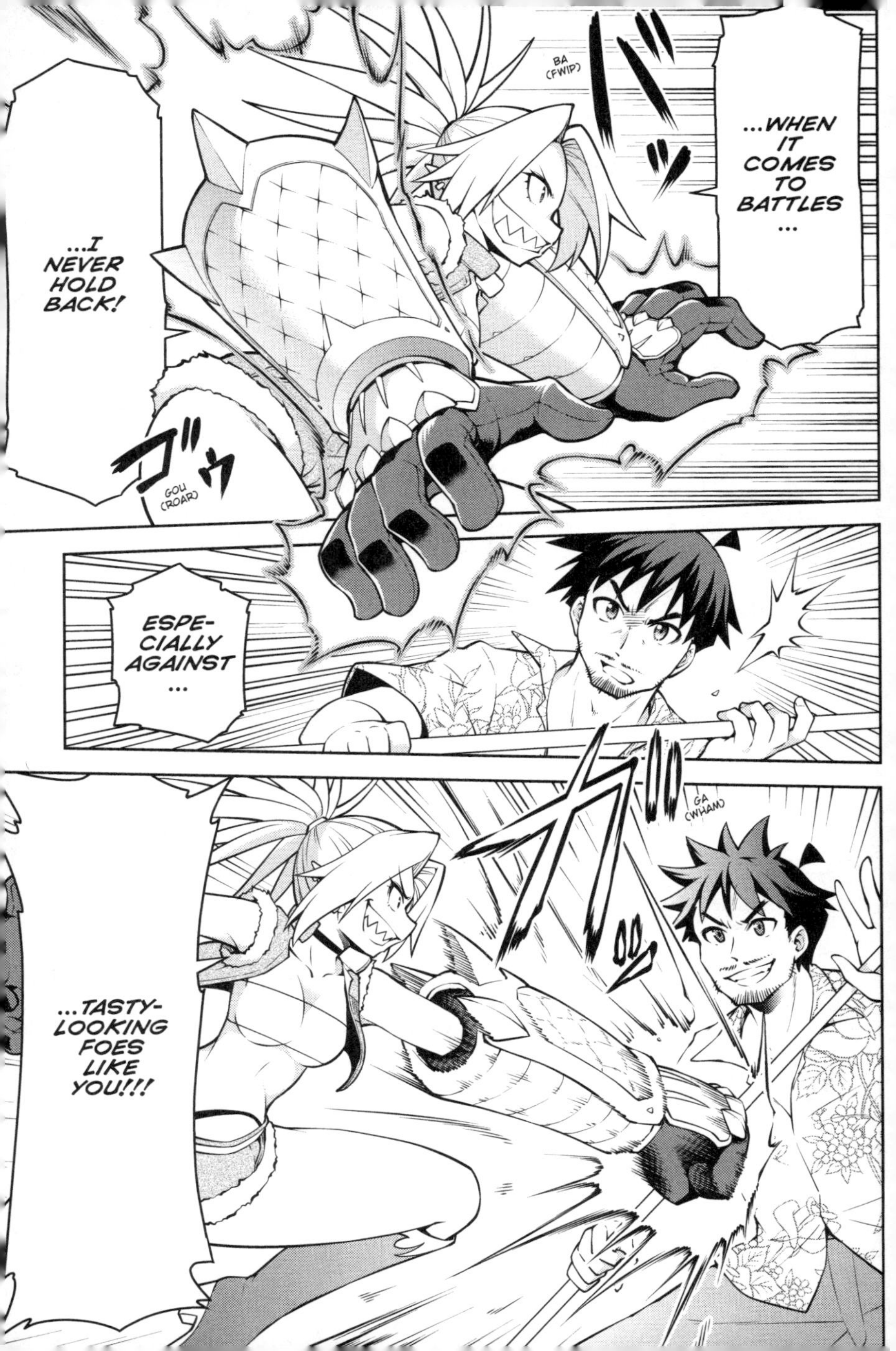
BA (FWIP)
...WHEN IT COMES TO BATTLES...
...I NEVER HOLD BACK!
GOU (ROAR)
ESPECIALLY AGAINST...
GA (WHAM)
...TASTY-LOOKING FOES LIKE YOU!!!

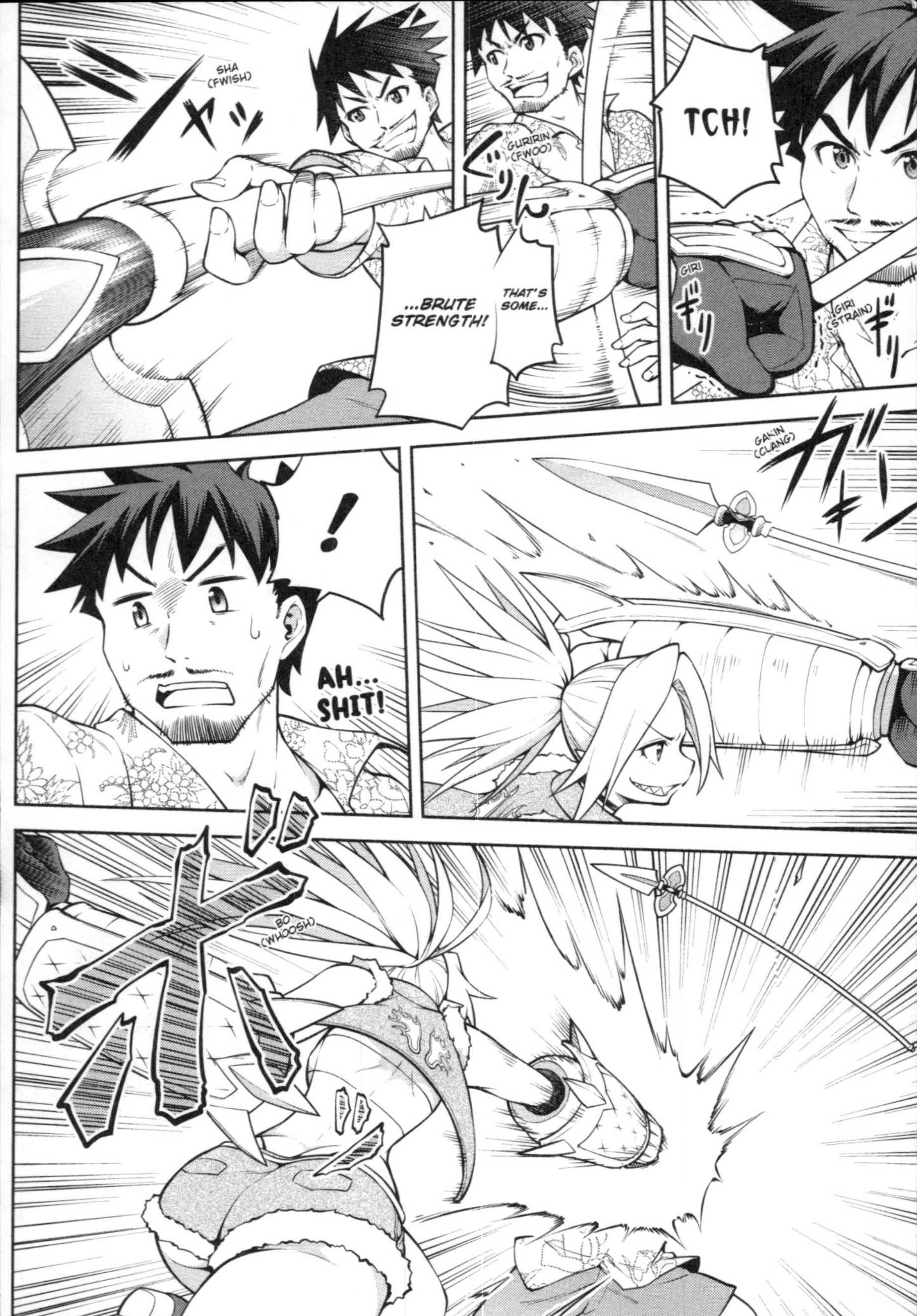
TCH!
GIRI
GIRI (STRAIN)
GURIRIN (FWOO)
THAT'S SOME...
SHA (FWISH)
...BRUTE STRENGTH!
GAKIN (CLANG)
!
AH... SHIT!
BO (WHOOSH)

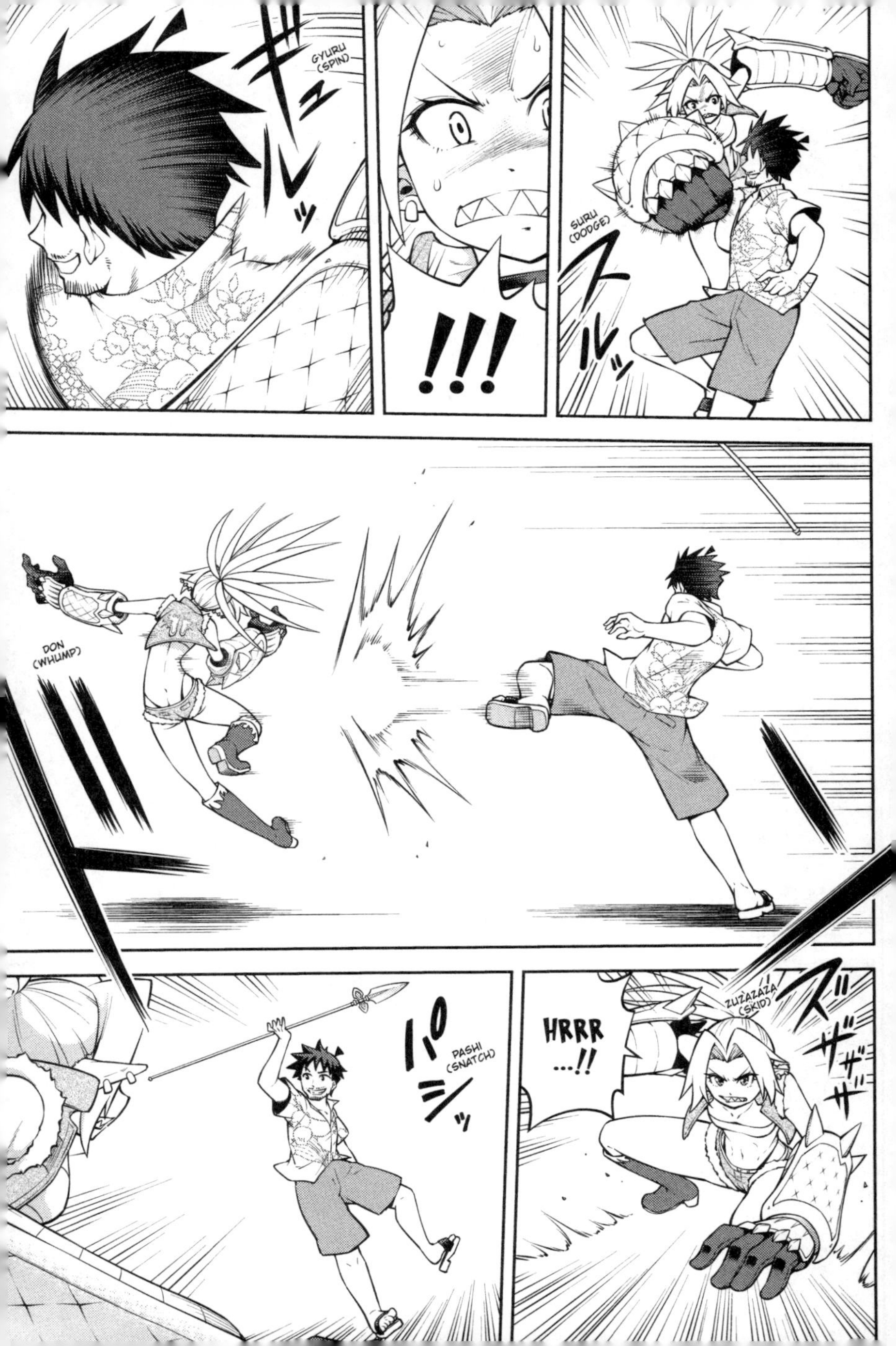
SURU (DODGE)
!!!
GYURU (SPIN)
DON (WHUMP)
ZUZAZAZA (SKID)
HRRR ...!!
PASHI (SNATCH)

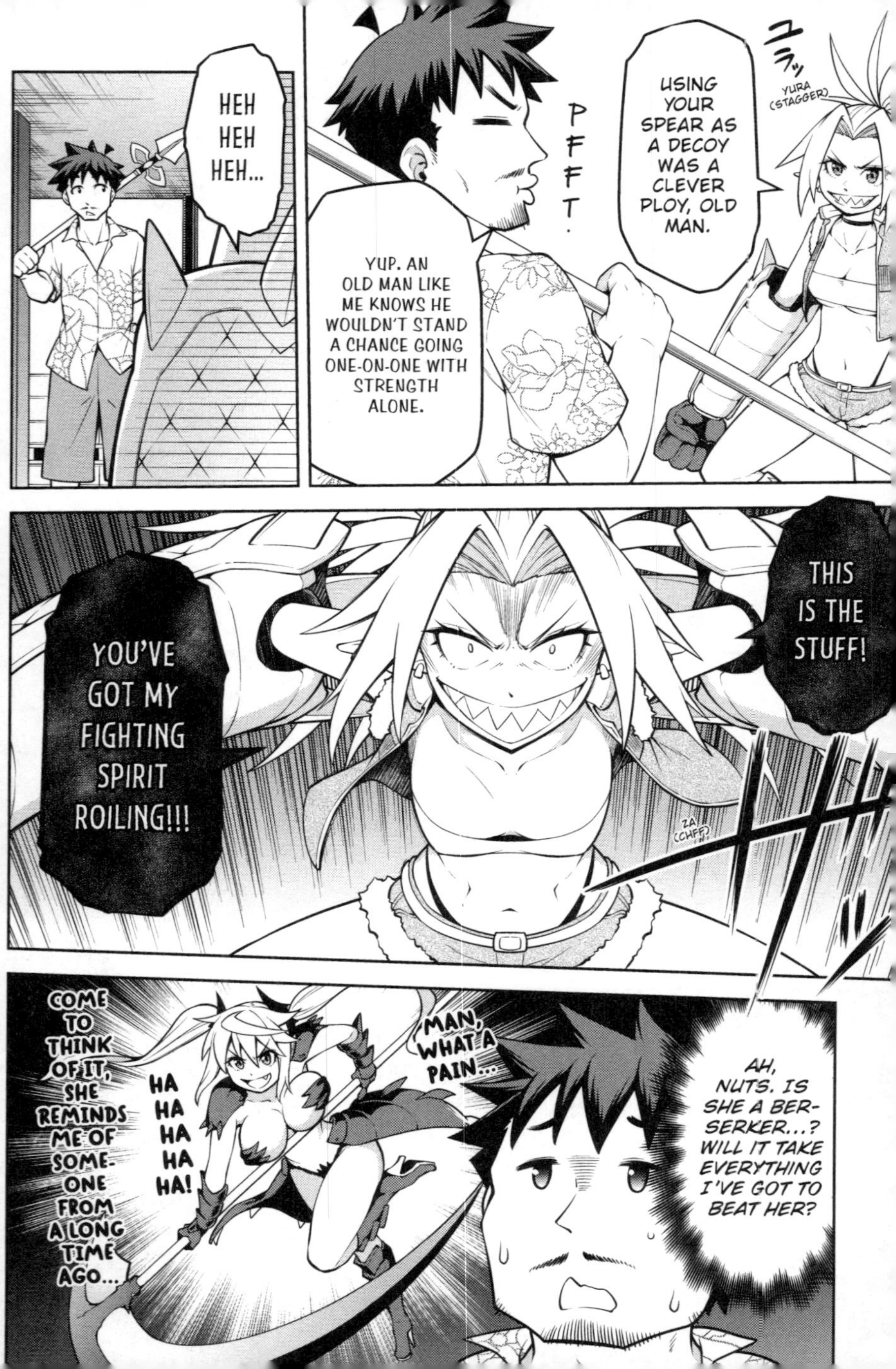
YURA (STAGGER)
USING YOUR SPEAR AS A DECOY WAS A CLEVER PLOY, OLD MAN.
PFFT.
YUP. AN OLD MAN LIKE ME KNOWS HE WOULDN'T STAND A CHANCE GOING ONE-ON-ONE WITH STRENGTH ALONE.
HEH HEH HEH...
THIS IS THE STUFF!
YOU'VE GOT MY FIGHTING SPIRIT ROILING!!!
ZA (CHFF)
AH, NUTS. IS SHE A BER-SERKER...? WILL IT TAKE EVERYTHING I'VE GOT TO BEAT HER?
MAN, WHAT A PAIN...
HA HA HA HA HA HA!
COME TO THINK OF IT, SHE REMINDS ME OF SOME-ONE FROM A LONG TIME AGO...

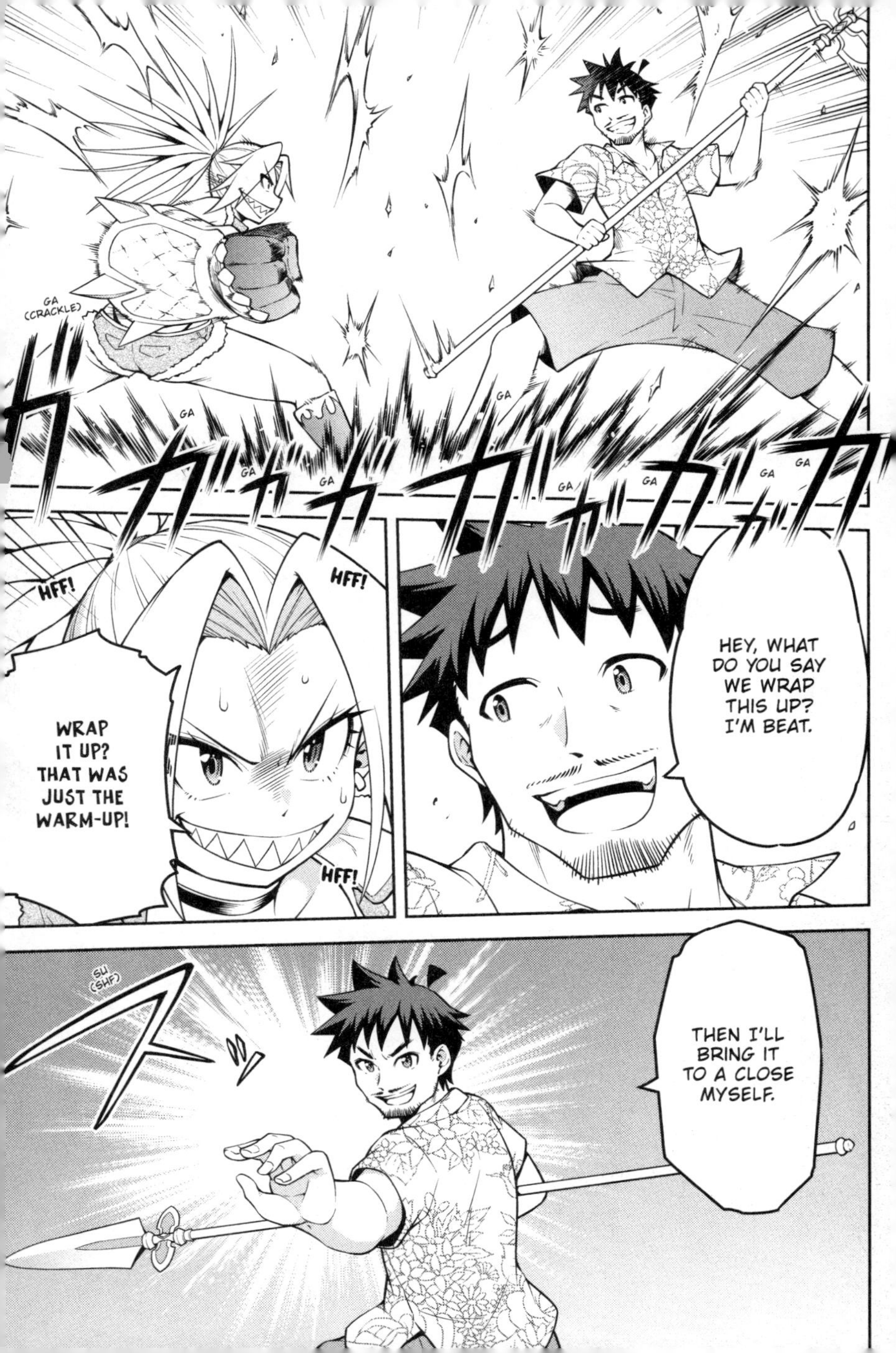
GA (CRACKLE)
GA
GA
GA
GA
GA
GA
GA
GA
HEY, WHAT DO YOU SAY WE WRAP THIS UP? I'M BEAT.
HFF!
HFF!
WRAP IT UP? THAT WAS JUST THE WARM-UP!
HFF!
SU (SHF)
THEN I'LL BRING IT TO A CLOSE MYSELF.

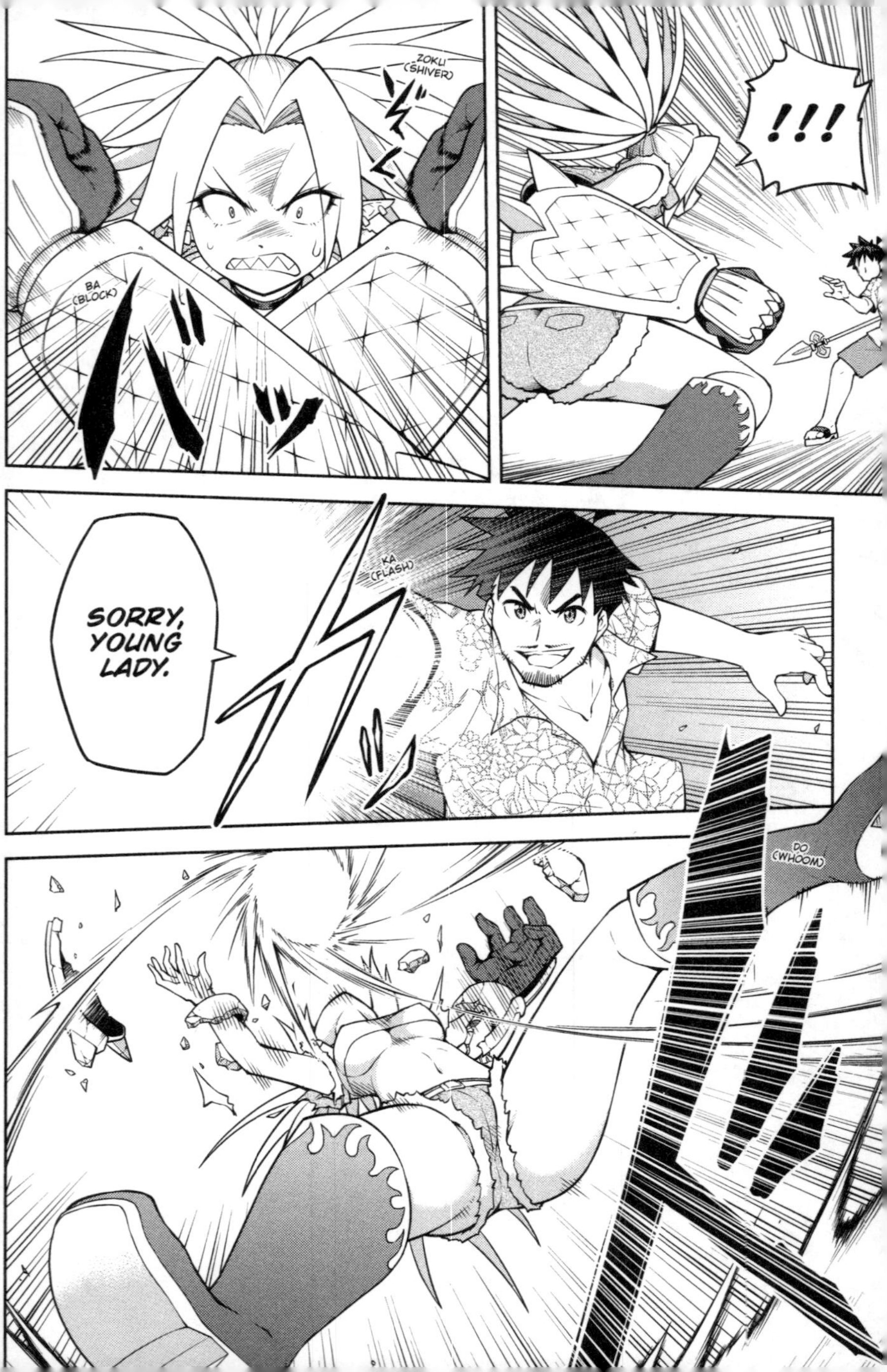
!!!
ZOKU (SHIVER)
BA (BLOCK)
KA (FLASH)
SORRY, YOUNG LADY.
DO (WHOOM)

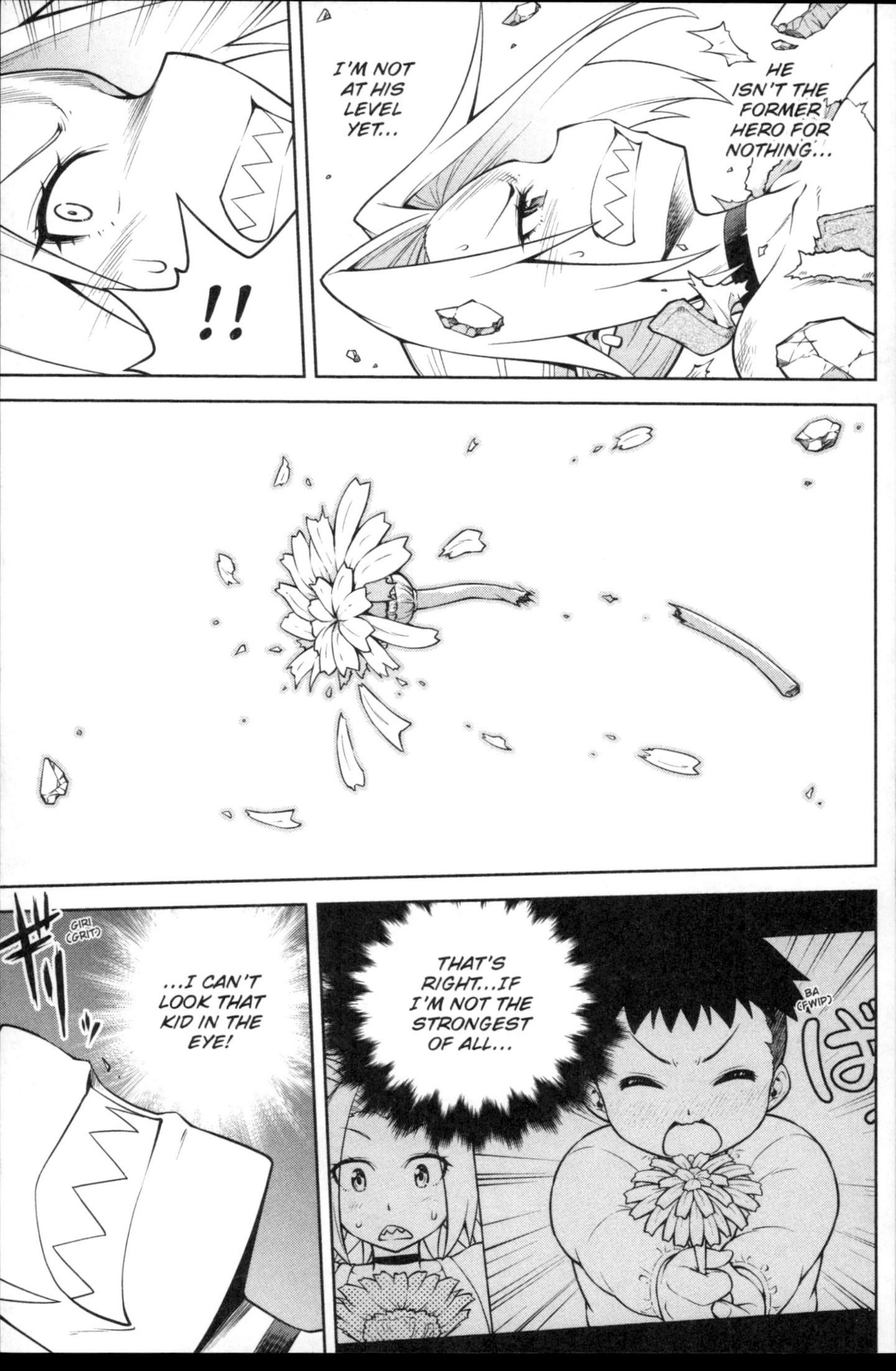
HE ISN'T THE FORMER HERO FOR NOTHING...
I'M NOT AT HIS LEVEL YET...
!!
THAT'S RIGHT...IF I'M NOT THE STRONGEST OF ALL...
BA (FWIP)
GIRI (GRIT)
...I CAN'T LOOK THAT KID IN THE EYE!

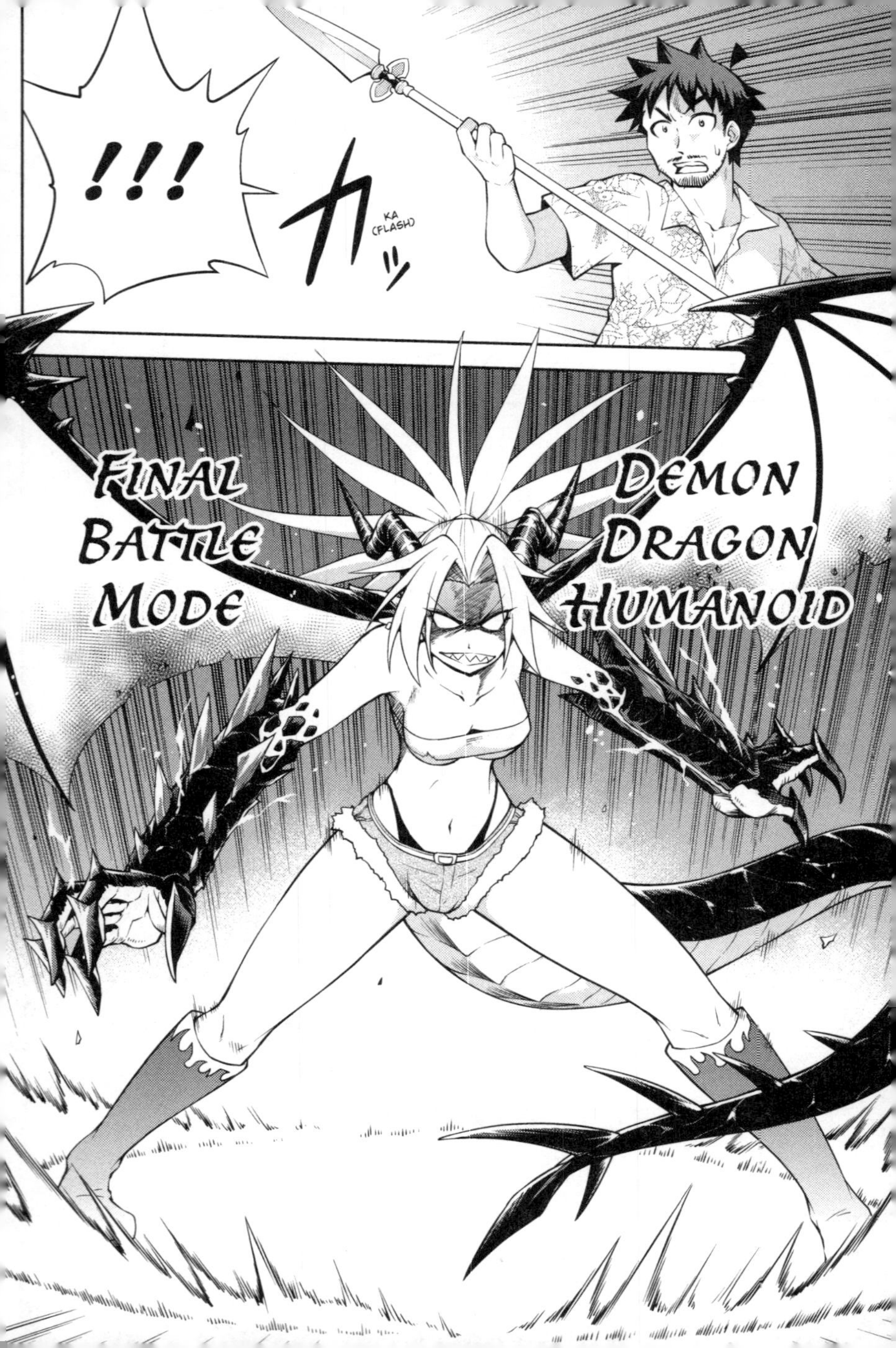
カッ
KA (FLASH)
!!!
DEMON DRAGON HUMANOID
FINAL BATTLE MODE

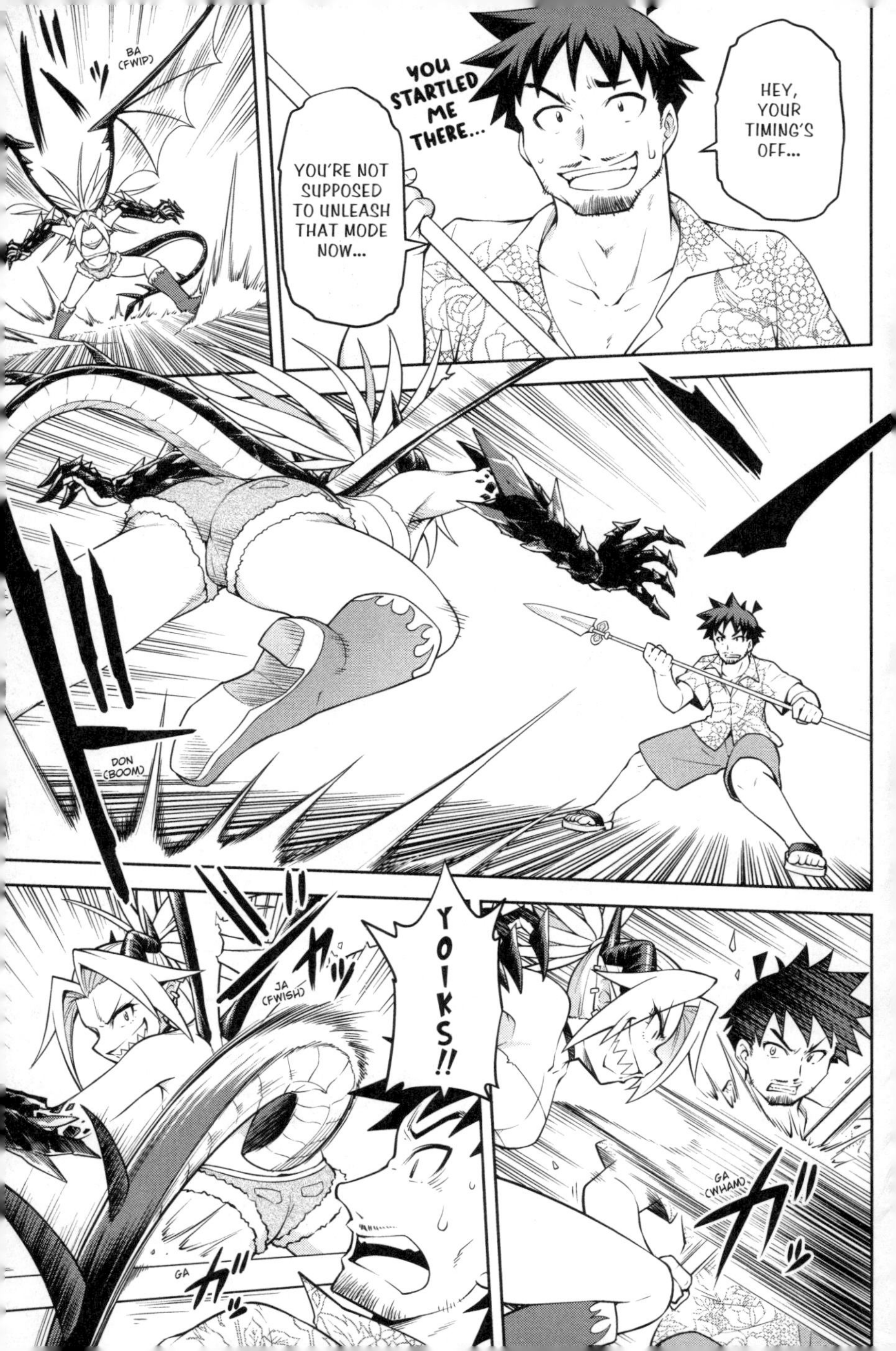
HEY, YOUR TIMING'S OFF...
YOU STARTLED ME THERE...
YOU'RE NOT SUPPOSED TO UNLEASH THAT MODE NOW...
BA (FWIP)
DON (BOOM)
GA (WHAM)
YOIKS!!
JA (FWISH)
GA

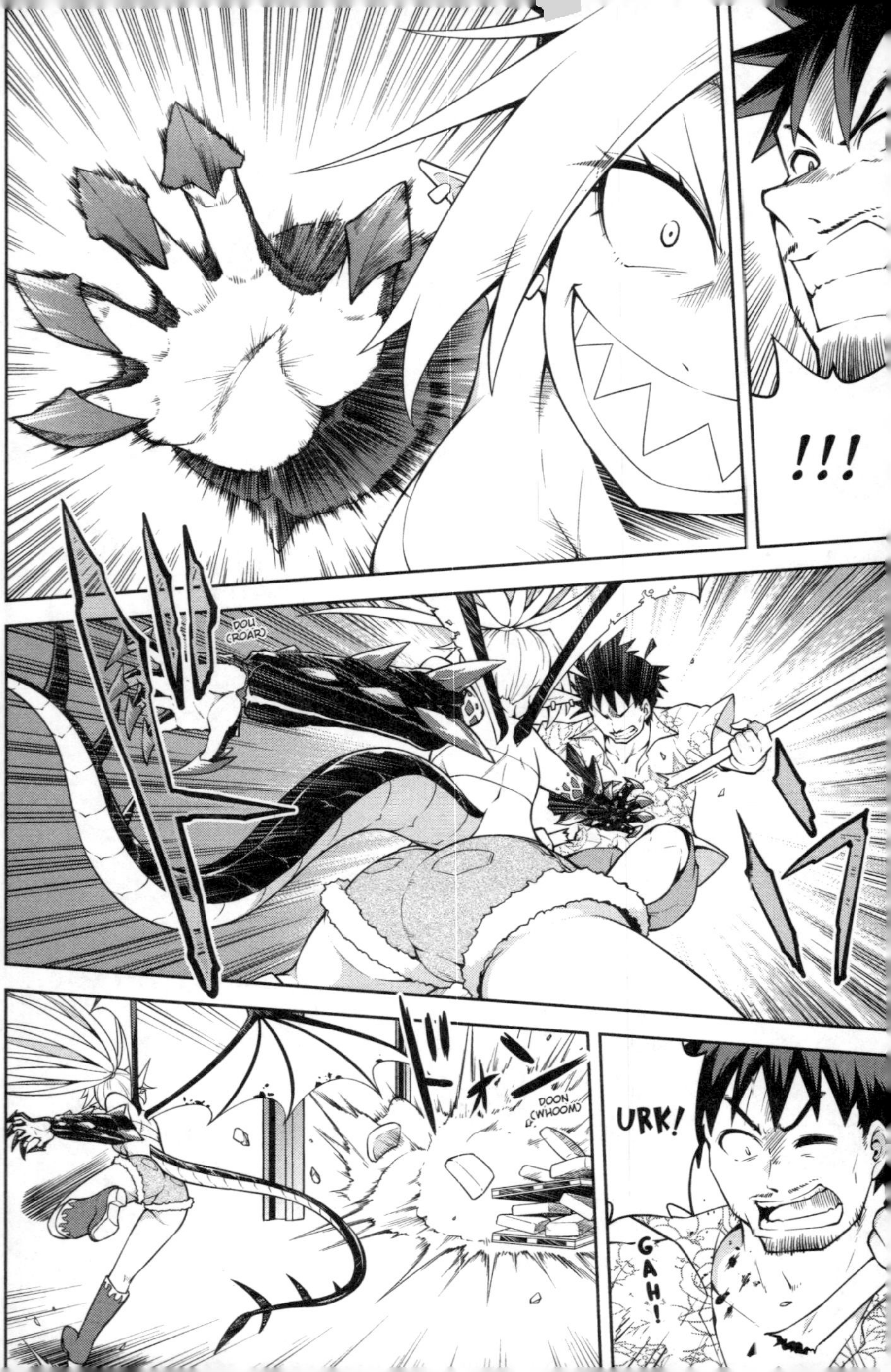
!!!
DOU (ROAR)
DOON (WHOOM)
URK!
GAH!

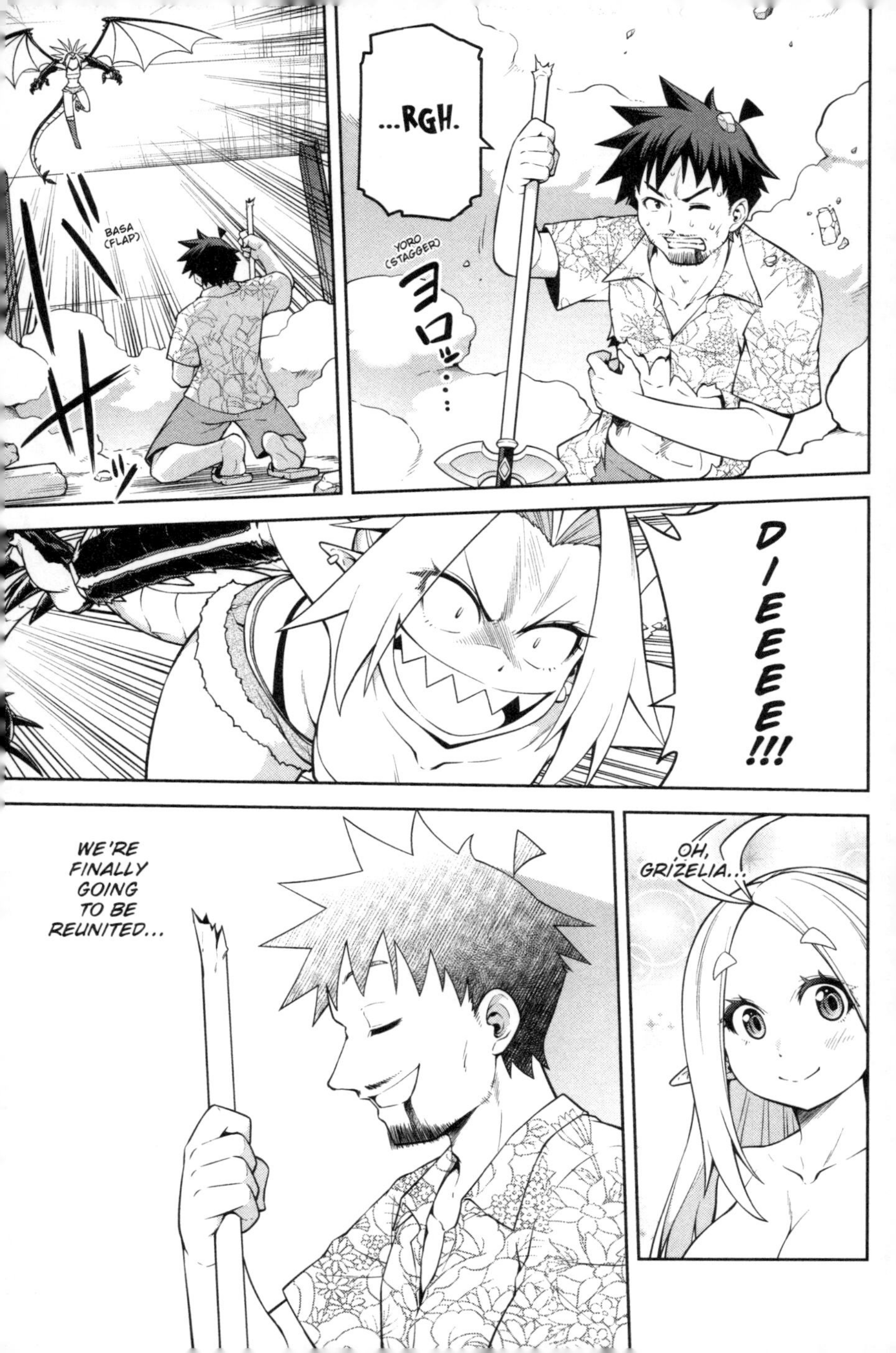
...RGH.
YORO (STAGGER)
ヨロッ…
BASA (FLAP)
バッ
DIEEEEE!!!
OH, GRIZELIA...
WE'RE FINALLY GOING TO BE REUNITED...

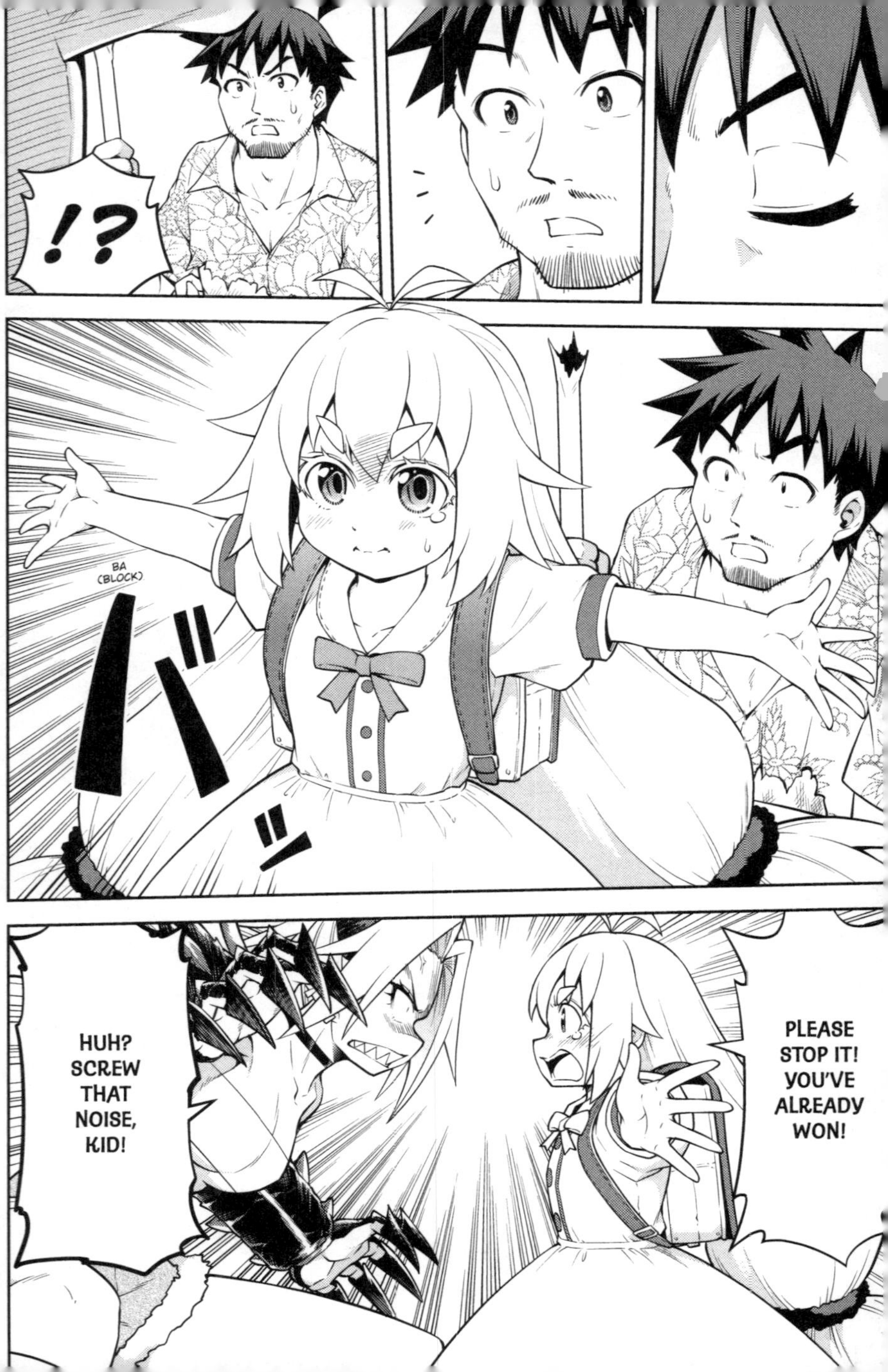
!?
BA
(BLOCK)
バッ
PLEASE STOP IT! YOU'VE ALREADY WON!
HUH? SCREW THAT NOISE, KID!

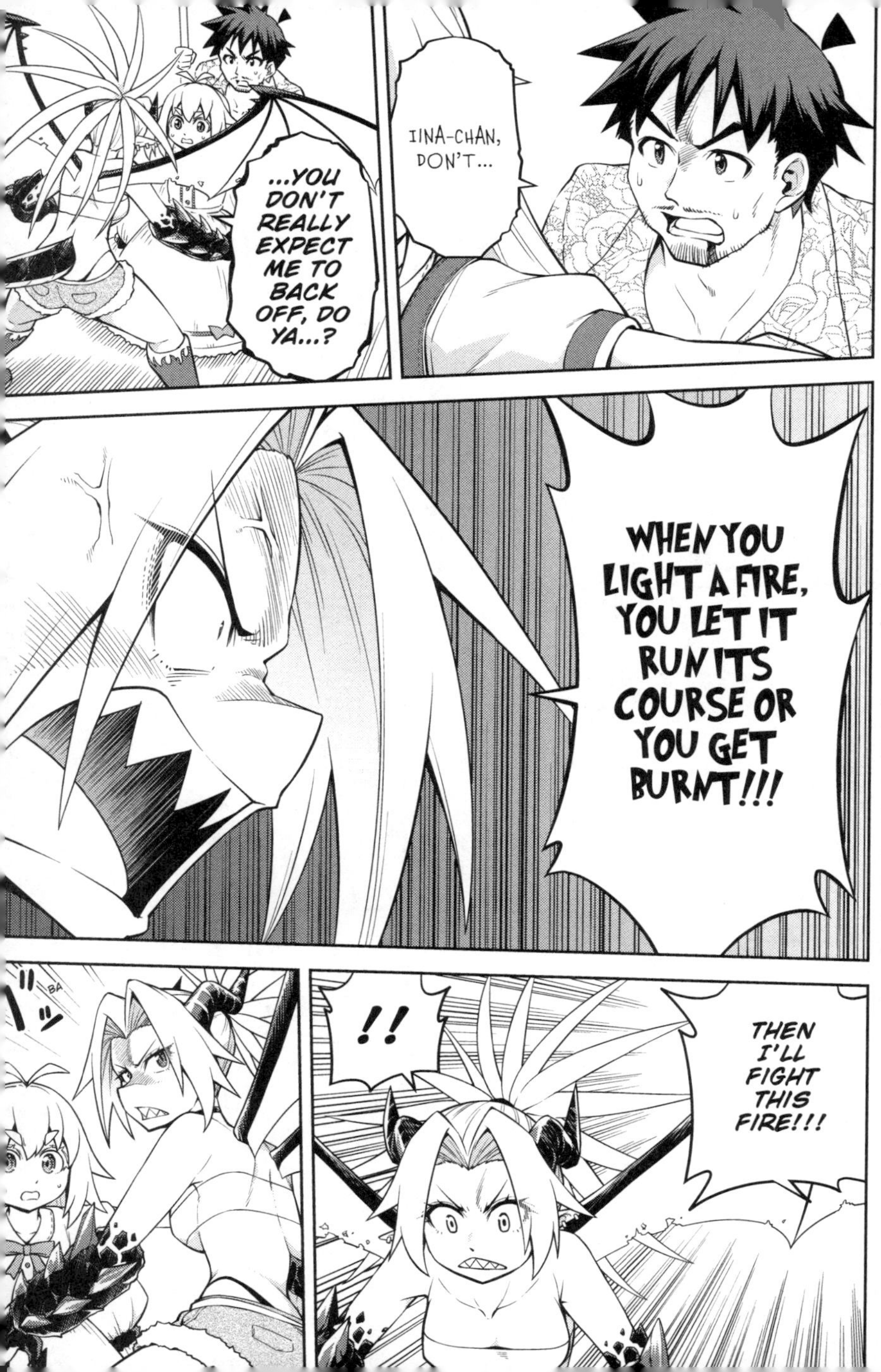
IINA-CHAN, DON'T...
...YOU DON'T REALLY EXPECT ME TO BACK OFF, DO YA...?
WHEN YOU LIGHT A FIRE, YOU LET IT RUN ITS COURSE OR YOU GET BURNT!!!
THEN I'LL FIGHT THIS FIRE!!!
!!
BA

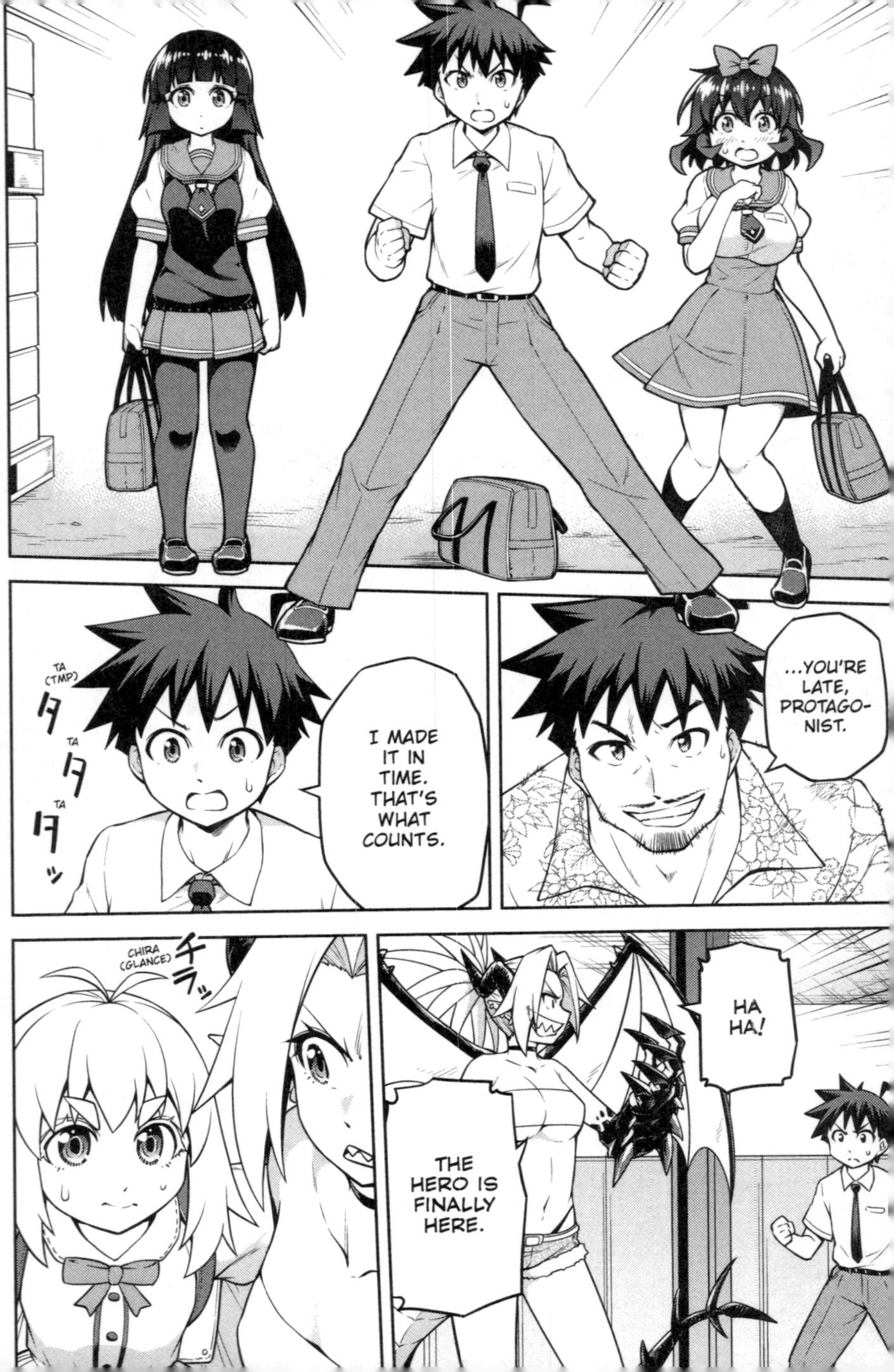
...YOU'RE LATE, PROTAGONIST.
TA (TMP)
タ
TA
タ
TA
タッ
I MADE IT IN TIME. THAT'S WHAT COUNTS.
HA HA!
THE HERO IS FINALLY HERE.
CHIRA (GLANCE)
チラッ

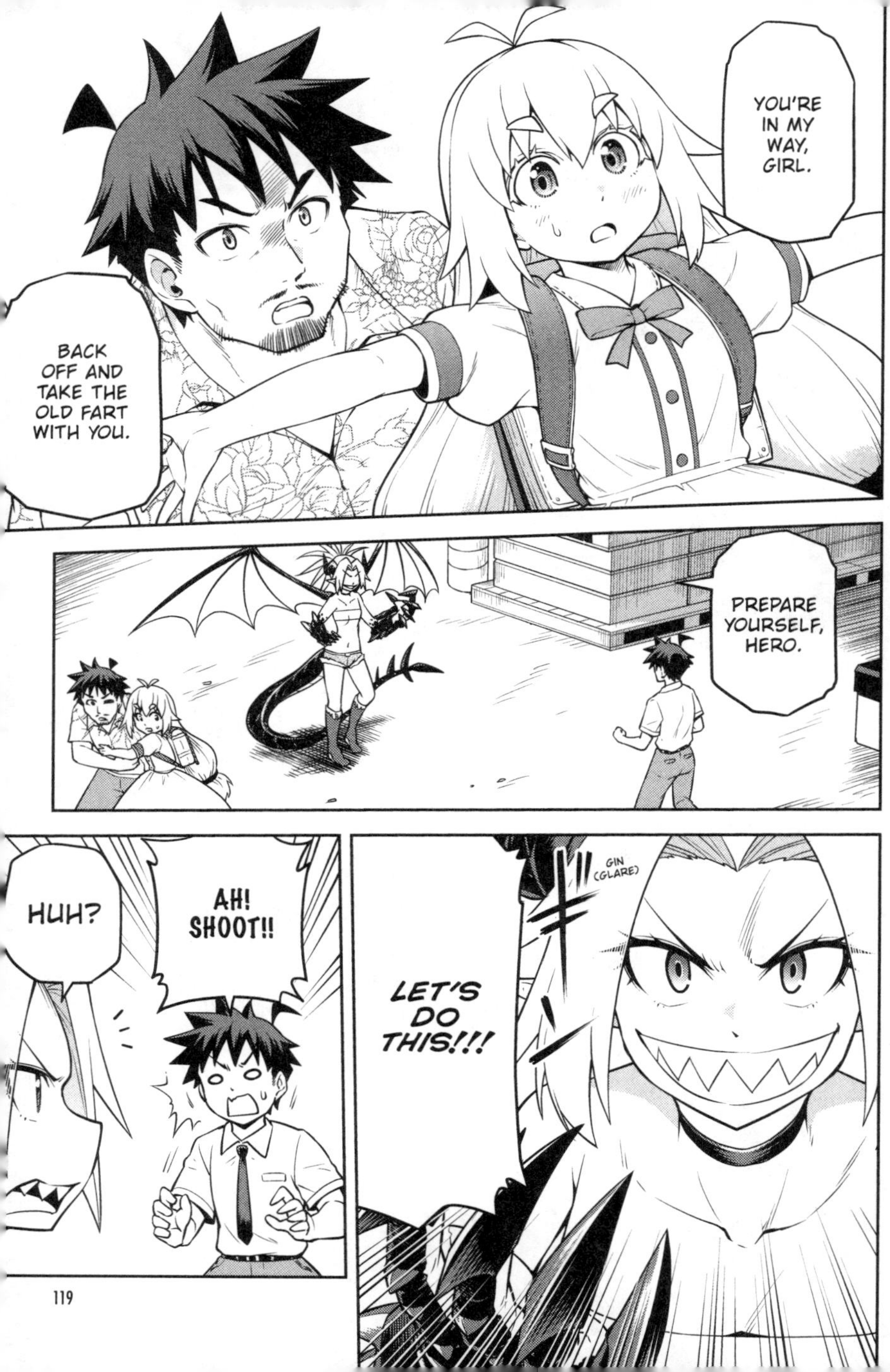
YOU'RE IN MY WAY, GIRL.
BACK OFF AND TAKE THE OLD FART WITH YOU.
PREPARE YOURSELF, HERO.
GIN (GLARE)
LET'S DO THIS!!!
AH! SHOOT!!
HUH?

HUH?

SORRY! I HAVE TO GET MY SACRED SWORD! WAIT HERE!

......

WHAT IS IT, YUUMA-KUN?

KANNA-CHAN!! I NEED YOU!!

TA (TMP) TA TA TA TA TA TAッ

HUH ...?

SACRED SWORD ...?

CAN WE GET THE SACRED SWORD OUT AGAIN?

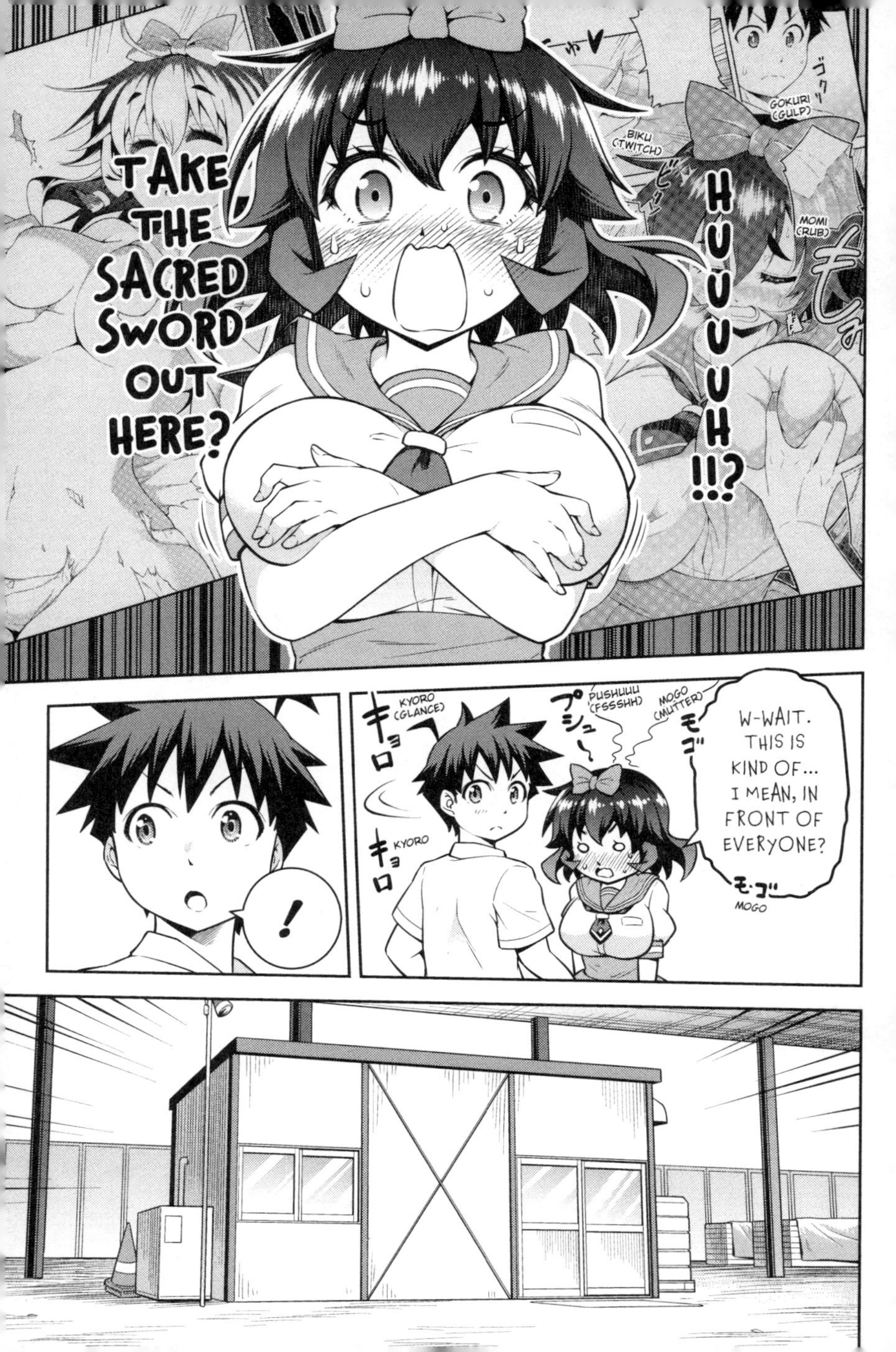
GOKURI (GULP)
BIKU (TWITCH)
MOMI (RUB)
HUUUUUH!!?
TAKE THE SACRED SWORD OUT HERE?
MOGO (MUTTER)
W-WAIT. THIS IS KIND OF... I MEAN, IN FRONT OF EVERYONE?
PUSHUUU (FSSSHH)
KYORO (GLANCE)
KYORO
MOGO
!

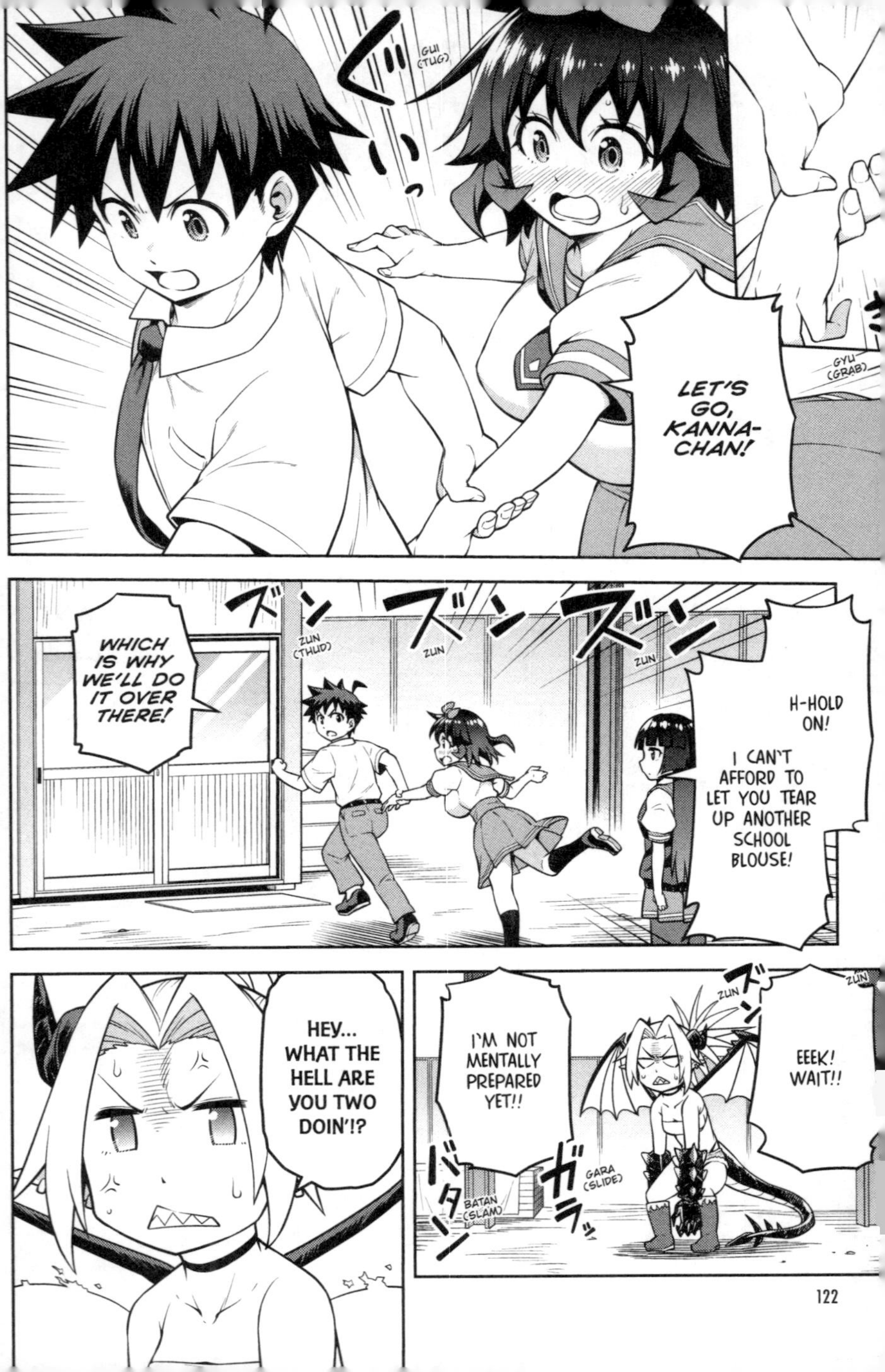
GYU (GRAB)
LET'S GO, KANNA-CHAN!
GUI (TUG)
H-HOLD ON!
I CAN'T AFFORD TO LET YOU TEAR UP ANOTHER SCHOOL BLOUSE!
ZUN
ZUN
ZUN (THUD)
WHICH IS WHY WE'LL DO IT OVER THERE!
ZUN
EEEK! WAIT!!
ZUN
I'M NOT MENTALLY PREPARED YET!!
GARA (SLIDE)
BATAN (SLAM)
HEY... WHAT THE HELL ARE YOU TWO DOIN'!?

ガタ
GATA (RATTLE)
AH! DON'T! I-I'LL DO IT!
ガタ
GATA
ガタ
GATA
I'LL TAKE IT OFF MYSELF!
ビクッ
BIKU (TWITCH)
HUH? TAKE IT OFF...?
ドキ
DOKI (BADUMP)
ドキ
DOKI
N... NOOOOO... ♡
ギシッ♡
GISHI (RUB)
ギシッ
GISHI
ギシッ♡
GISHI
プル
PURU (SHIVER)
YOU SHOULDN'T HEAR THIS, IINA-CHAN.
?
KYAAA!
プル
PURU
プル
PURU
ひょこ
HYOKO (PEEK)

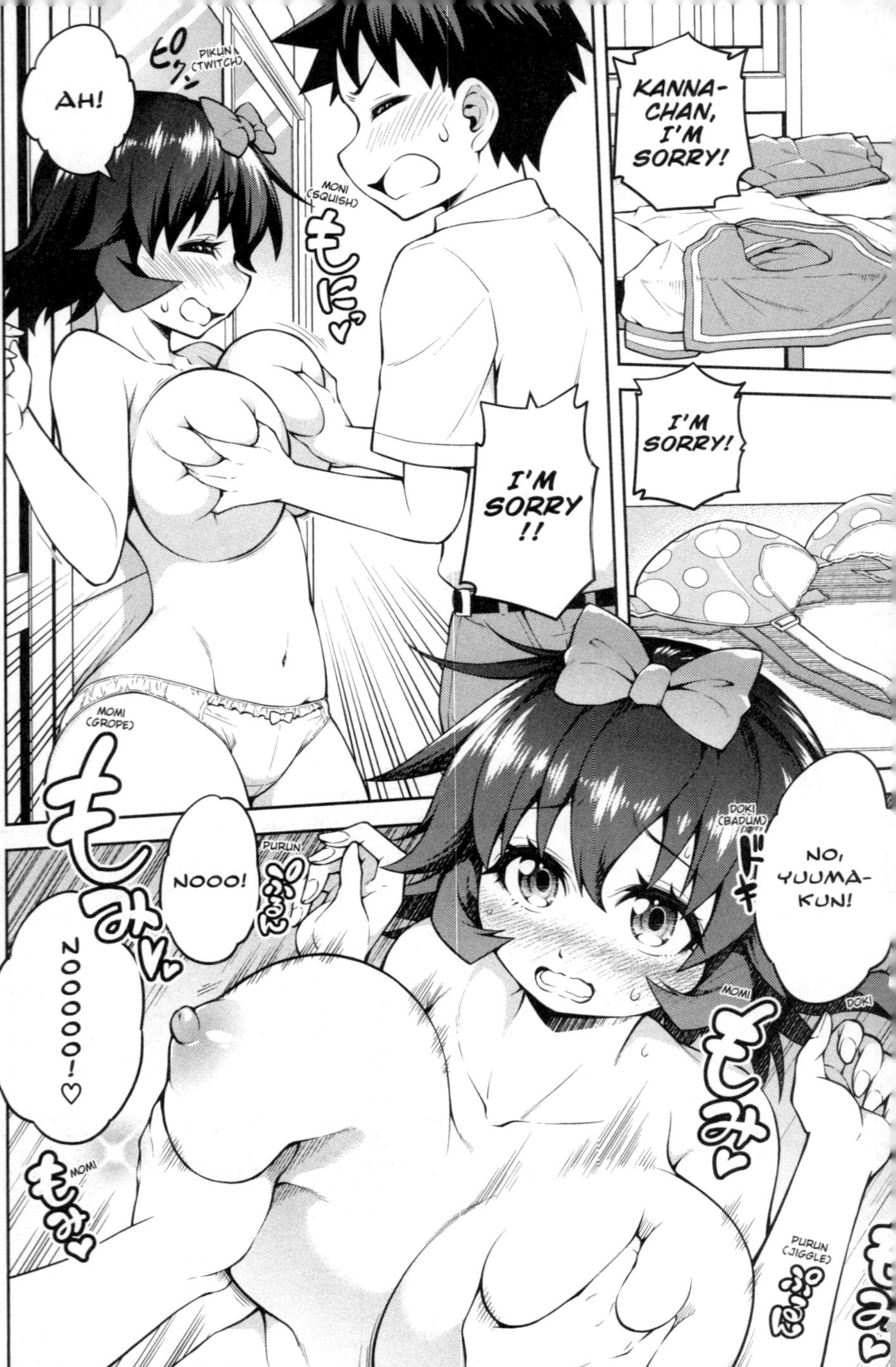
KANNA-CHAN, I'M SORRY!
I'M SORRY!
PIKUN (TWITCH)
AH!
MONI (SQUISH)
I'M SORRY !!
DOKI (BADUM)
NO, YUUMA-KUN!
MOMI
DOKI
PURUN (JIGGLE)
PURUN
NOOO!
MOMI (GROPE)
NOOOOOO!♡
MOMI

OHHHH...
もみ
MOMI
MOMI
もみ
SACRED SWORD! COME ON OUT!!
MOMI
もみ
ピクッ
PIKU
IT'S COMING ...
IT'S COMI------NG!!!
PAAA (GLOW)
!!
カッ
KA (FLASH)

HFF...

HFF...

SORRY FOR THE WAIT!

GARA (SLIDE)

ガラッ

HOKAA (STEAM)

ホカァ♥

I AM YOUR OPPO-NENT!

DOKI (BADUM)

ドキ

DOKI

DOKI

OKAY... AS LONG AS YOU'RE READY NOW...

YAY! THE SACRED SWORD!

PACHI

PACHI (CLAP)

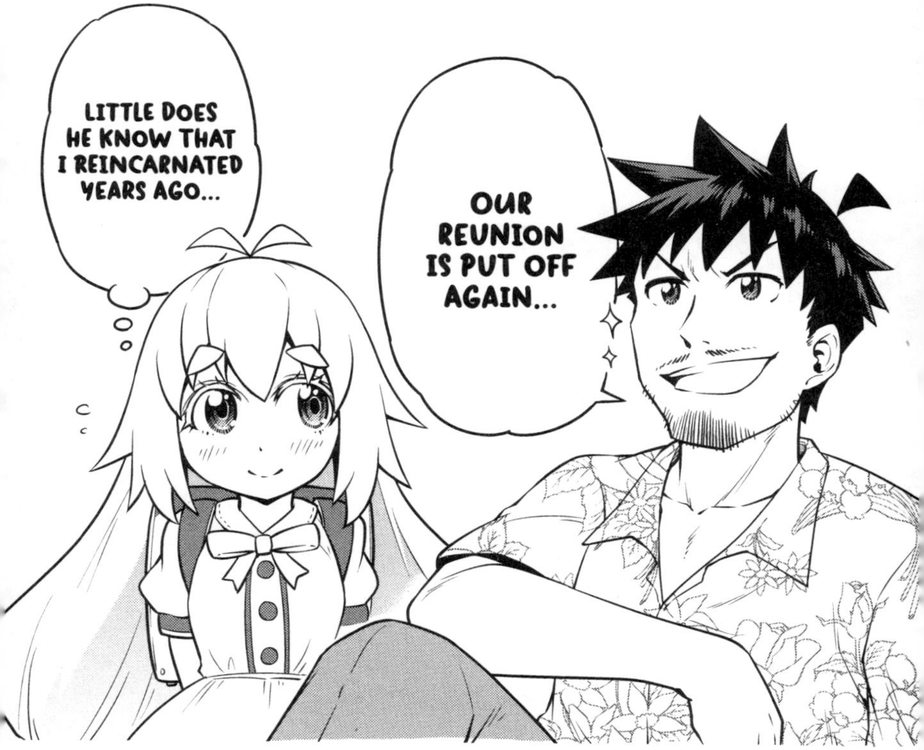
OUR REUNION IS PUT OFF AGAIN...
LITTLE DOES HE KNOW THAT I REINCARNATED YEARS AGO...

I'm the HERO, but the DEMON LORD's Also Me

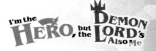

# Chapter 15

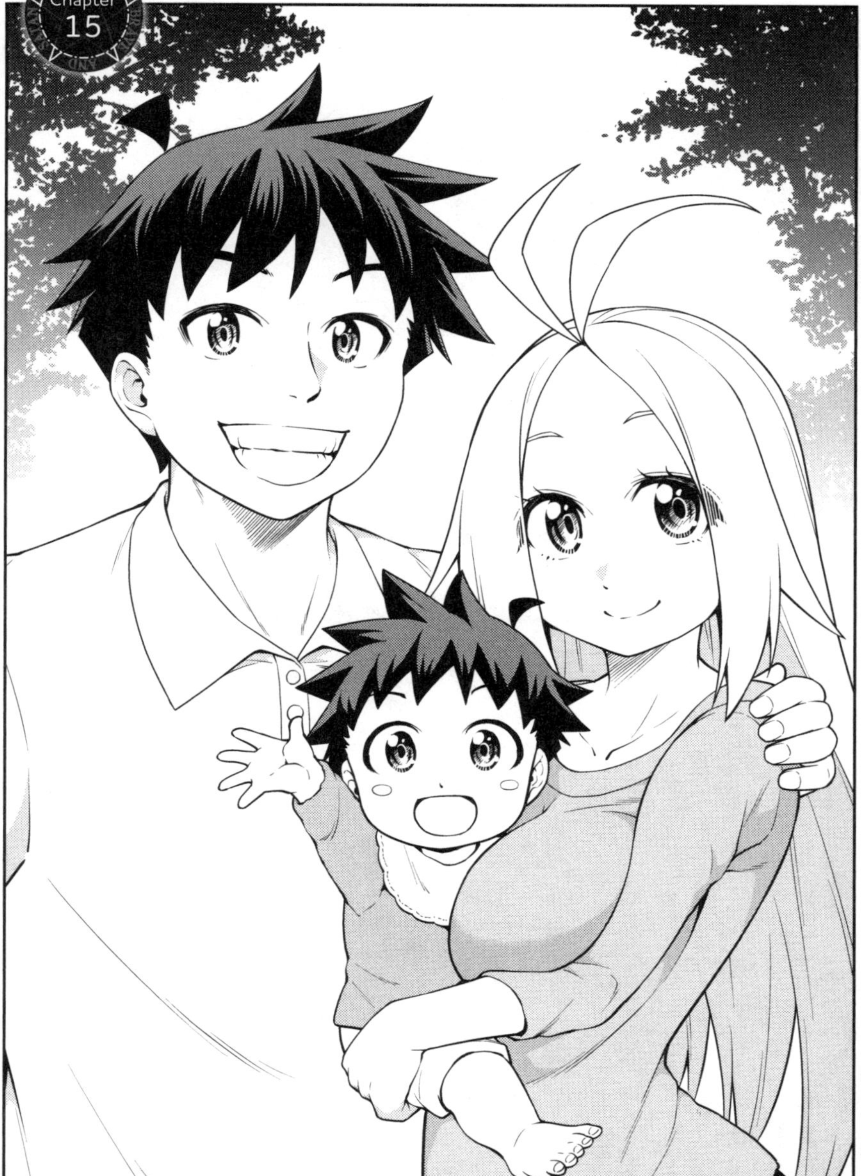

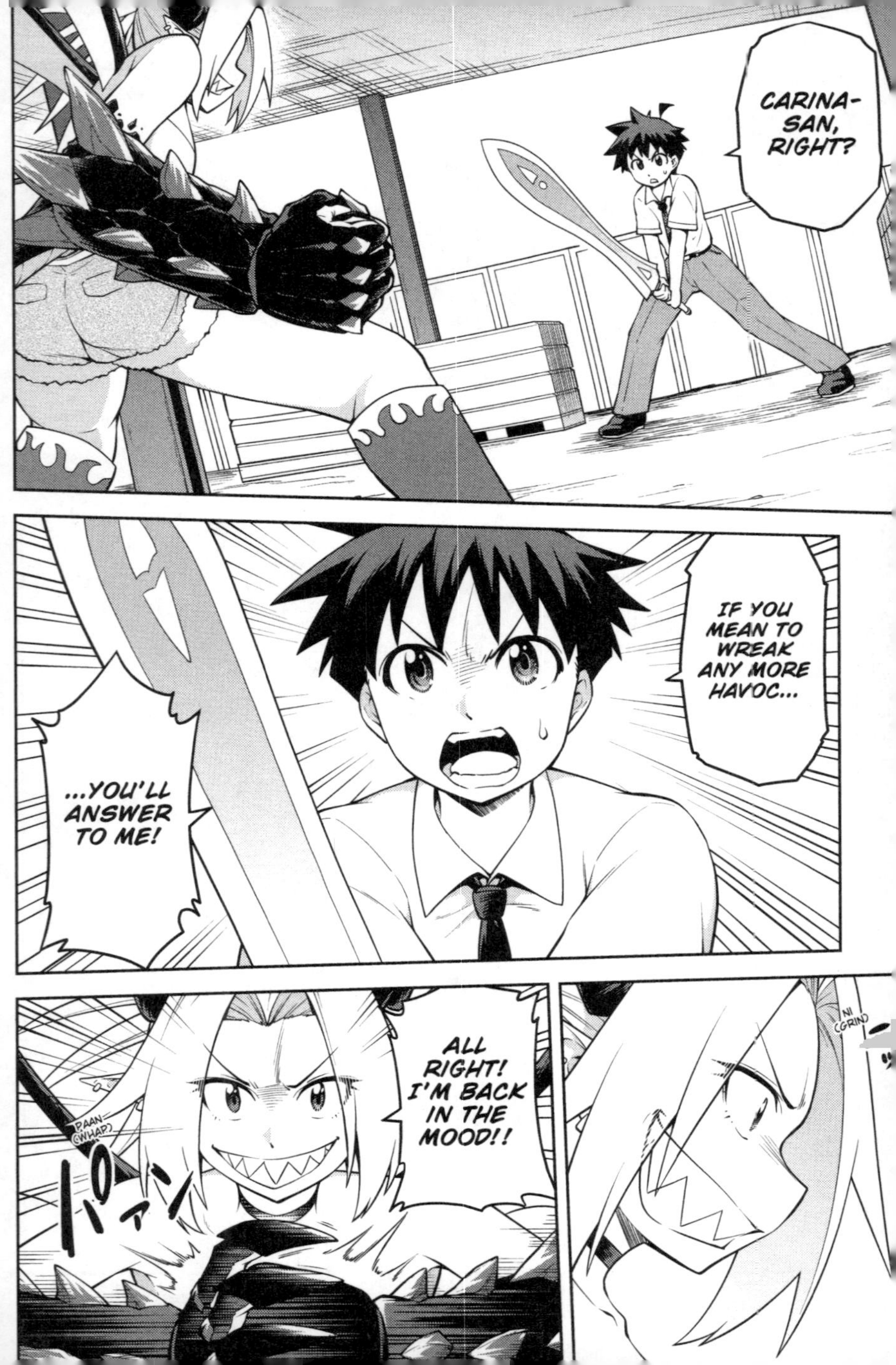
CARINA-SAN, RIGHT?
IF YOU MEAN TO WREAK ANY MORE HAVOC...
...YOU'LL ANSWER TO ME!
NI (GRIN)
ALL RIGHT! I'M BACK IN THE MOOD!!
PAAN (WHAP)

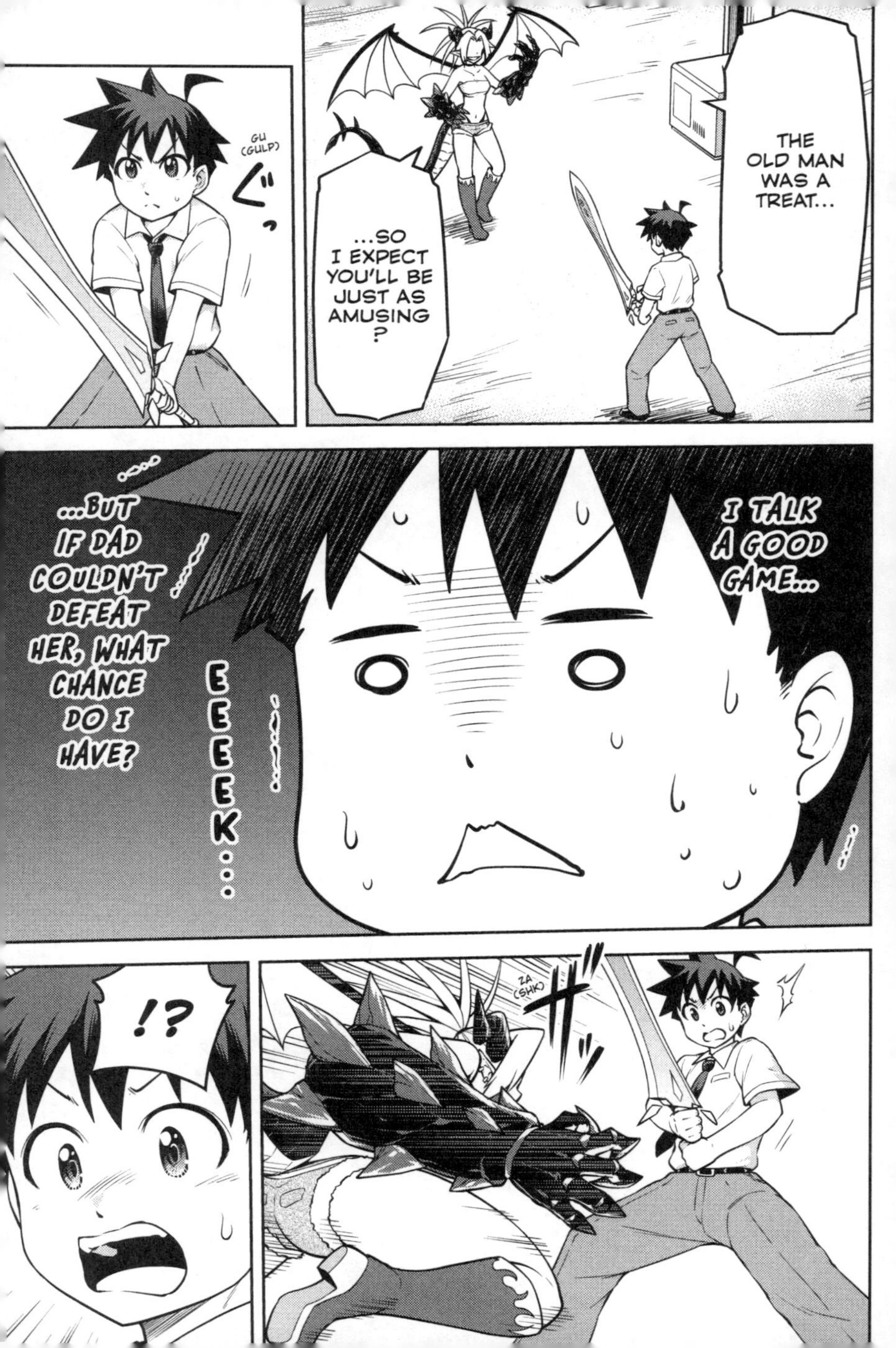
THE OLD MAN WAS A TREAT...
...SO I EXPECT YOU'LL BE JUST AS AMUSING?
GU (GULP)
I TALK A GOOD GAME...
...BUT IF DAD COULDN'T DEFEAT HER, WHAT CHANCE DO I HAVE?
EEEEK...
ZA (SHK)
!?

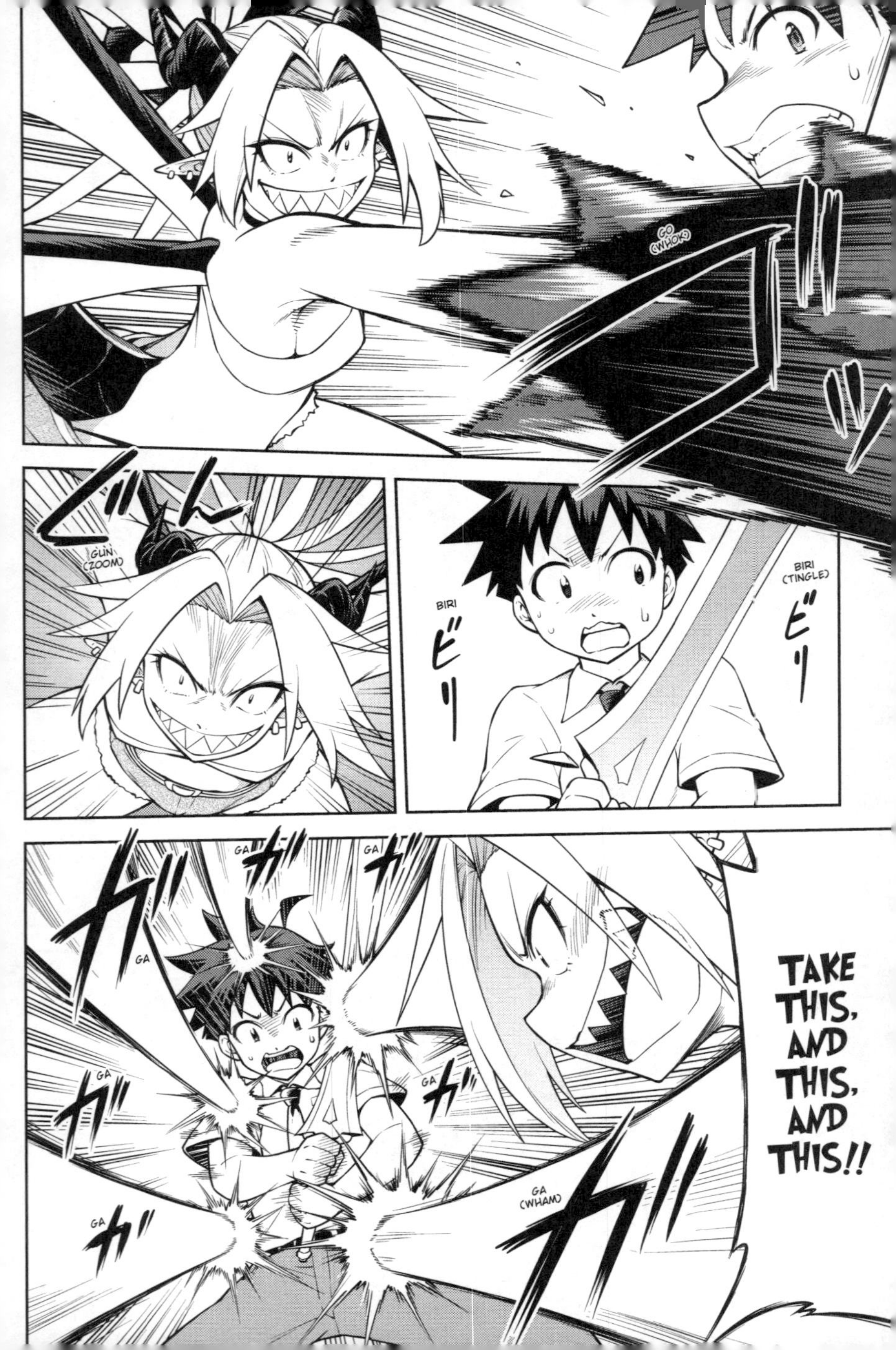
GO (WHOK)
BIRI (TINGLE)
BIRI
GUN (ZOOM)
TAKE THIS, AND THIS, AND THIS!!
GA
GA
GA
GA
GA
GA (WHAM)
GA

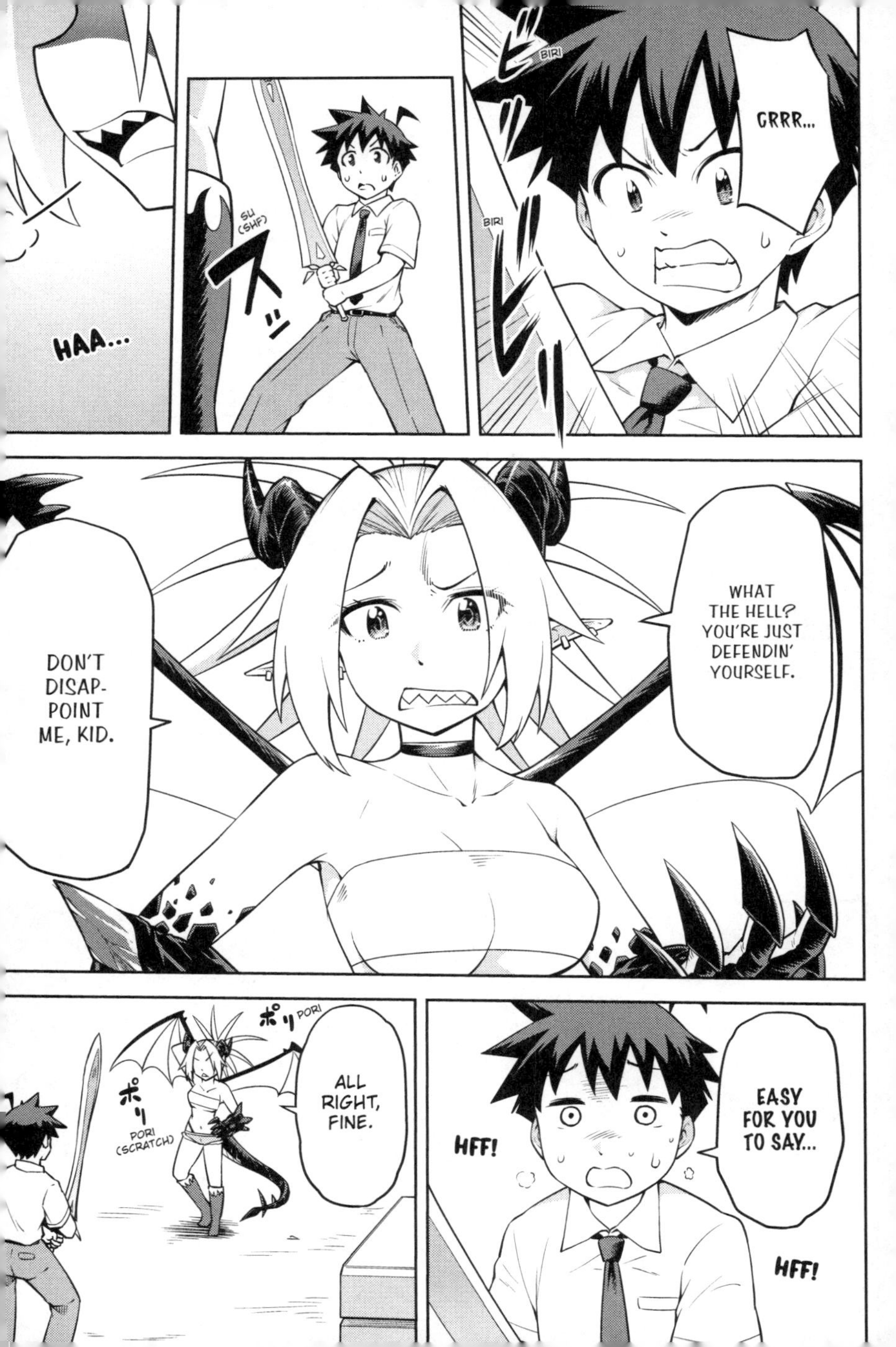
GRRR...
BIRI
BIRI
SU (SHF)
HAA...
WHAT THE HELL? YOU'RE JUST DEFENDIN' YOURSELF.
DON'T DISAP-POINT ME, KID.
EASY FOR YOU TO SAY...
HFF!
HFF!
PORI
ALL RIGHT, FINE.
PORI (SCRATCH)

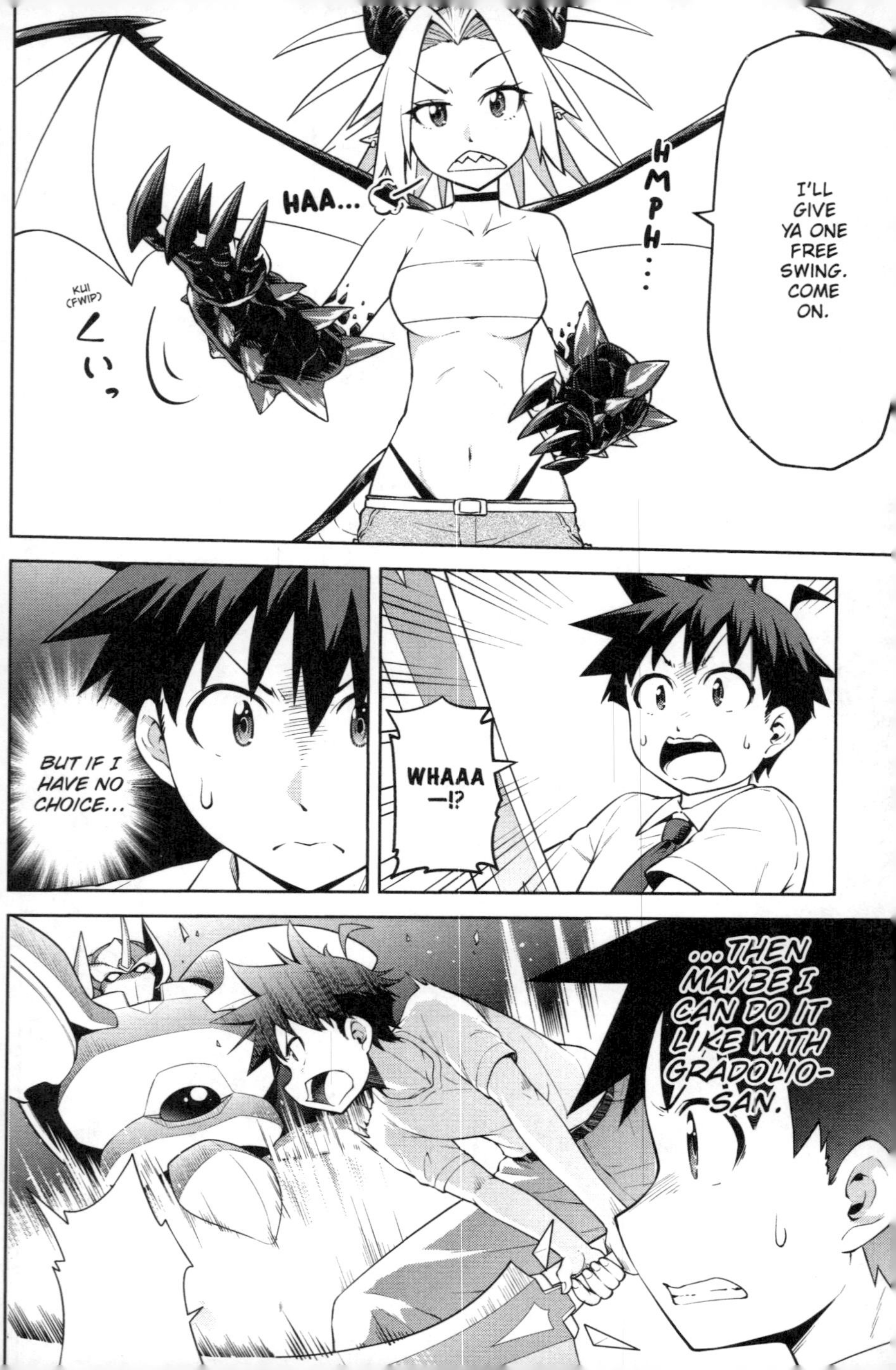
I'LL GIVE YA ONE FREE SWING. COME ON.
HMPH...
HAA...
KUI (FWIP)
くいっ
WHAAA—!?
BUT IF I HAVE NO CHOICE...
...THEN MAYBE I CAN DO IT LIKE WITH GRADOLIO-SAN.

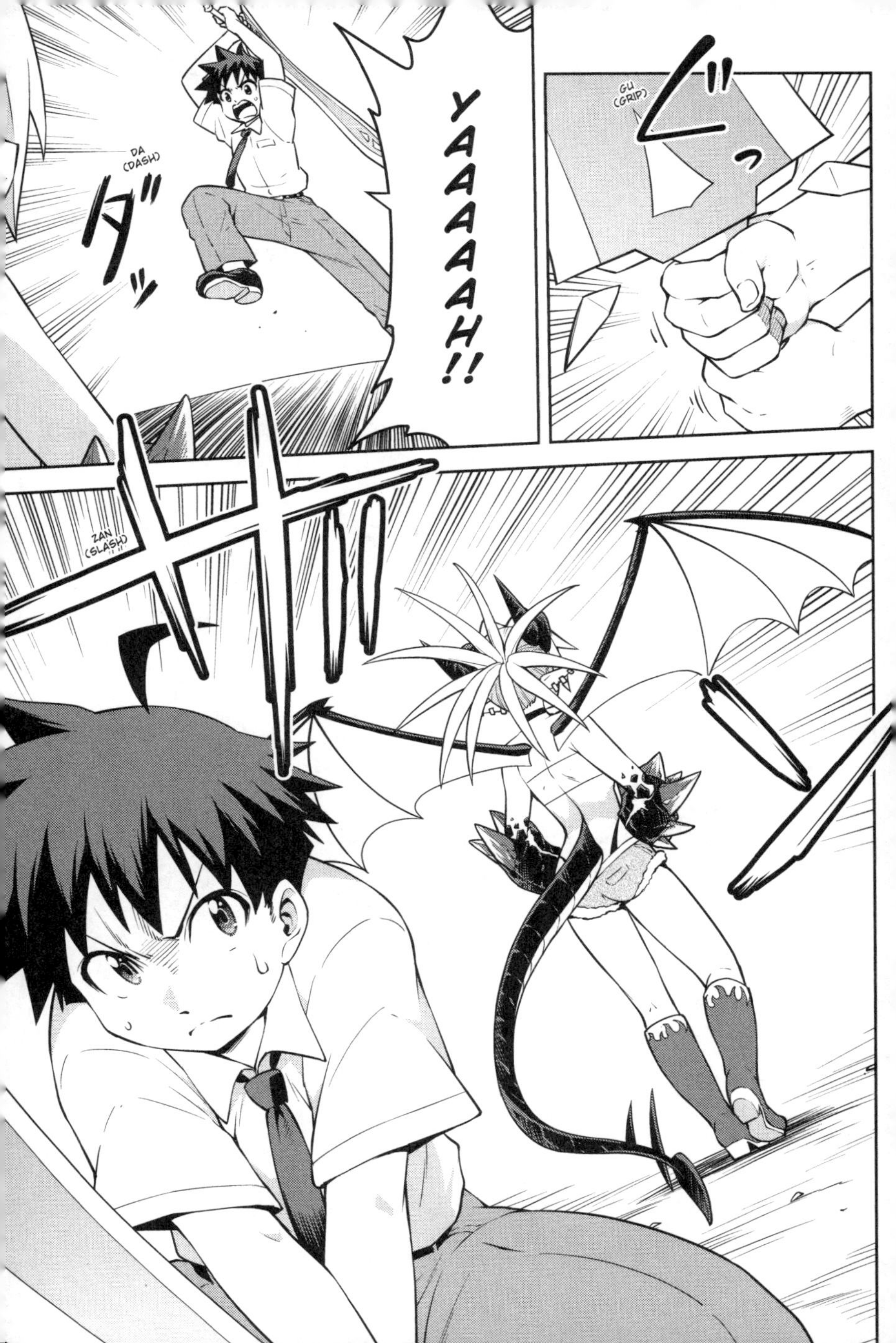
ぐっ
GU (GRIP)
YAAAAAAH!!
ダッ
DA (DASH)
ZAN (SLASH)

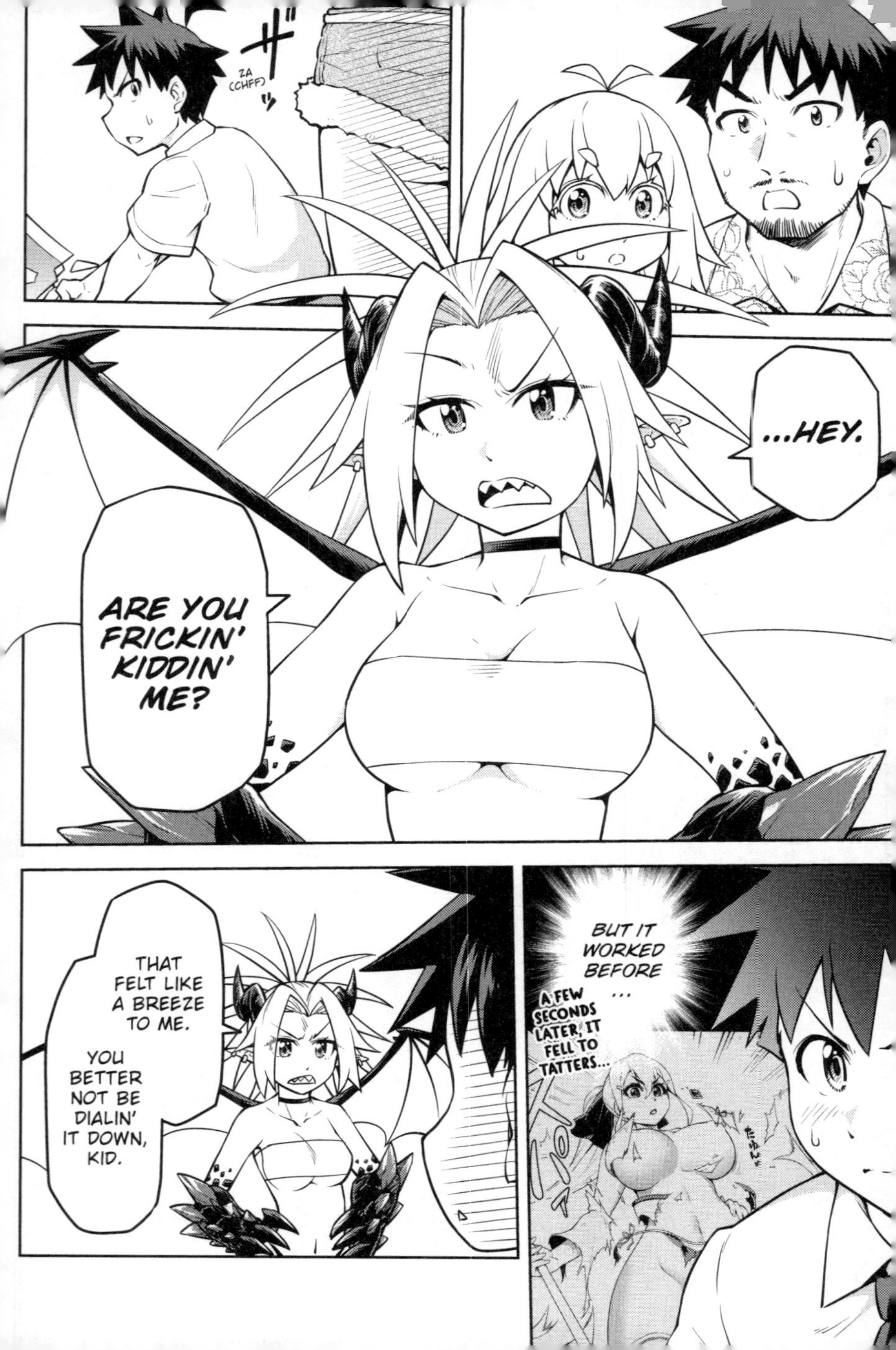
ZA (CHFF)
...HEY.
ARE YOU FRICKIN' KIDDIN' ME?
BUT IT WORKED BEFORE ...
A FEW SECONDS LATER, IT FELL TO TATTERS...
THAT FELT LIKE A BREEZE TO ME.
YOU BETTER NOT BE DIALIN' IT DOWN, KID.

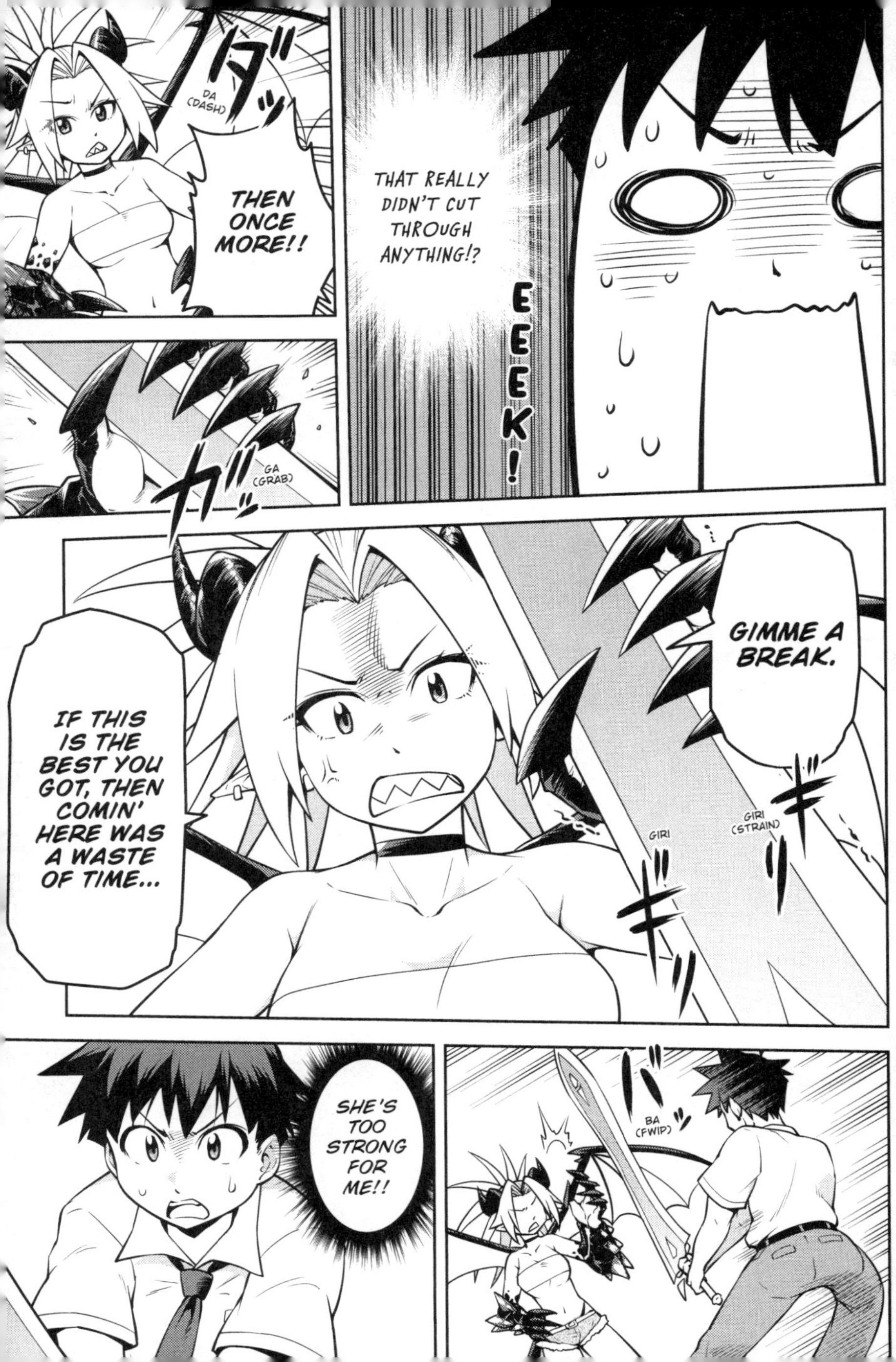
THAT REALLY DIDN'T CUT THROUGH ANYTHING!?
EEEK!
DA (DASH)
THEN ONCE MORE!!
GA (GRAB)
GIMME A BREAK.
GIRI (STRAIN)
GIRI
IF THIS IS THE BEST YOU GOT, THEN COMIN' HERE WAS A WASTE OF TIME...
BA (FWIP)
SHE'S TOO STRONG FOR ME!!

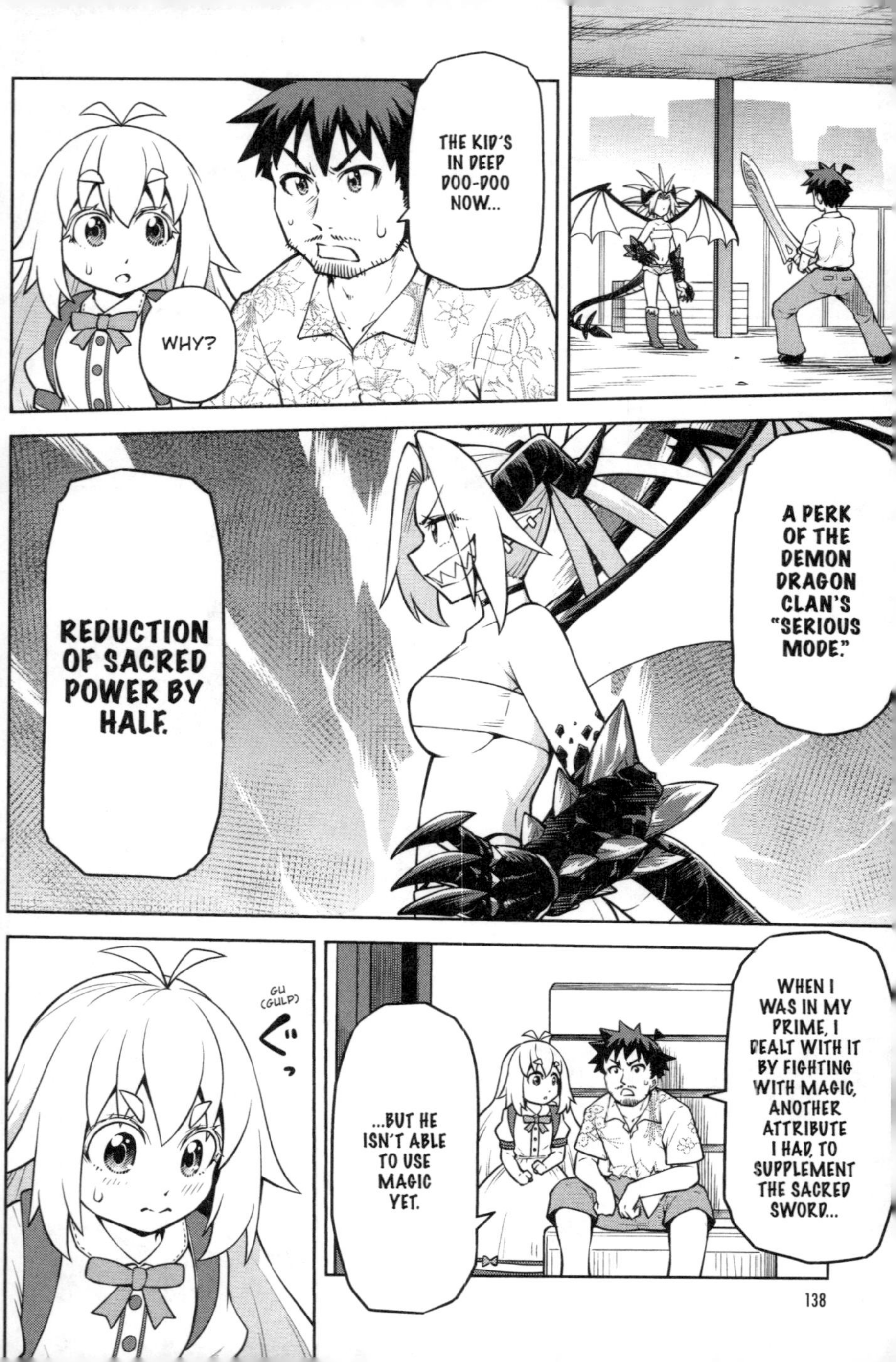
THE KID'S IN DEEP DOO-DOO NOW...
WHY?
A PERK OF THE DEMON DRAGON CLAN'S "SERIOUS MODE."
REDUCTION OF SACRED POWER BY HALF.
WHEN I WAS IN MY PRIME, I DEALT WITH IT BY FIGHTING WITH MAGIC, ANOTHER ATTRIBUTE I HAD, TO SUPPLEMENT THE SACRED SWORD...
...BUT HE ISN'T ABLE TO USE MAGIC YET.
GU (GULP)
ぐっ

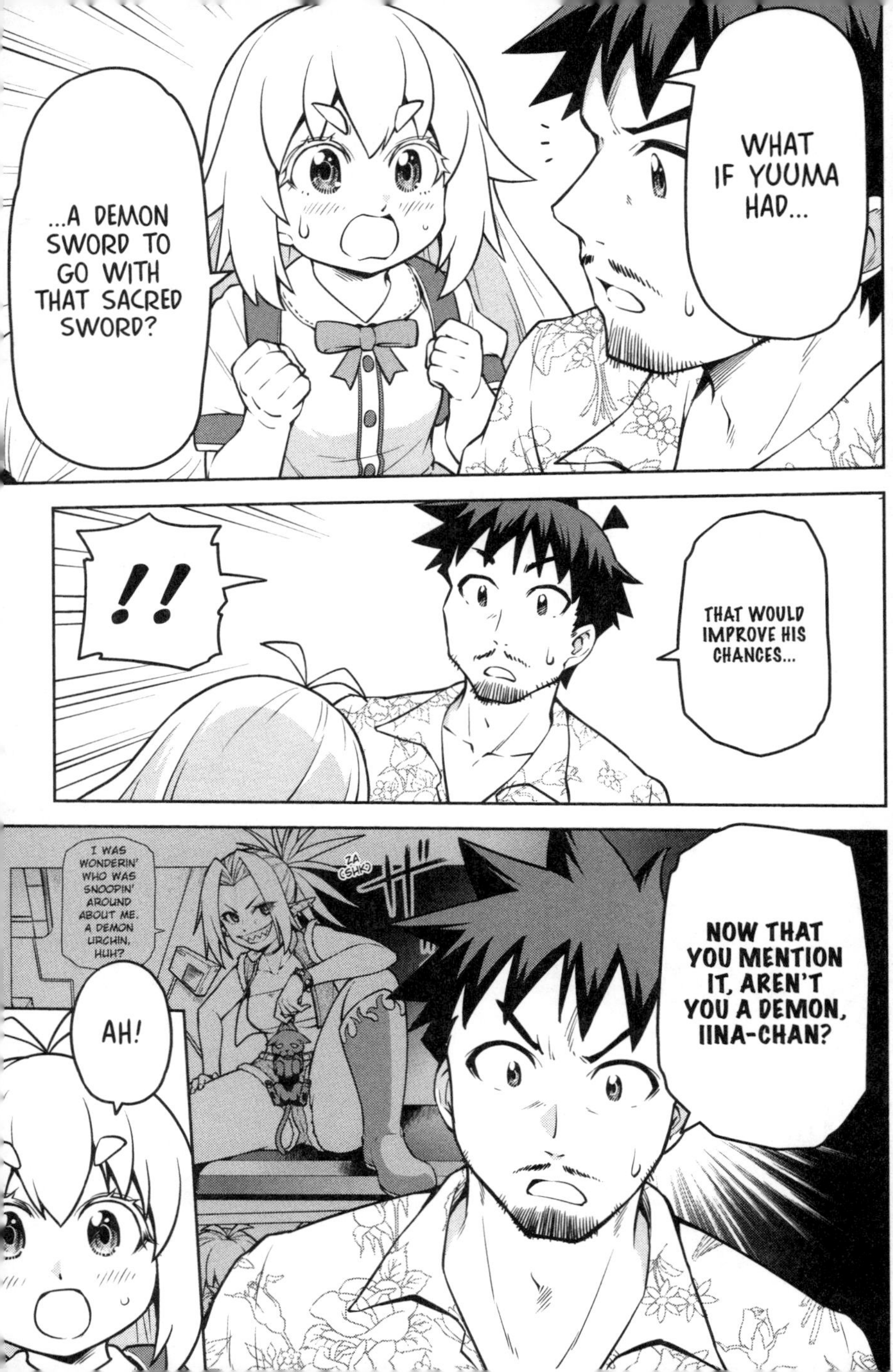
WHAT IF YUUMA HAD...
...A DEMON SWORD TO GO WITH THAT SACRED SWORD?
THAT WOULD IMPROVE HIS CHANCES...
!!
NOW THAT YOU MENTION IT, AREN'T YOU A DEMON, IINA-CHAN?
ZA (SHK)
I WAS WONDERIN' WHO WAS SNOOPIN' AROUND ABOUT ME. A DEMON URCHIN, HUH?
AH!

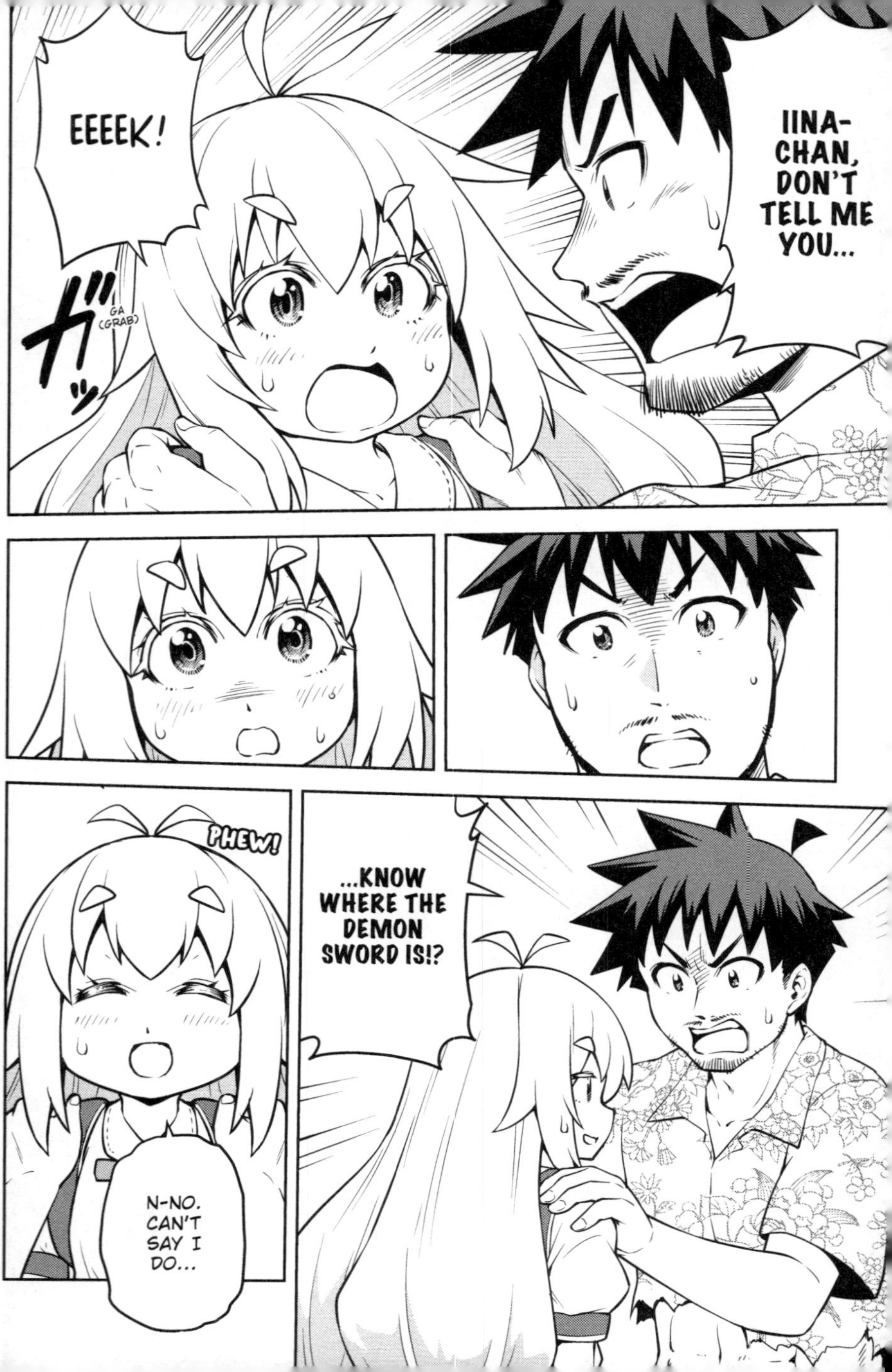
IINA-CHAN, DON'T TELL ME YOU...
EEEEK!
ガッ
GA (GRAB)
...KNOW WHERE THE DEMON SWORD IS!?
PHEW!
N-NO. CAN'T SAY I DO...

PHEW. FOR A SECOND THERE, I THOUGHT...

SORRY...

HAA...

DIDN'T THINK SO...

LIKE I'D EVER BE THAT LUCKY...

!!!

ぽむ
POMU
(PAT)

ビク
BIKU
(TWITCH)

NAH, YOU DIDN'T DO ANYTHING WRONG, IINA-CHAN.

I APOLO-GIZE FOR STARTLING YOU.

ドキ
DOKI

DOKI

ドキ
DOKI
(BADUM)

ドキ

UH... IT'S OKAY.

ドキ
DOKI

ド
キ

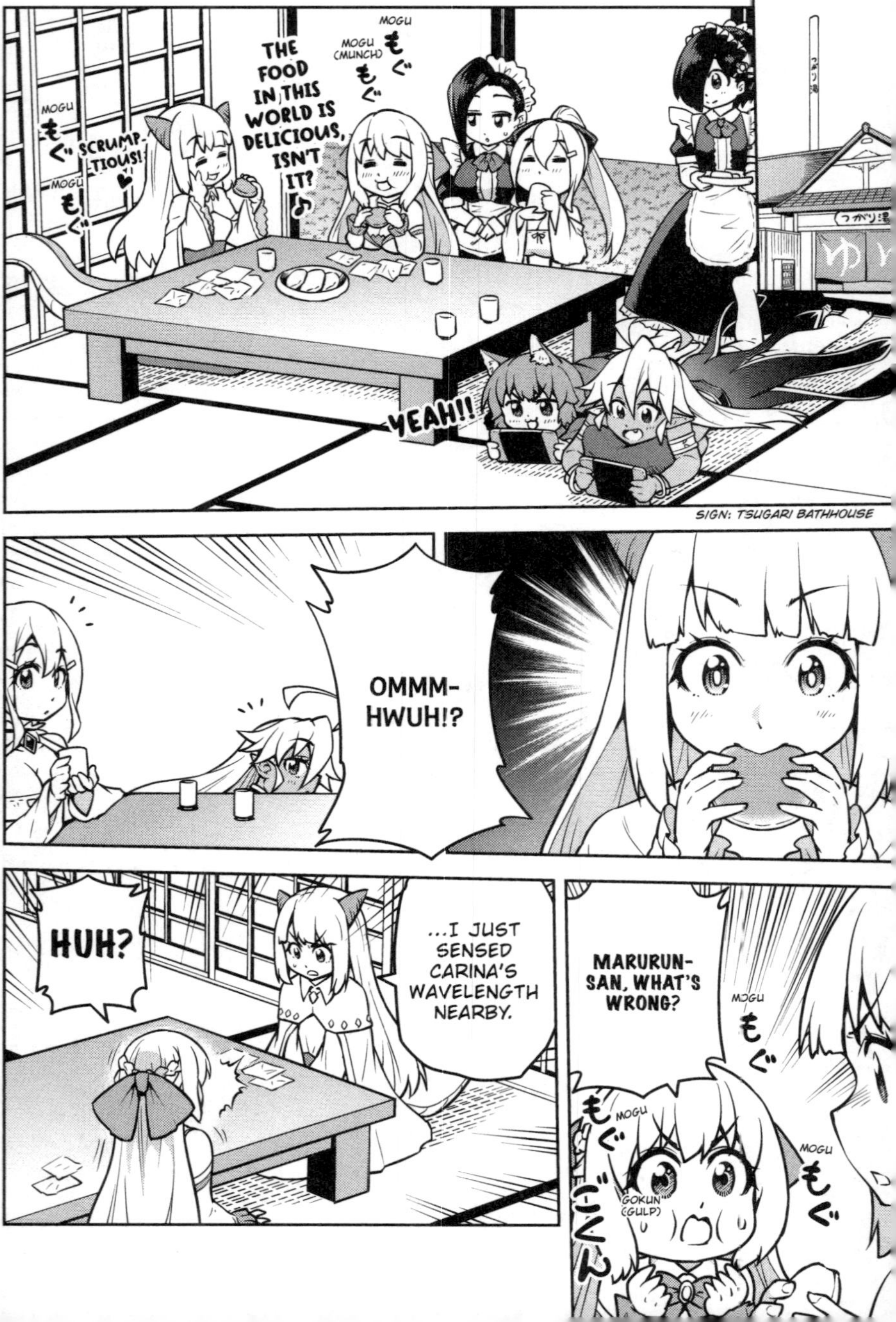
MOGU
もぐ
MOGU (MUNCH)
もぐ
THE FOOD IN THIS WORLD IS DELICIOUS, ISN'T IT? ♪
MOGU
もぐ
SCRUMPTIOUS! ♥
MOGU
もぐ
YEAH!!
SIGN: TSUGARI BATHHOUSE
OMMM-HWUH!?
MARURUN-SAN, WHAT'S WRONG?
MOGU
もぐ
MOGU
もぐ
MOGU
もぐ
GOKUN (GULP)
ごくん
...I JUST SENSED CARINA'S WAVELENGTH NEARBY.
HUH?

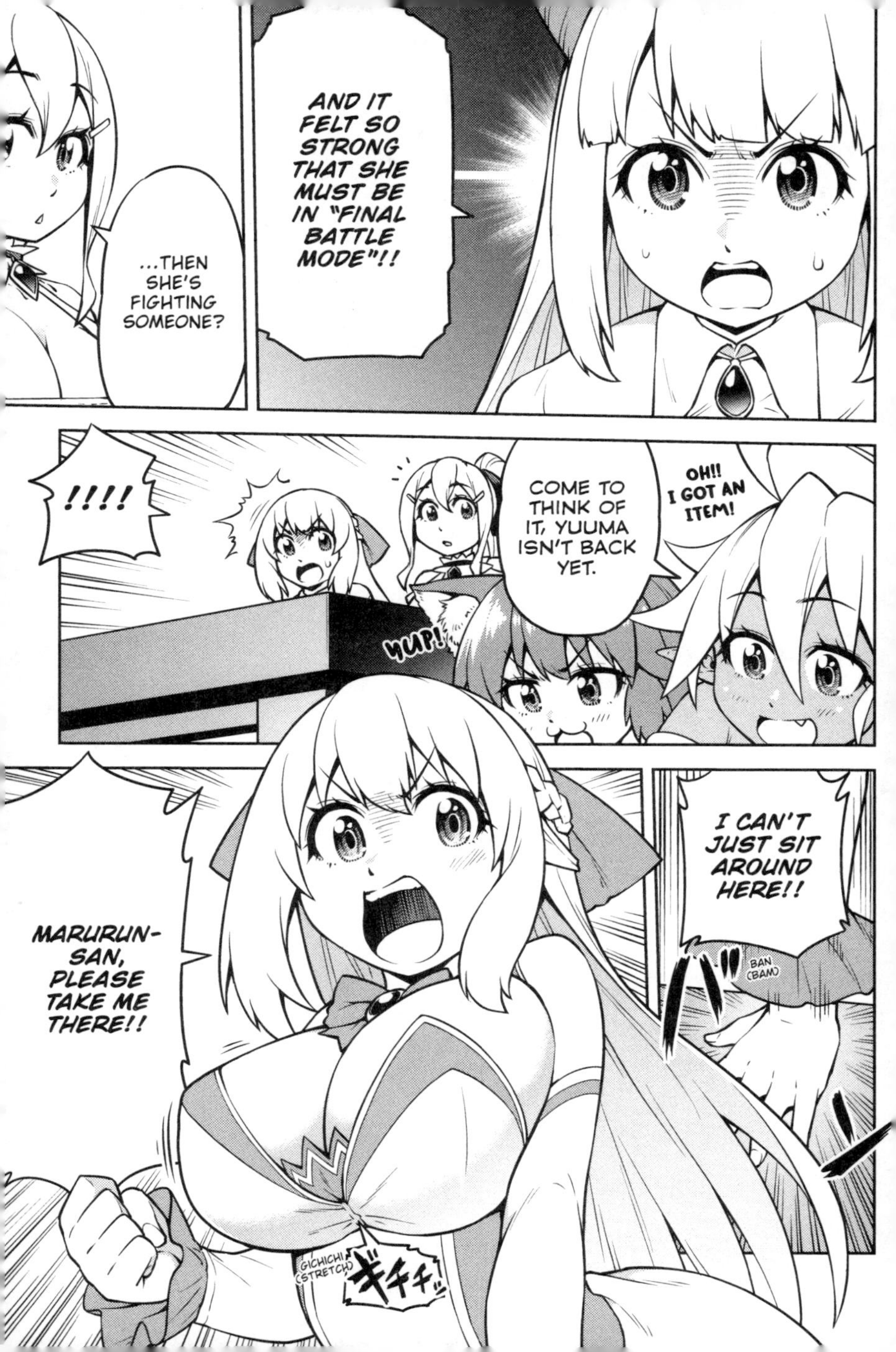
AND IT FELT SO STRONG THAT SHE MUST BE IN "FINAL BATTLE MODE"!!
...THEN SHE'S FIGHTING SOMEONE?
OH!! I GOT AN ITEM!
COME TO THINK OF IT, YUUMA ISN'T BACK YET.
YUP!
!!!!
I CAN'T JUST SIT AROUND HERE!!
BAN (BAM)
MARURUN-SAN, PLEASE TAKE ME THERE!!
GICHICHI (STRETCH)
ギチチ

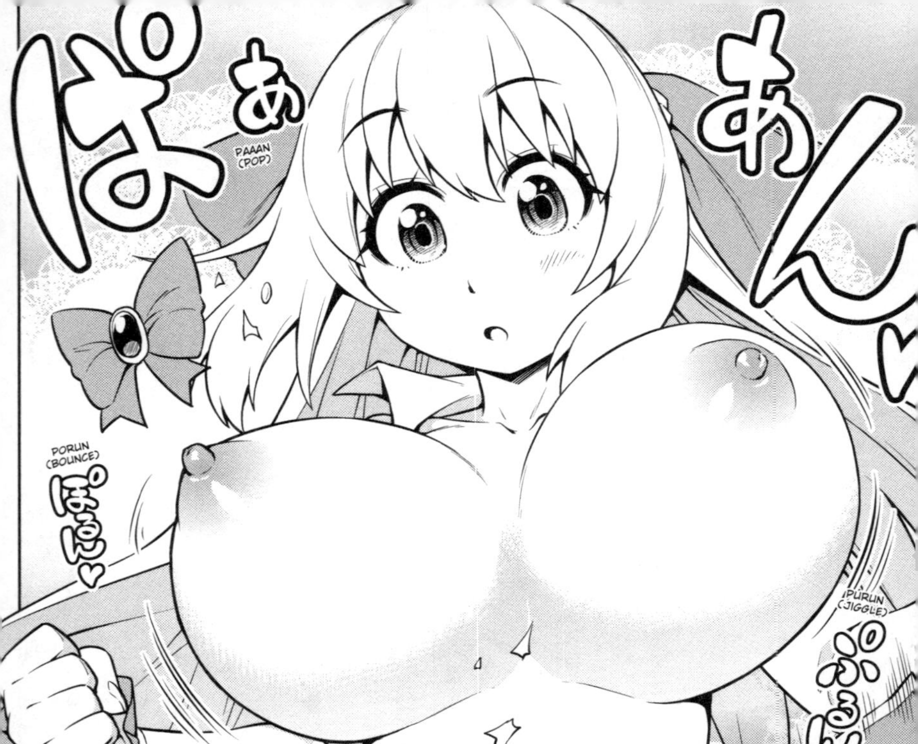
ぱぁあん♥
PAAAN (POP)
ぷるん♥
PURUN (JIGGLE)
ぽるん♥
PORUN (BOUNCE)
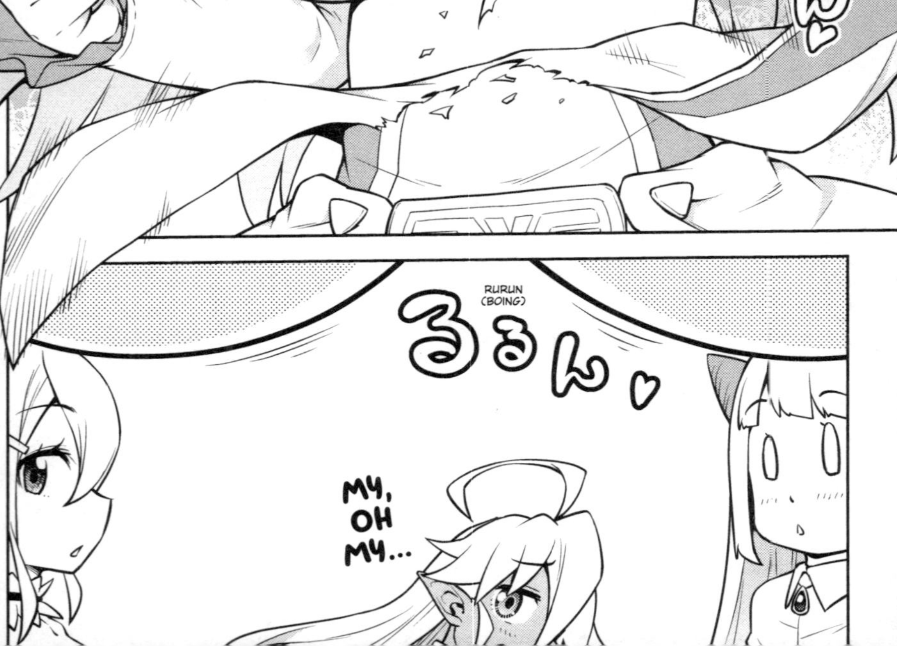
るるん♥
RURUN (BOING)
MY, OH MY...

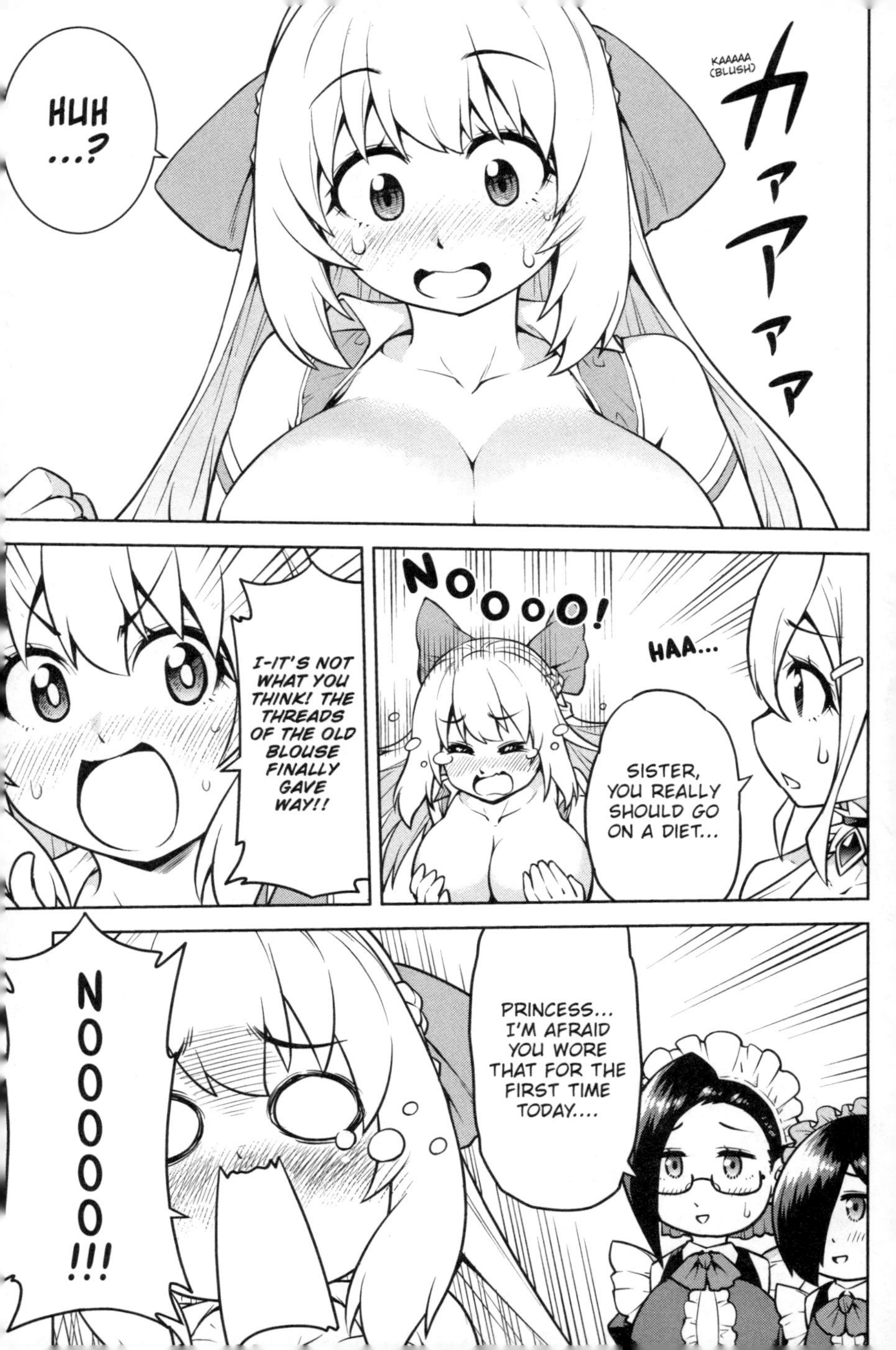
KAAAAA (BLUSH)
カァアーァァ
HUH ...?
HAA...
SISTER, YOU REALLY SHOULD GO ON A DIET...
NOOOO!
I-IT'S NOT WHAT YOU THINK! THE THREADS OF THE OLD BLOUSE FINALLY GAVE WAY!!
PRINCESS... I'M AFRAID YOU WORE THAT FOR THE FIRST TIME TODAY....
NOOOOOO!!!

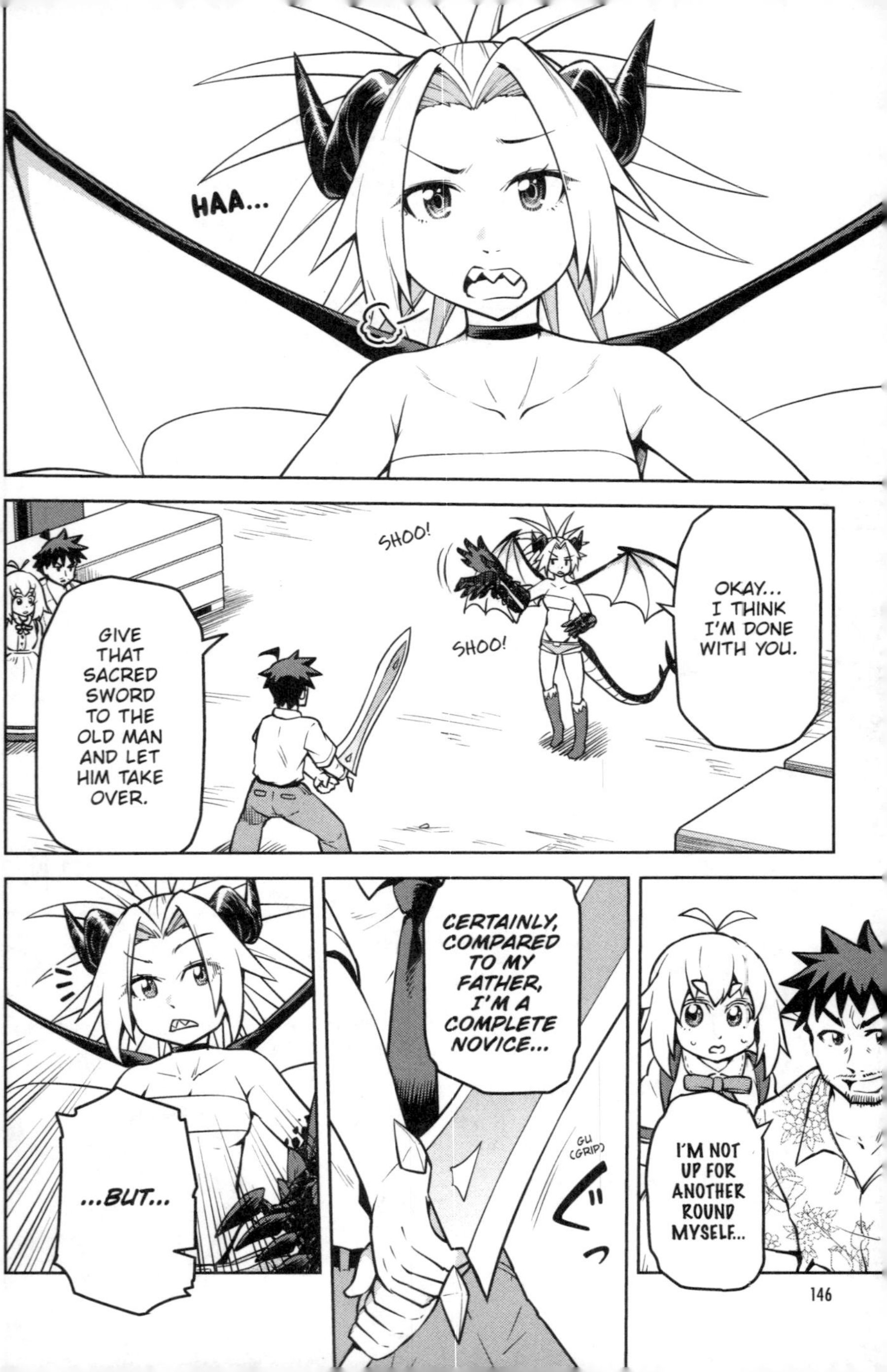
HAA...
OKAY... I THINK I'M DONE WITH YOU.
SHOO!
SHOO!
GIVE THAT SACRED SWORD TO THE OLD MAN AND LET HIM TAKE OVER.
I'M NOT UP FOR ANOTHER ROUND MYSELF...
CERTAINLY, COMPARED TO MY FATHER, I'M A COMPLETE NOVICE...
GU (GRIP)
...BUT...

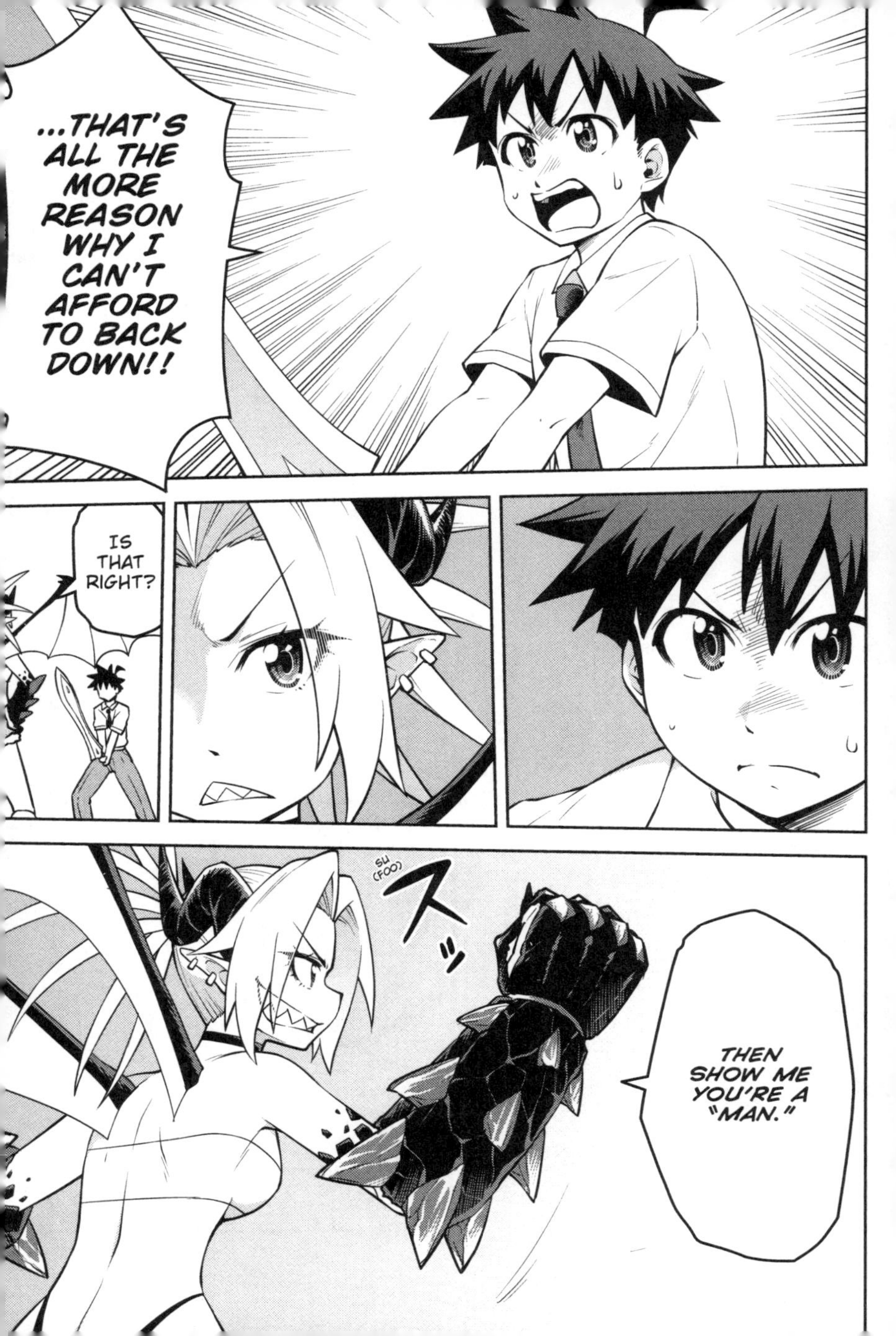
...THAT'S ALL THE MORE REASON WHY I CAN'T AFFORD TO BACK DOWN!!
IS THAT RIGHT?
SU (FOO)
THEN SHOW ME YOU'RE A "MAN."

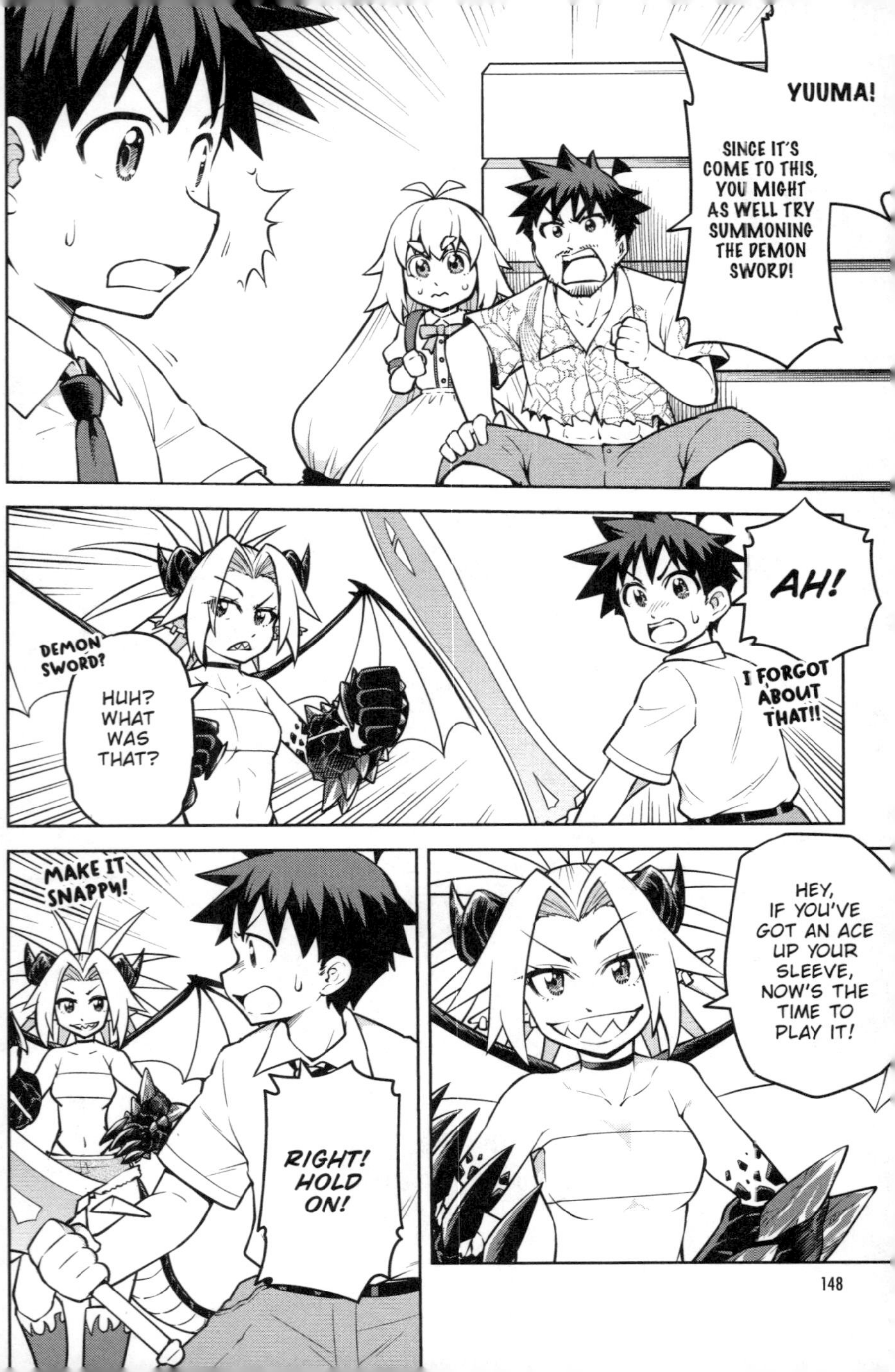
YUUMA!
SINCE IT'S COME TO THIS, YOU MIGHT AS WELL TRY SUMMONING THE DEMON SWORD!
AH!
I FORGOT ABOUT THAT!!
DEMON SWORD?
HUH? WHAT WAS THAT?
HEY, IF YOU'VE GOT AN ACE UP YOUR SLEEVE, NOW'S THE TIME TO PLAY IT!
RIGHT! HOLD ON!
MAKE IT SNAPPY!

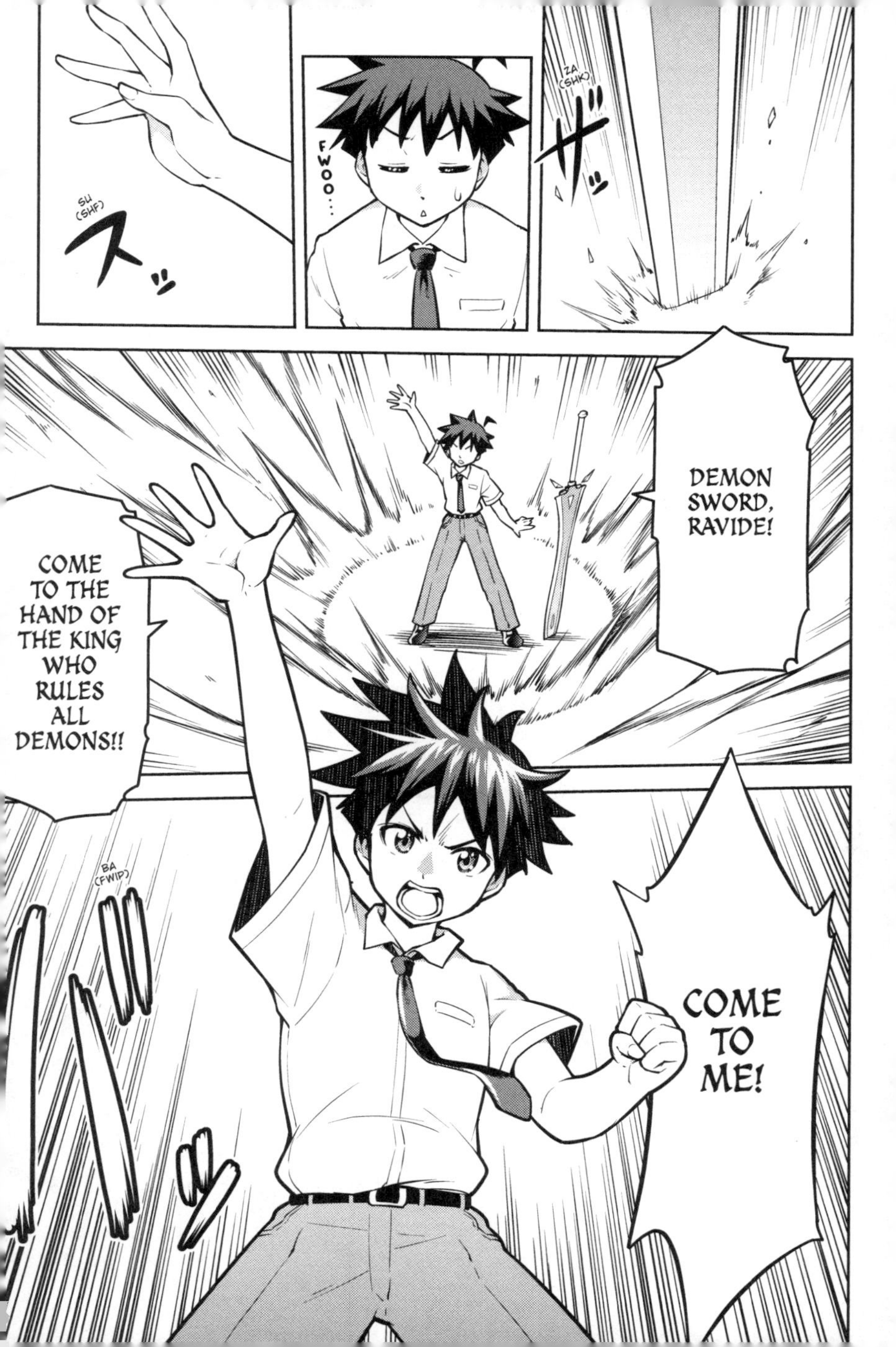
ZA (SHK)
FWOO...
SU (SHF)
DEMON SWORD, RAVIDE!
COME TO THE HAND OF THE KING WHO RULES ALL DEMONS!!
COME TO ME!
BA (FWIP)

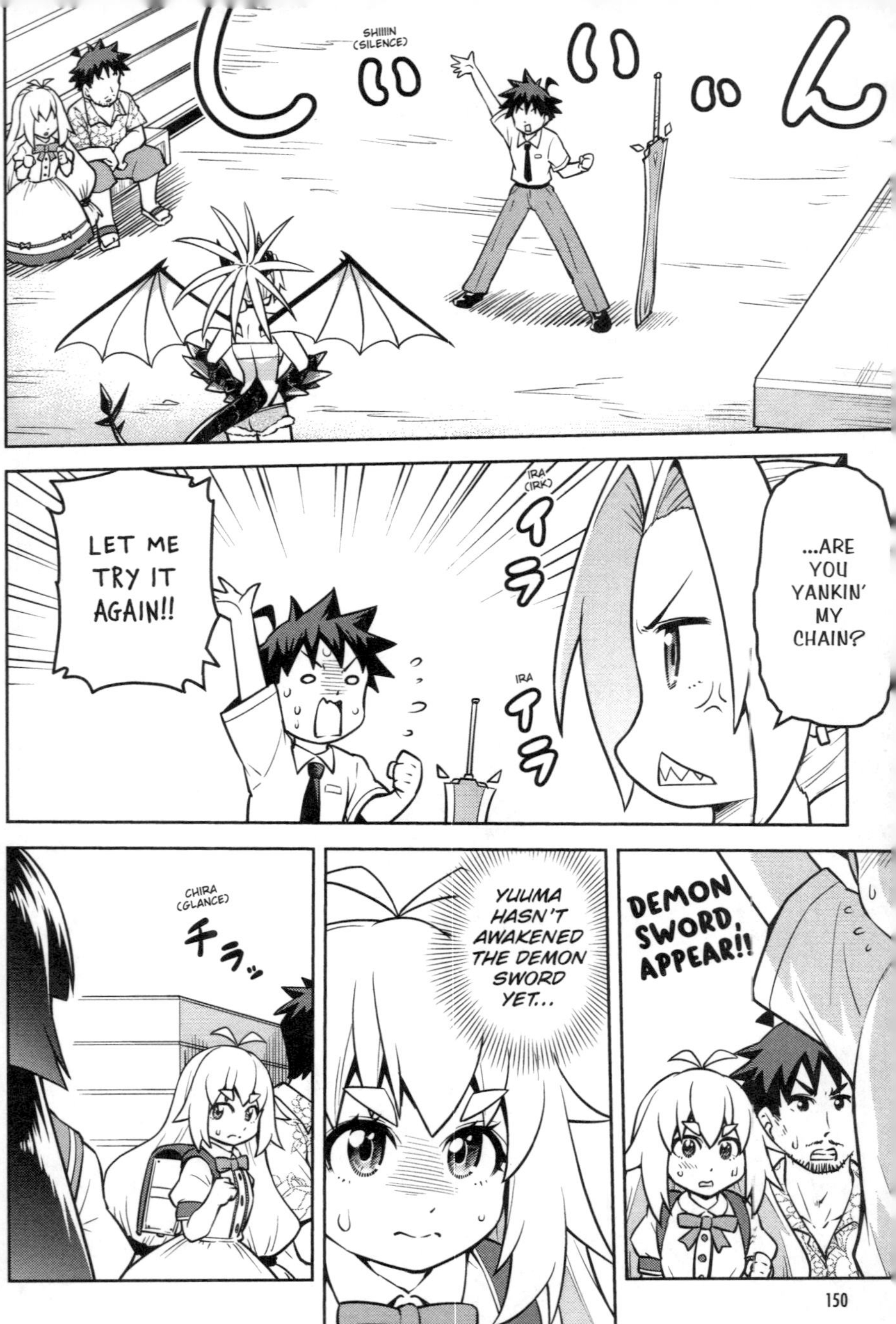
SHIIIIN (SILENCE)
しぃぃぃん
...ARE YOU YANKIN' MY CHAIN?
IRA (IRK)
イラ
IRA
イラ
LET ME TRY IT AGAIN!!
DEMON SWORD, APPEAR!!
YUUMA HASN'T AWAKENED THE DEMON SWORD YET...
CHIRA (GLANCE)
チラッ

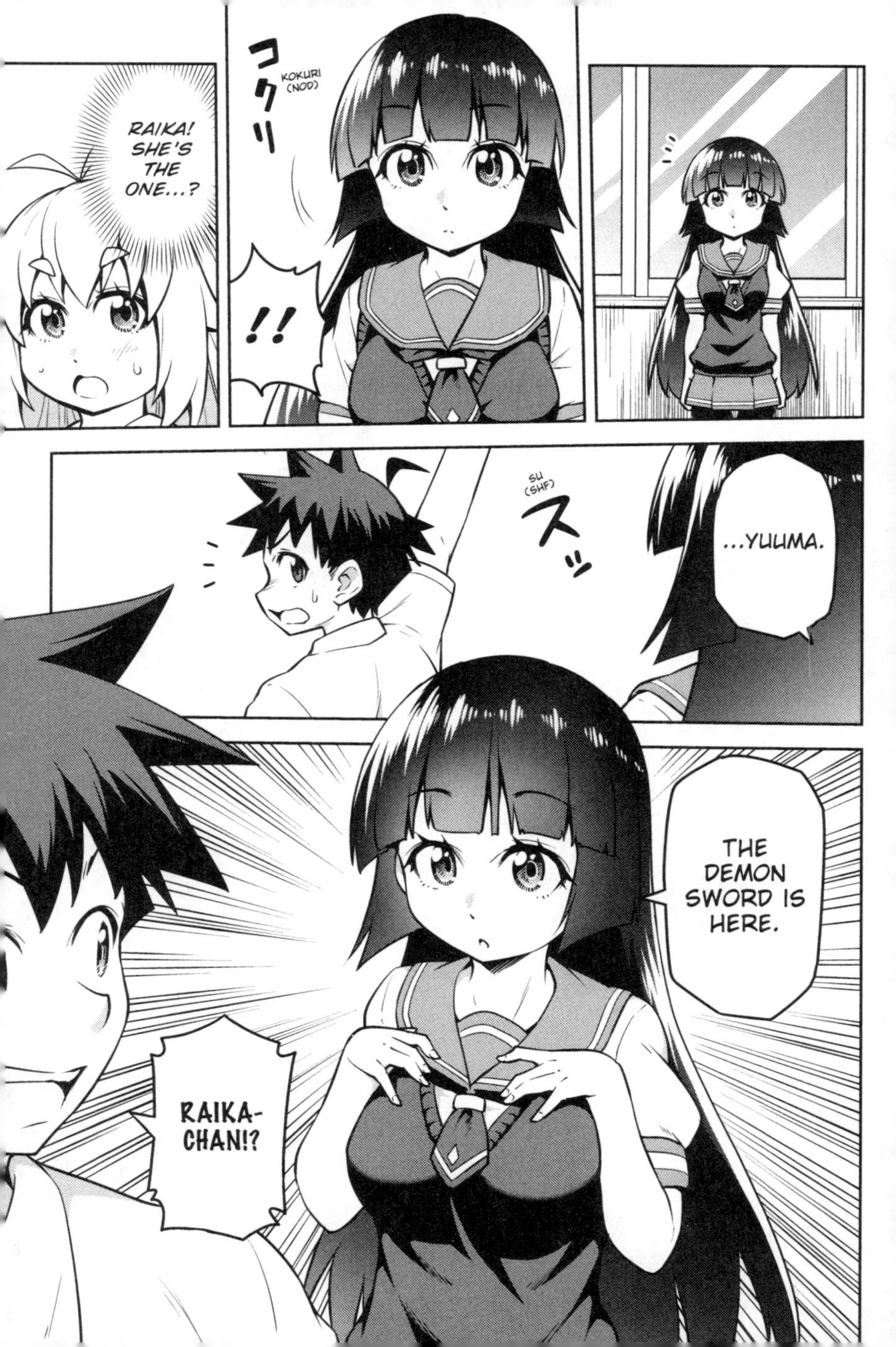
コクリ
KOKURI (NOD)
!!
RAIKA! SHE'S THE ONE...?
...YUUMA.
スッ
SU (SHF)
THE DEMON SWORD IS HERE.
RAIKA-CHAN!?

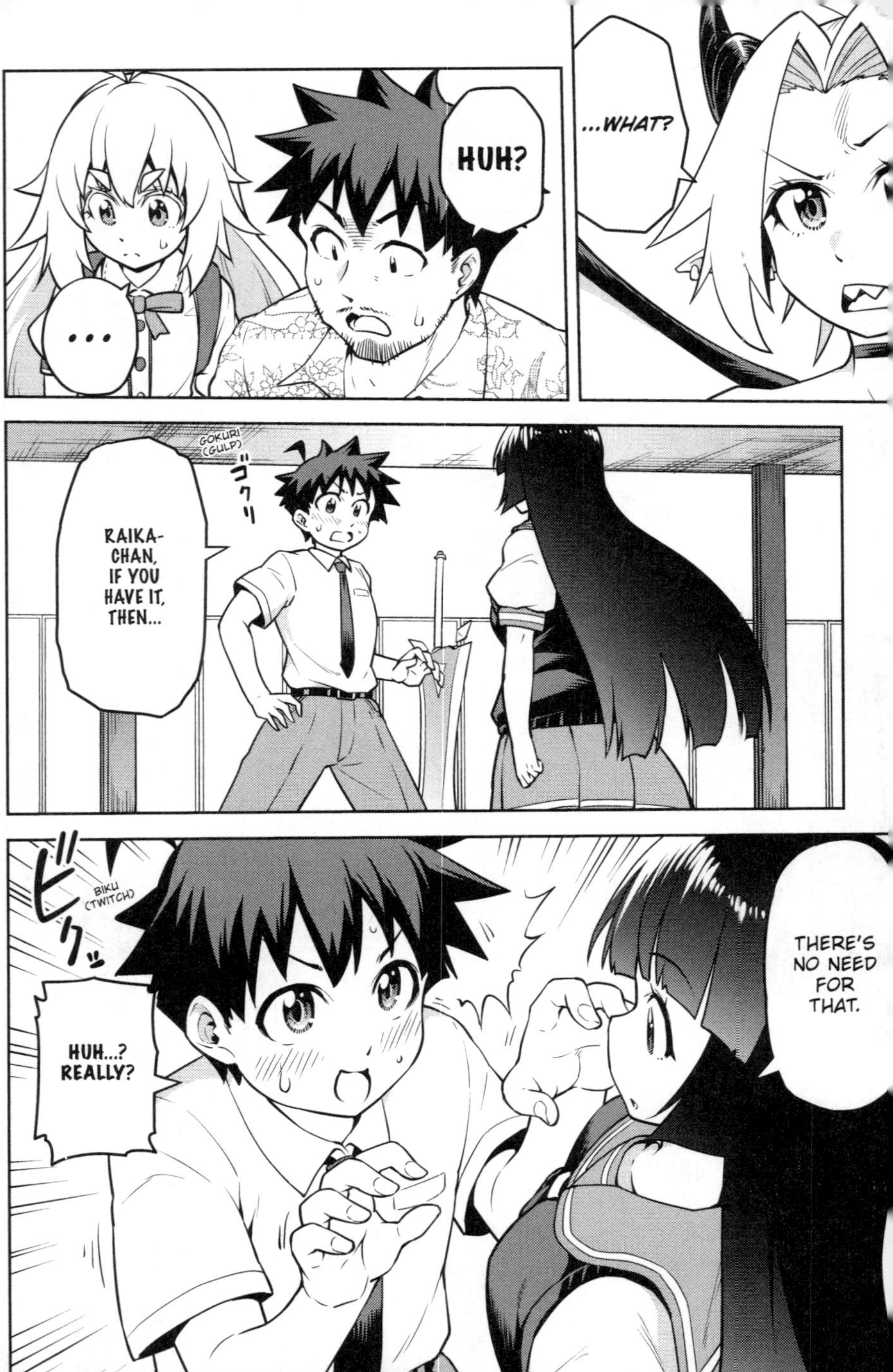
...WHAT?
HUH?
...
GOKURI (GULP)
ゴクリ
RAIKA-CHAN, IF YOU HAVE IT, THEN...
THERE'S NO NEED FOR THAT.
BIKU (TWITCH)
ビクッ
HUH...? REALLY?

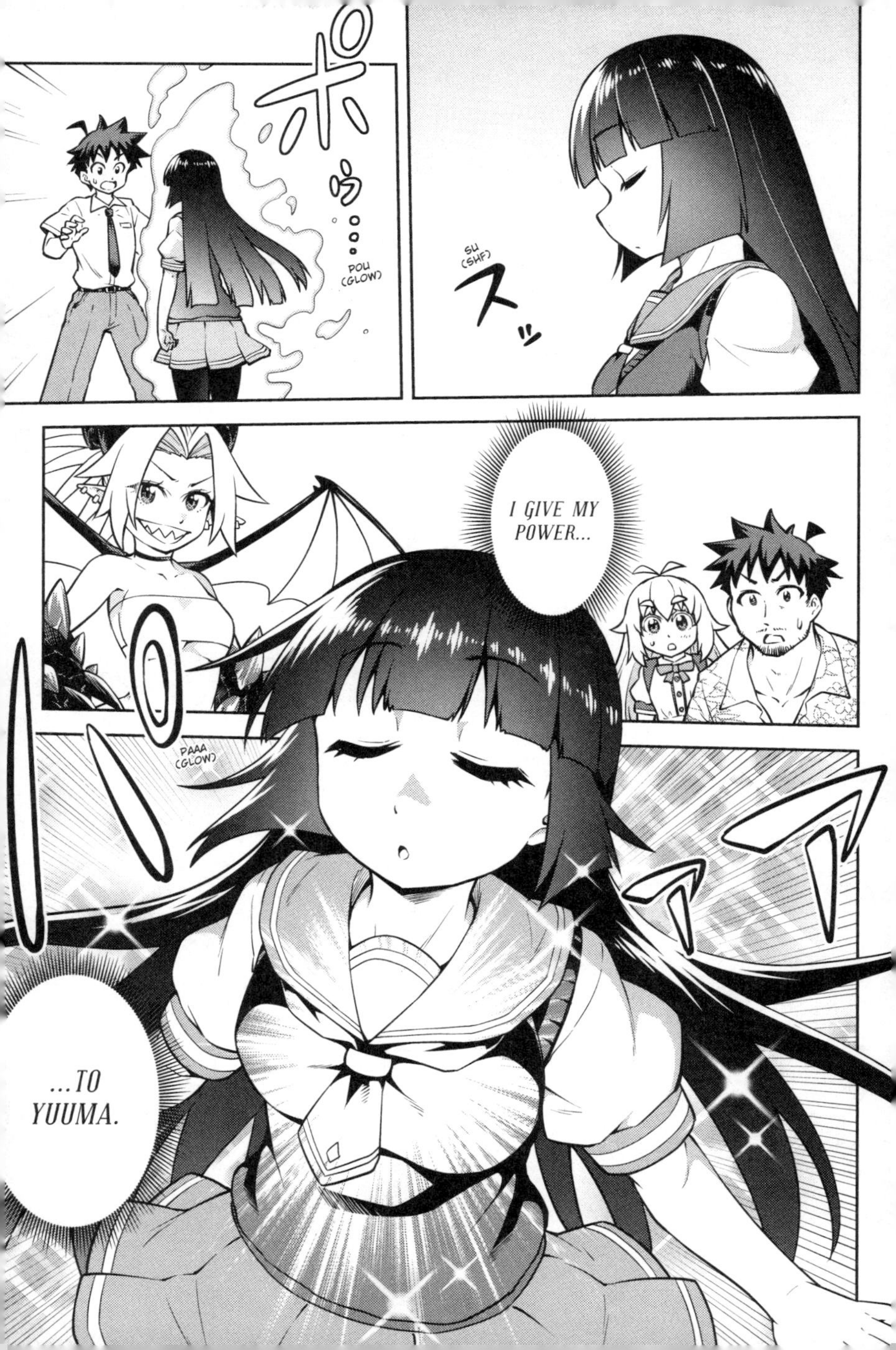
SU (SHF)
POU (GLOW)
I GIVE MY POWER...
PAAA (GLOW)
...TO YUUMA.

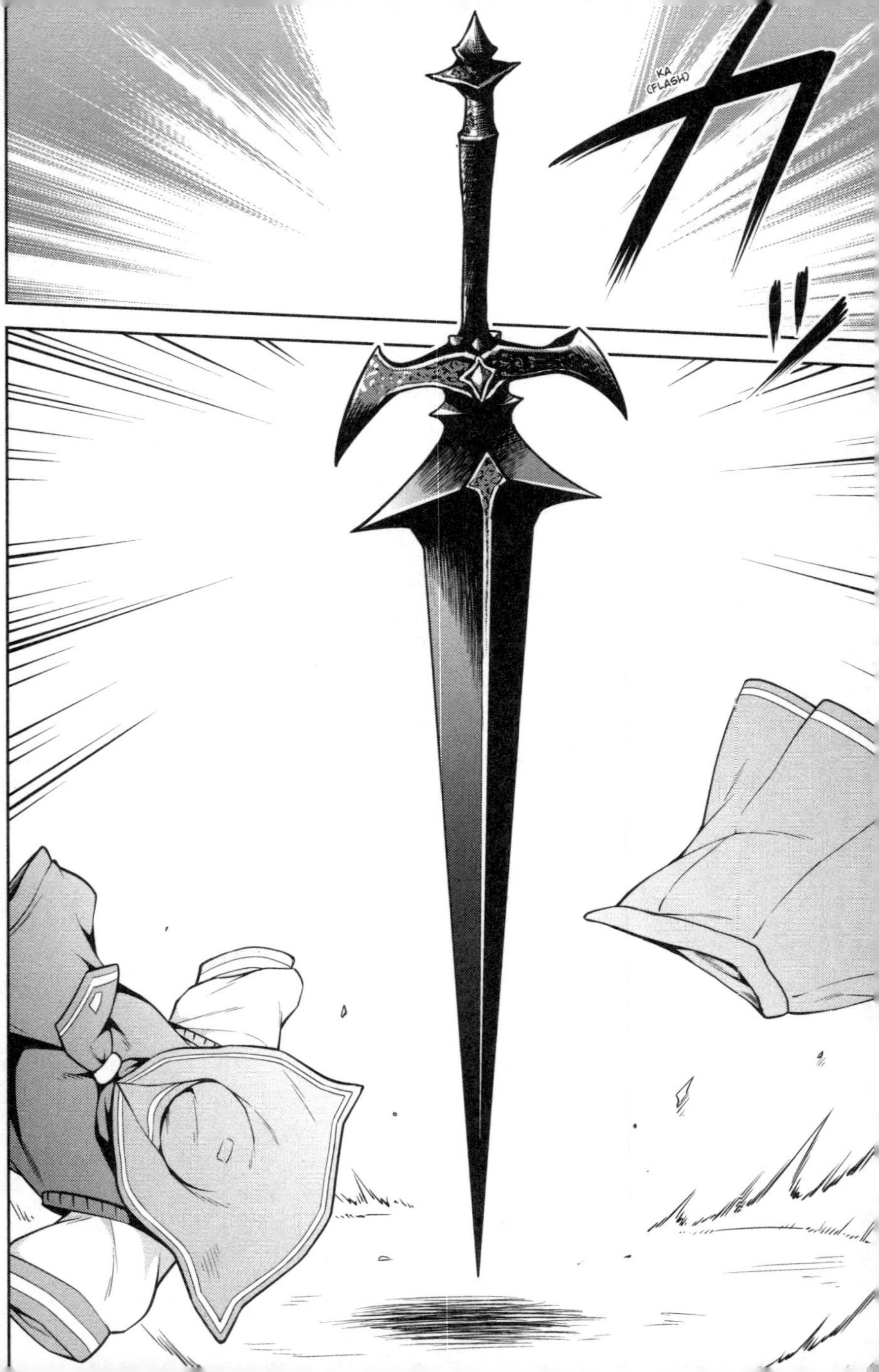
KA
(FLASH)

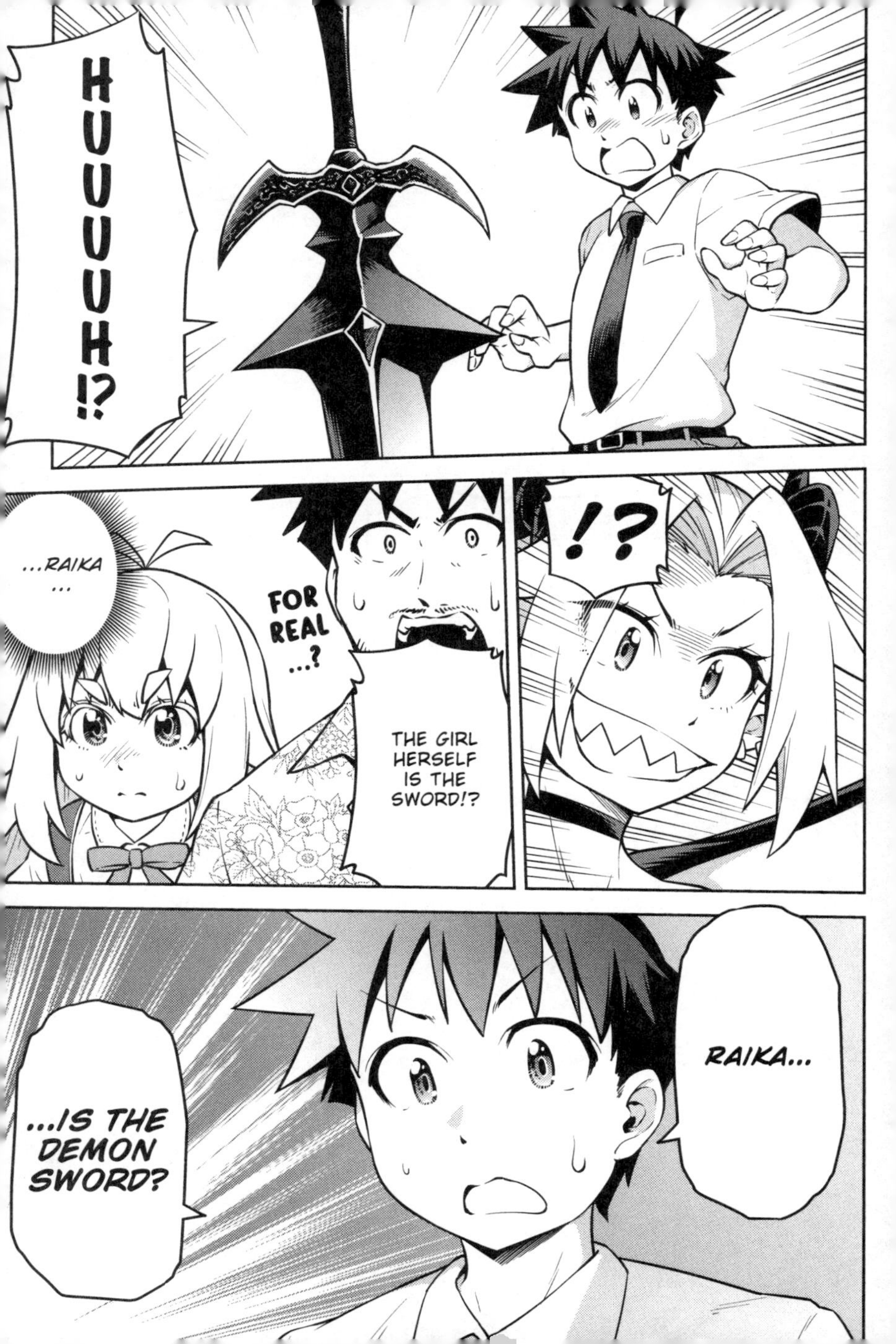
HUUUUUUH!?
!?
FOR REAL ...?
THE GIRL HERSELF IS THE SWORD!?
...RAIKA ...
RAIKA...
...IS THE DEMON SWORD?

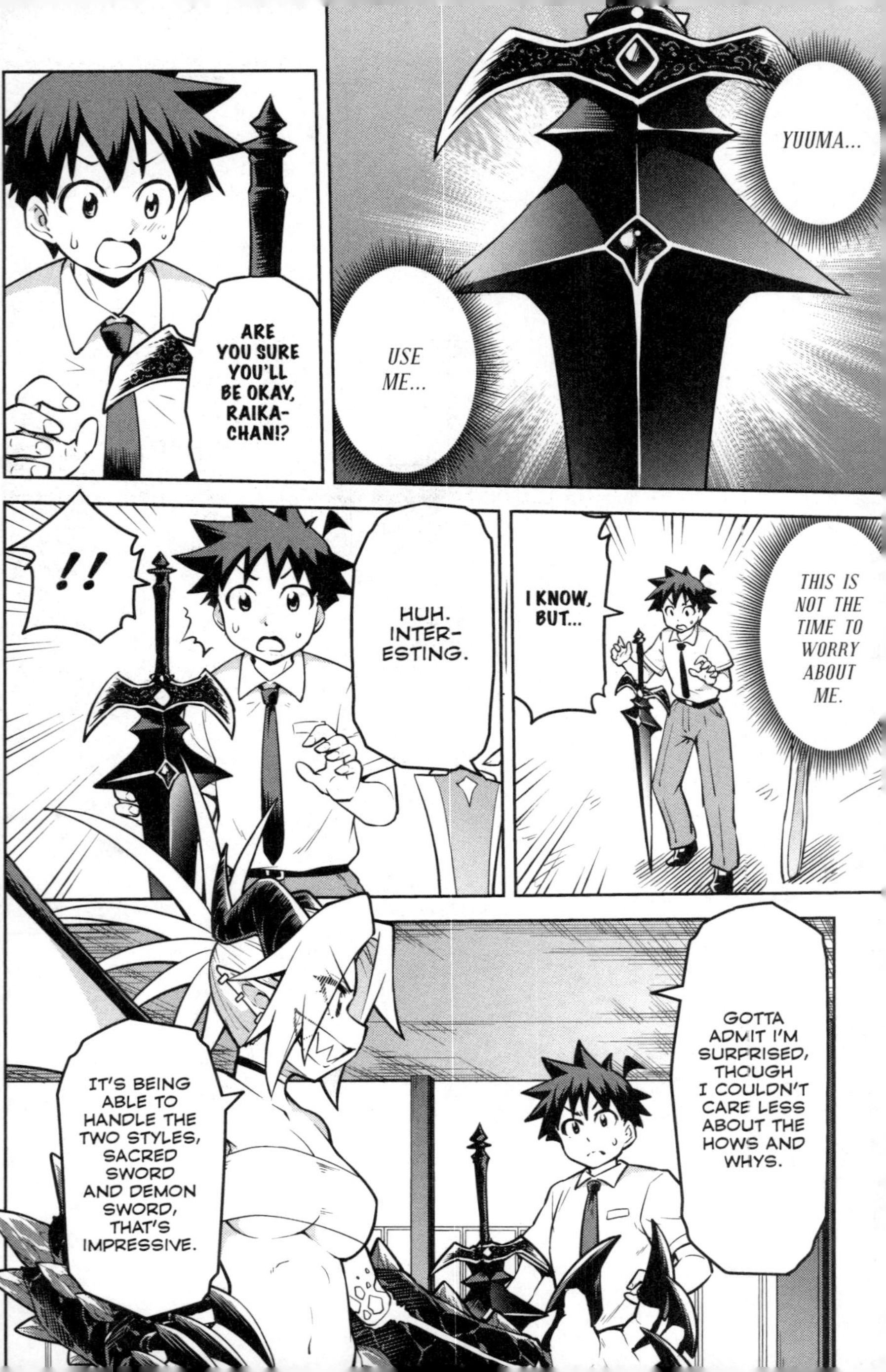
YUUMA...
USE ME...
ARE YOU SURE YOU'LL BE OKAY, RAIKA-CHAN!?
THIS IS NOT THE TIME TO WORRY ABOUT ME.
I KNOW, BUT...
HUH. INTERESTING.
!!
GOTTA ADMIT I'M SURPRISED, THOUGH I COULDN'T CARE LESS ABOUT THE HOWS AND WHYS.
IT'S BEING ABLE TO HANDLE THE TWO STYLES, SACRED SWORD AND DEMON SWORD, THAT'S IMPRESSIVE.

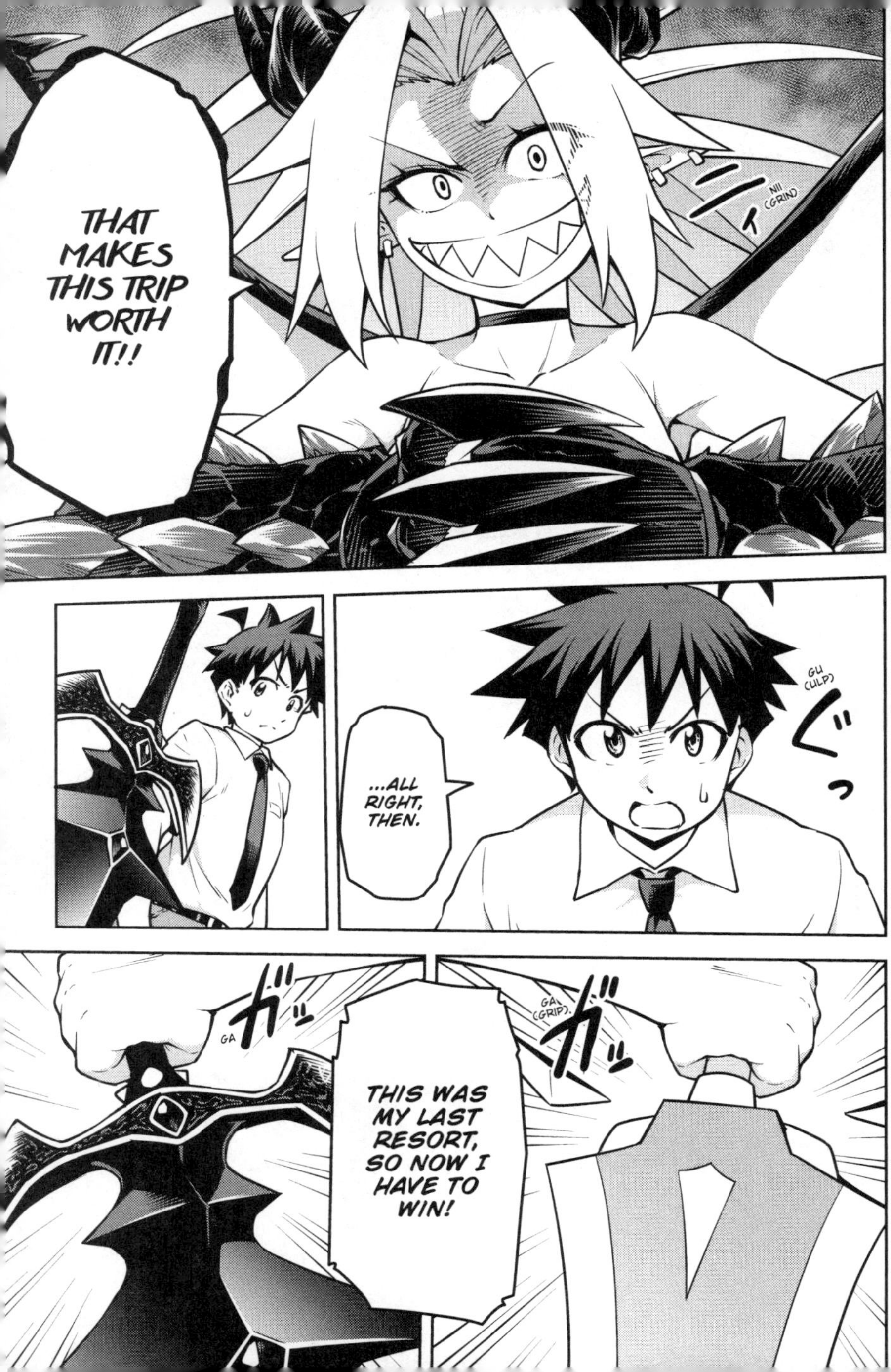
ニイ
NII (GRIN)
THAT MAKES THIS TRIP WORTH IT!!
ぐっ
GU (ULP)
...ALL RIGHT, THEN.
ガッ
GA (GRIP)
ガッ
GA
THIS WAS MY LAST RESORT, SO NOW I HAVE TO WIN!

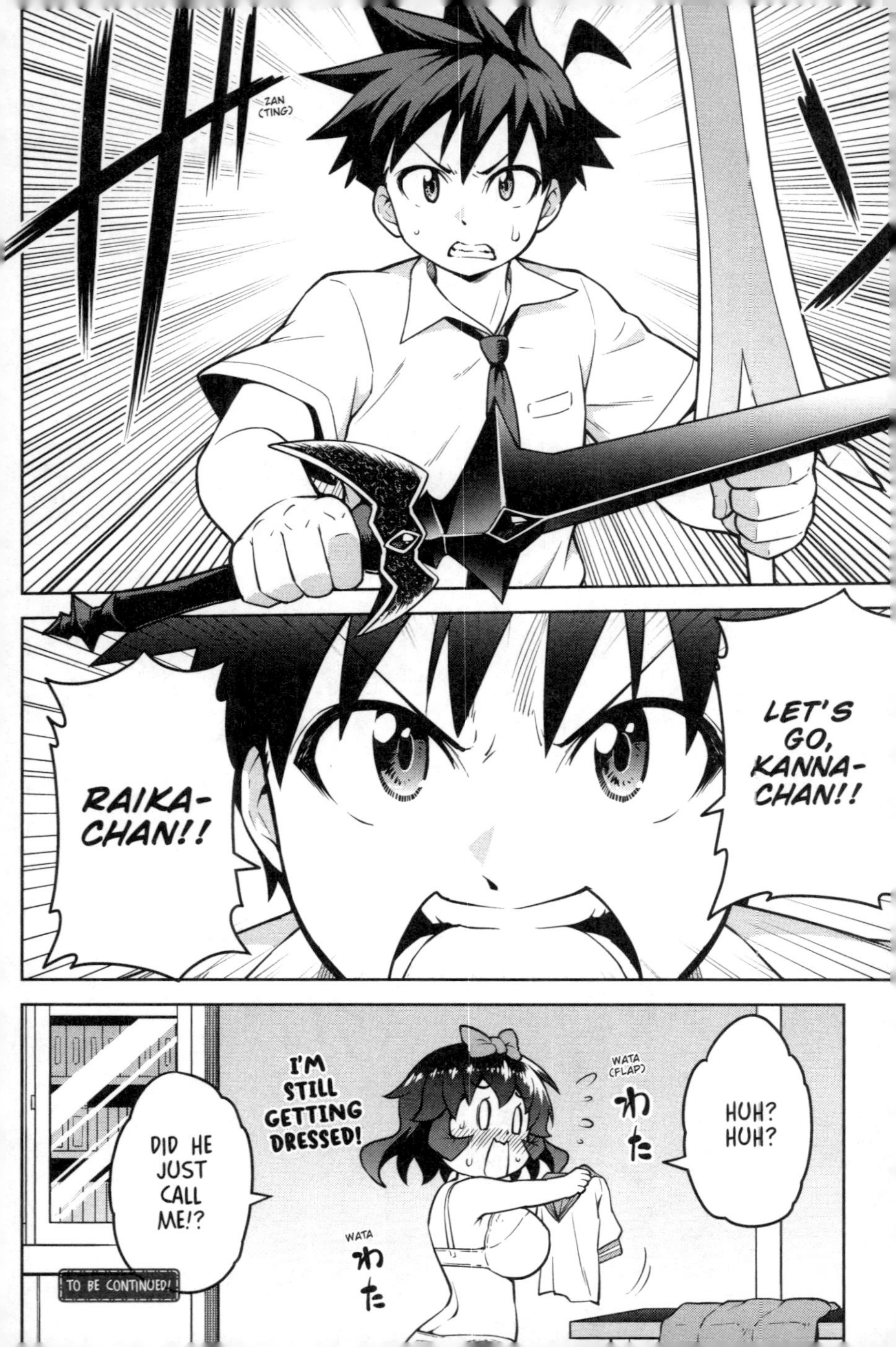
ZAN (TING)
LET'S GO, KANNA-CHAN!!
RAIKA-CHAN!!
HUH? HUH?
WATA (FLAP) わた
I'M STILL GETTING DRESSED!
WATA わた
DID HE JUST CALL ME!?
TO BE CONTINUED!

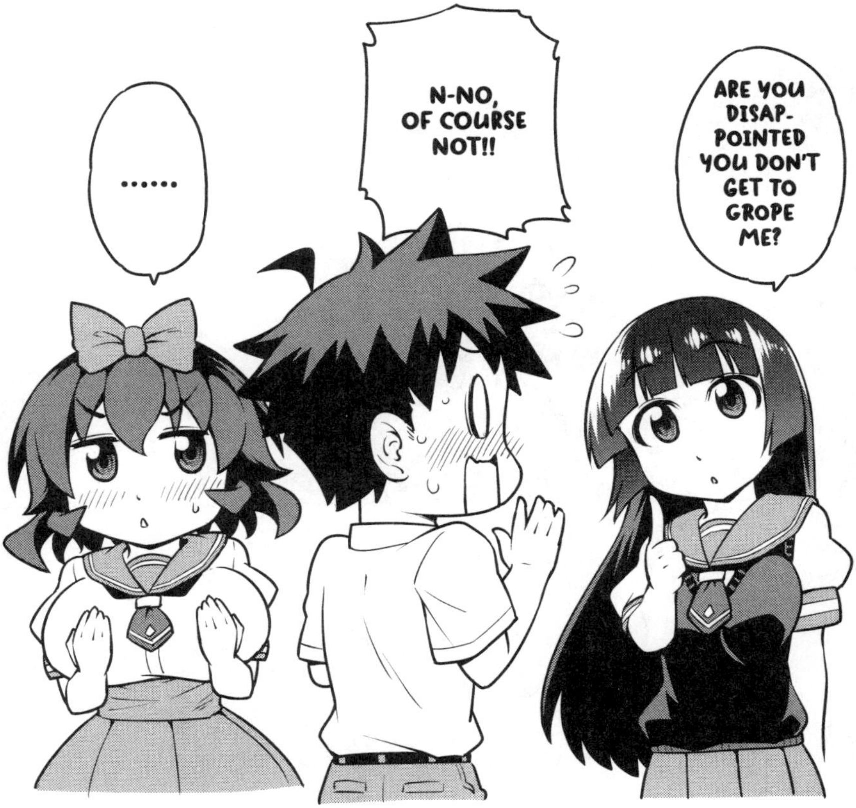
ARE YOU DISAP-POINTED YOU DON'T GET TO GROPE ME?
N-NO, OF COURSE NOT!!
......

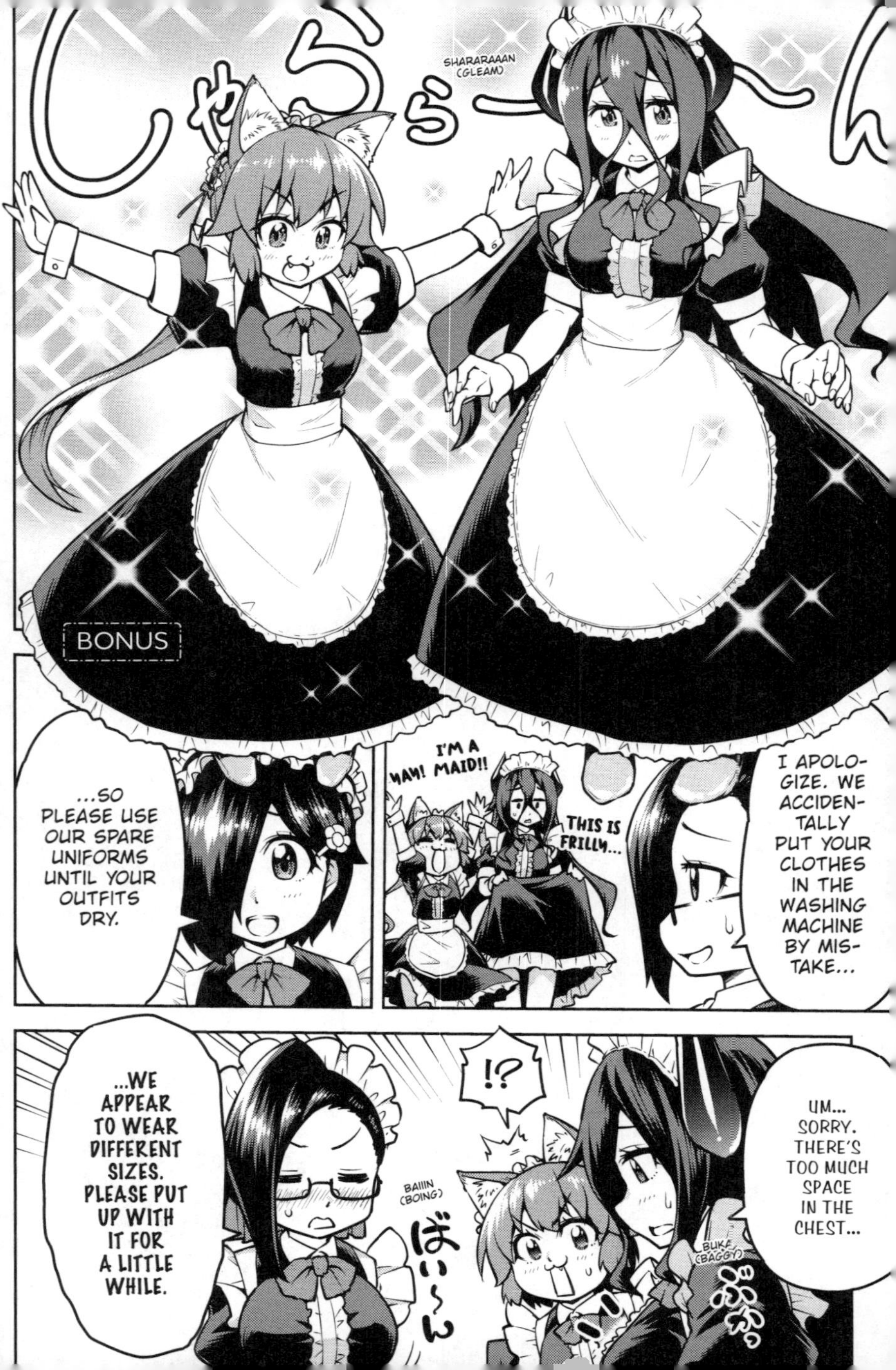
しゃらら～ん
SHARARAAAN (GLEAM)
BONUS
I APOLOGIZE. WE ACCIDENTALLY PUT YOUR CLOTHES IN THE WASHING MACHINE BY MISTAKE...
I'M A MAID!!
YAY!
THIS IS FRILLY...
...SO PLEASE USE OUR SPARE UNIFORMS UNTIL YOUR OUTFITS DRY.
UM... SORRY. THERE'S TOO MUCH SPACE IN THE CHEST...
BUKA (BAGGY)
!?
ばい～ん
BAIIN (BOING)
...WE APPEAR TO WEAR DIFFERENT SIZES. PLEASE PUT UP WITH IT FOR A LITTLE WHILE.

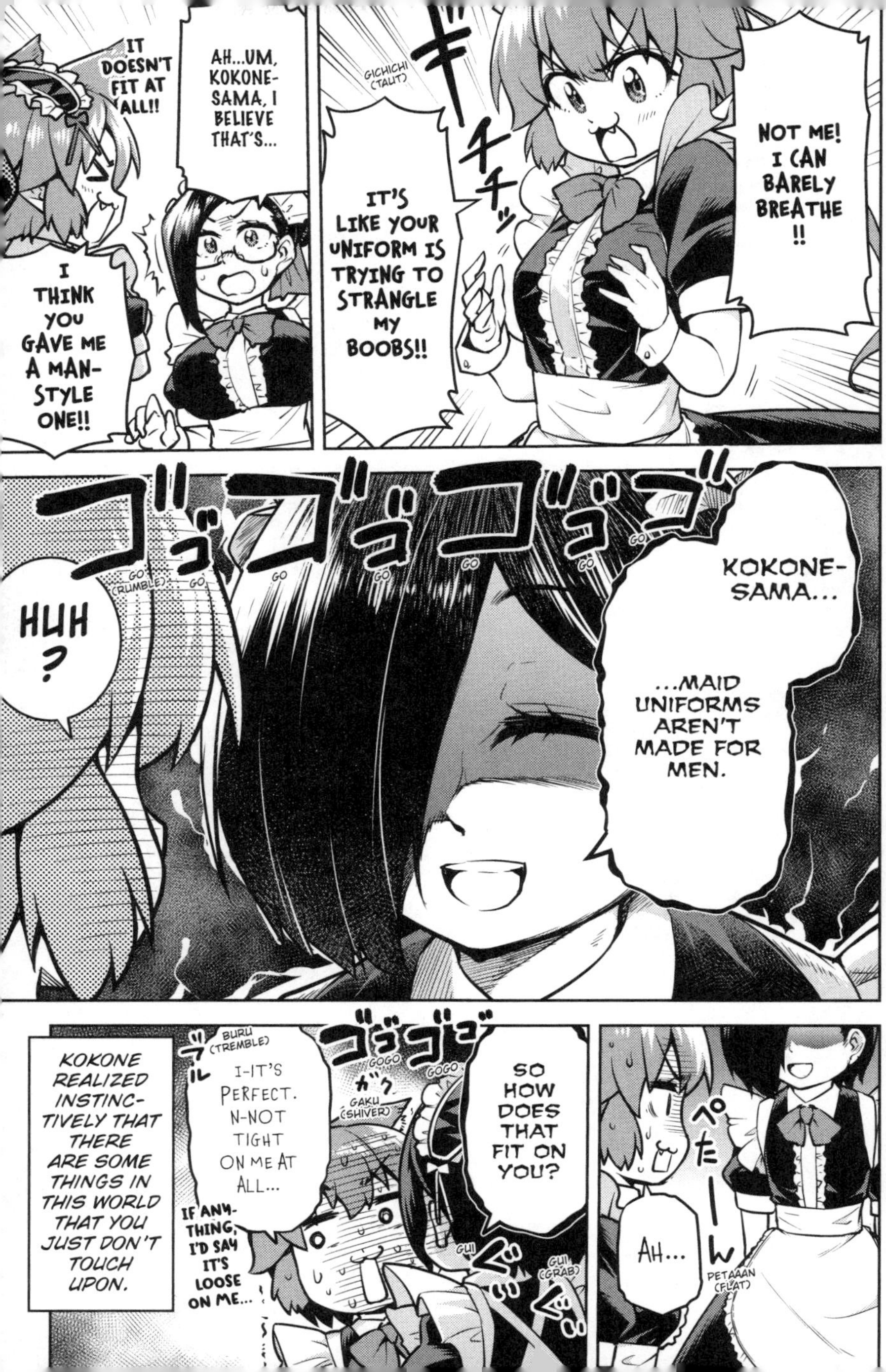
GICHICHI (TAUT)
NOT ME! I CAN BARELY BREATHE!!
IT'S LIKE YOUR UNIFORM IS TRYING TO STRANGLE MY BOOBS!!
AH...UM, KOKONE-SAMA, I BELIEVE THAT'S...
IT DOESN'T FIT AT ALL!!
I THINK YOU GAVE ME A MAN-STYLE ONE!!
KOKONE-SAMA...
...MAID UNIFORMS AREN'T MADE FOR MEN.
GO GO GO GO GO GO GO (RUMBLE)
HUH?
AH...
PETAAAN (FLAT)
SO HOW DOES THAT FIT ON YOU?
GOGO GOGO
BURU (TREMBLE)
I-IT'S PERFECT. N-NOT TIGHT ON ME AT ALL...
GAKU (SHIVER)
IF ANYTHING, I'D SAY IT'S LOOSE ON ME...
GUI GUI (GRAB)
KOKONE REALIZED INSTINCTIVELY THAT THERE ARE SOME THINGS IN THIS WORLD THAT YOU JUST DON'T TOUCH UPON.

# TRANSLATION NOTES ........................................

## COMMON HONORIFICS

**no honorific**: Indicates familiarity or closeness; if used without permission or reason, addressing someone in this manner would constitute an insult.

**-san**: The Japanese equivalent of Mr./Mrs./Miss. If a situation calls for politeness, this is the fail-safe honorific.

**-sama**: Conveys great respect; may also indicate that the social status of the speaker is lower than that of the addressee.

**-shi**: An impersonal honorific used in formal speech or writing, e.g. legal documents.

**-dono**: Roughly equivalent to "master" or "milord."

**-kun**: Used most often when referring to boys, this indicates affection or familiarity. Occasionally used by older men among their peers, but it may also be used by anyone referring to a person of lower standing.

**-chan**: An affectionate honorific indicating familiarity used mostly in reference to girls; also used in reference to cute persons or animals of either gender.

**-tan**: A cutesy version of -chan.

**-(o)nii/(o)nee**: Meaning "big brother"/ "big sister," it can also refer to those older but relatively close in age to the speaker. It is typically followed by -san, -chan, or -sama.

**-senpai**: An honorific for one's senior classmate, colleague, etc., although not as senior or respected as a *sensei* ("teacher").

## GENERAL

One hundred yen is roughly equal to one U.S. dollar.

## PAGE 9

The "**cat robot**" Yuuma's referring to is Doraemon, perhaps the most well-known character in Japan, who also sleeps in a closet.

## PAGE 27

The pun here in Japanese is on the word *maki*, or "roll." Yuuma's dad uses an expression to say that a dragon's coming means it's time to finish things (*maki ga hairu*, literally "a roll enters"). Kokone responds with the kinds of *maki* she wants—*harumaki* (a spring roll), and *nikumaki*, a type of roll where the outside is actually a thinly sliced layer of beef.

# AFTERWORD

HERE WE ARE WITH
VOLUME 3 ALREADY!
CARINA-SAN IS TAKING
A MORE ACTIVE ROLE
THAN I HAD IMAGINED.
IT'S FUN DRAWING THE
DRAGON CHARACTERS!!
SEE YOU NEXT VOLUME!

TATSUYA ENDO

I'M AKIYOSHI OTA, THE
CREATOR OF THIS SERIES.

I HOPE YOU ENJOYED
VOLUME 3 OF BOKUYUMA.
WE REALLY BUILT UP TO
A CLIMAX AT THE END,
SO DON'T MISS THE NEXT
VOLUME TO SEE HOW IT
PLAYS OUT!

I'D LIKE TO MAKE THE STORY
AS EXCITING, BUT ALSO AS
LEWD, AS I CAN, SO THANK
YOU FOR YOUR SUPPORT!

# I'm the HERO, but the DEMON LORD's Also Me

## 3
**ART** TATSUYA ENDO
**STORY** AKIYOSHI OTA

**Translation: Sheldon Drzka | Lettering: Phil Christie**

This book is a work of fiction. Names, characters, places, and incidents are the product of the author's imagination or are used fictitiously. Any resemblance to actual events, locales, or persons, living or dead, is coincidental.

BOKU GA YUSHA DE MAO MO BOKUDE Vol. 3
©Tatsuya Endo 2020 ©Akiyoshi Ota 2020
First published in Japan in 2020 by KADOKAWA CORPORATION, Tokyo.
English translation rights arranged with KADOKAWA CORPORATION, Tokyo through TUTTLE-MORI AGENCY, INC., Tokyo.

English translation © 2022 by Yen Press, LLC

Yen Press
150 West 30th Street, 19th Floor
New York, NY 10001

Visit us!
yenpress.com • facebook.com/yenpress • twitter.com/yenpress
yenpress.tumblr.com • instagram.com/yenpress

First Yen Press Edition: January 2022

Yen Press is an imprint of Yen Press, LLC.
The Yen Press name and logo are trademarks of Yen Press, LLC.

The publisher is not responsible for websites (or their content) that are not owned by the publisher.

Library of Congress Control Number: 2021932182

ISBNs: 978-1-9753-3621-9 (paperback)
978-1-9753-3622-6 (ebook)

10 9 8 7 6 5 4 3 2 1

LSC-C

Printed in the United States of America